A Field Guide to Genetic Programming

Riccardo Poli
Department of Computing and Electronic Systems
University of Essex – UK
rpoli@essex.ac.uk

William B. Langdon
Departments of Biological and Mathematical Sciences
University of Essex – UK
wlangdon@essex.ac.uk

Nicholas F. McPhee
Division of Science and Mathematics
University of Minnesota, Morris – USA
mcphee@morris.umn.edu

with contributions by
John R. Koza
Stanford University – USA
john@johnkoza.com

March 2008

To cite this book, please see the entry for (Poli, Langdon, and McPhee, 2008) in the bibliography.

ISBN 978-1-4092-0073-4 (softcover)

Preface

Genetic programming (GP) is a collection of evolutionary computation techniques that allow computers to solve problems automatically. Since its inception twenty years ago, GP has been used to solve a wide range of practical problems, producing a number of human-competitive results and even patentable new inventions. Like many other areas of computer science, GP is evolving rapidly, with new ideas, techniques and applications being constantly proposed. While this shows how wonderfully prolific GP is, it also makes it difficult for newcomers to become acquainted with the main ideas in the field, and form a mental map of its different branches. Even for people who have been interested in GP for a while, it is difficult to keep up with the pace of new developments.

Many books have been written which describe aspects of GP. Some provide general introductions to the field as a whole. However, no new introductory book on GP has been produced in the last decade, and anyone wanting to learn about GP is forced to map the terrain painfully on their own. This book attempts to fill that gap, by providing a modern field guide to GP for both newcomers and old-timers.

It would have been straightforward to find a traditional publisher for such a book. However, we want our book to be as accessible as possible to everyone interested in learning about GP. Therefore, we have chosen to make it freely available on-line, while also allowing printed copies to be ordered inexpensively from http://lulu.com. Visit http://www.gp-field-guide.org.uk for the details.

The book has undergone numerous iterations and revisions. It began as a book-chapter overview of GP (more on this below), which quickly grew to almost 100 pages. A technical report version of it was circulated on the GP mailing list. People responded very positively, and some encouraged us to continue and expand that survey into a book. We took their advice and this field guide is the result.

Acknowledgements

We would like to thank the University of Essex and the University of Minnesota, Morris, for their support.

Many thanks to Tyler Hutchison for the use of his cool drawing on the cover (and elsewhere!), and for finding those scary pinks and greens.

We had the invaluable assistance of many people, and we are very grateful for their individual and collective efforts, often on very short timelines. Rick Riolo, Matthew Walker, Christian Gagne, Bob McKay, Giovanni Pazienza, and Lee Spector all provided useful suggestions based on an early technical report version. Yossi Borenstein, Caterina Cinel, Ellery Crane, Cecilia Di Chio, Stephen Dignum, Edgar Galván-López, Keisha Harriott, David Hunter, Lonny Johnson, Ahmed Kattan, Robert Keller, Andy Korth, Yevgeniya Kovalchuk, Simon Lucas, Wayne Manselle, Alberto Moraglio, Oliver Oechsle, Francisco Sepulveda, Elias Tawil, Edward Tsang, William Tozier and Christian Wagner all contributed to the final proofreading festival. Their sharp eyes and hard work did much to make the book better; any remaining errors or omissions are obviously the sole responsibility of the authors.

We would also like to thank Prof. Xin Yao and the School of Computer Science of The University of Birmingham and Prof. Bernard Buxton of University College, London, for continuing support, particularly of the genetic programming bibliography. We also thank Schloss Dagstuhl, where some of the integration of this book took place.

Most of the tools used in the construction of this book are open source,[1] and we are very grateful to all the developers whose efforts have gone into building those tools over the years.

As mentioned above, this book started life as a chapter. This was for a forthcoming handbook on computational intelligence[2] edited by John Fulcher and Lakhmi C. Jain. We are grateful to John Fulcher for his useful comments and edits on that book chapter. We would also like to thank most warmly John Koza, who co-authored the aforementioned chapter with us, and for allowing us to reuse some of his original material in this book.

This book is a summary of nearly two decades of intensive research in the field of genetic programming, and we obviously owe a great debt to all the researchers whose hard work, ideas, and interactions ultimately made this book possible. Their work runs through every page, from an idea made somewhat clearer by a conversation at a conference, to a specific concept or diagram. It has been a pleasure to be part of the GP community over the years, and we greatly appreciate having so much interesting work to summarise!

March 2008

Riccardo Poli
William B. Langdon
Nicholas Freitag McPhee

---

[1] See the colophon (page 235) for more details.

[2] Tentatively entitled *Computational Intelligence: A Compendium* and to be published by Springer in 2008.

What's in this book

The book is divided up into four parts.

Part I covers the basics of genetic programming (GP). This starts with a gentle introduction which describes how a population of programs is stored in the computer so that they can evolve with time. We explain how programs are represented, how random programs are initially created, and how GP creates a new generation by mutating the better existing programs or combining pairs of good parent programs to produce offspring programs. This is followed by a simple explanation of how to apply GP and an illustrative example of using GP.

In Part II, we describe a variety of alternative representations for programs and some advanced GP techniques. These include: the evolution of machine-code and parallel programs, the use of grammars and probability distributions for the generation of programs, variants of GP which allow the solution of problems with multiple objectives, many speed-up techniques and some useful theoretical tools.

Part III provides valuable information for anyone interested in using GP in practical applications. To illustrate genetic programming's scope, this part contains a review of many real-world applications of GP. These include: curve fitting, data modelling, symbolic regression, image analysis, signal processing, financial trading, time series prediction, economic modelling, industrial process control, medicine, biology, bioinformatics, hyperheuristics, artistic applications, computer games, entertainment, compression and human-competitive results. This is followed by a series of recommendations and suggestions to obtain the most from a GP system. We then provide some conclusions.

Part IV completes the book. In addition to a bibliography and an index, this part includes two appendices that provide many pointers to resources, further reading and a simple GP implementation in Java.

About the authors

The authors are experts in genetic programming with long and distinguished track records, and over 50 years of combined experience in both theory and practice in GP, with collaborations extending over a decade.

Riccardo Poli is a Professor in the Department of Computing and Electronic Systems at Essex. He started his academic career as an electronic engineer doing a PhD in biomedical image analysis to later become an expert in the field of EC. He has published around 240 refereed papers and a book (Langdon and Poli, 2002) on the theory and applications of genetic programming, evolutionary algorithms, particle swarm optimisation, biomedical engineering, brain-computer interfaces, neural networks, image/signal processing, biology and psychology. He is a Fellow of the International Society for Genetic and Evolutionary Computation (2003–), a recipient of the EvoStar award for outstanding contributions to this field (2007), and an ACM SIGEVO executive board member (2007–2013). He was co-founder and co-chair of the European Conference on GP (1998–2000, 2003). He was general chair (2004), track chair (2002, 2007), business committee member (2005), and competition chair (2006) of ACM's Genetic and Evolutionary Computation Conference, co-chair of the Foundations of Genetic Algorithms Workshop (2002) and technical chair of the International Workshop on Ant Colony Optimisation and Swarm Intelligence (2006). He is an associate editor of *Genetic Programming and Evolvable Machines*, *Evolutionary Computation* and the *International Journal of Computational Intelligence Research*. He is an advisory board member of the *Journal on Artificial Evolution and Applications* and an editorial board member of *Swarm Intelligence*. He is a member of the EPSRC Peer Review College, an EU expert evaluator and a grant-proposal referee for Irish, Swiss and Italian funding bodies.

W. B. Langdon was research officer for the Central Electricity Research Laboratories and project manager and technical coordinator for Logica before becoming a prolific, internationally recognised researcher (working at UCL, Birmingham, CWI and Essex). He has written two books, edited six more, and published over 80 papers in international conferences and journals. He is the resource review editor for *Genetic Programming and Evolvable Machines* and a member of the editorial board of *Evolutionary*

Computation. He has been a co-organiser of eight international conferences and workshops, and has given nine tutorials at international conferences. He was elected ISGEC Fellow for his contributions to EC. Dr Langdon has extensive experience designing and implementing GP systems, and is a leader in both the empirical and theoretical analysis of evolutionary systems. He also has broad experience both in industry and academic settings in biomedical engineering, drug design, and bioinformatics.

Nicholas F. McPhee is a Full Professor in Computer Science in the Division of Science and Mathematics, University of Minnesota, Morris. He is an associate editor of the *Journal on Artificial Evolution and Applications*, an editorial board member of *Genetic Programming and Evolvable Machines*, and has served on the program committees for dozens of international events. He has extensive expertise in the design of GP systems, and in the theoretical analysis of their behaviours. His joint work with Poli on the theoretical analysis of GP (McPhee and Poli, 2001; Poli and McPhee, 2001) received the best paper award at the 2001 European Conference on Genetic Programming, and several of his other foundational studies continue to be widely cited. He has also worked closely with biologists on a number of projects, building individual-based models to illuminate genetic interactions and changes in the genotypic and phenotypic diversity of populations.

To

Caterina, Ludovico, Rachele and Leonardo R.P.

Susan and Thomas N.F.M.

Contents

Chapter 1

Introduction

The goal of having computers automatically solve problems is central to artificial intelligence, machine learning, and the broad area encompassed by what Turing called "machine intelligence" (Turing, 1948). Machine learning pioneer Arthur Samuel, in his 1983 talk entitled "AI: Where It Has Been and Where It Is Going" (Samuel, 1983), stated that the main goal of the fields of machine learning and artificial intelligence is:

> "to get machines to exhibit behaviour, which if done by humans, would be assumed to involve the use of intelligence."

Genetic programming (GP) is an evolutionary computation (EC)[1] technique that automatically solves problems without requiring the user to know or specify the form or structure of the solution in advance. At the most abstract level GP is a *systematic, domain-independent* method for getting computers to solve problems *automatically* starting from a *high-level statement* of what needs to be done.

Since its inception, GP has attracted the interest of myriads of people around the globe. This book gives an overview of the basics of GP, summarised important work that gave direction and impetus to the field and discusses some interesting new directions and applications. Things continue to change rapidly in genetic programming as investigators and practitioners discover new methods and applications. This makes it impossible to cover all aspects of GP, and this book should be seen as a snapshot of a particular moment in the history of the field.

---

[1] These are also known as *evolutionary algorithms* or EAs.

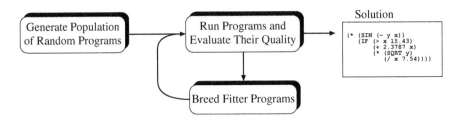

Figure 1.1: The basic control flow for genetic programming, where survival of the fittest is used to find solutions.

1.1   Genetic Programming in a Nutshell

In genetic programming we evolve a population of *computer programs*. That is, generation by generation, GP *stochastically* transforms populations of programs into new, hopefully better, populations of programs, cf. Figure 1.1. GP, like nature, is a random process, and it can never guarantee results. GP's essential randomness, however, can lead it to escape traps which deterministic methods may be captured by. Like nature, GP has been very successful at evolving novel and unexpected ways of solving problems. (See Chapter 12 for numerous examples.)

The basic steps in a GP system are shown in Algorithm 1.1. GP finds out how well a program works by running it, and then comparing its behaviour to some ideal (line 3). We might be interested, for example, in how well a program predicts a time series or controls an industrial process. This comparison is quantified to give a numeric value called *fitness*. Those programs that do well are chosen to breed (line 4) and produce new programs for the next generation (line 5). The primary genetic operations that are used to create new programs from existing ones are:

- **Crossover:** The creation of a child program by combining randomly chosen parts from two selected parent programs.

- **Mutation:** The creation of a new child program by randomly altering a randomly chosen part of a selected parent program.

1.2   Getting Started

Two key questions for those first exploring GP are:

1. What should I read to get started in GP?

2. Should I implement my own GP system or should I use an existing package? If so, what package should I use?

1: Randomly create an *initial population* of programs from the available primitives (more on this in Section 2.2).

2: **repeat**

3: *Execute* each program and ascertain its fitness.

4: *Select* one or two program(s) from the population with a probability based on fitness to participate in genetic operations (Section 2.3).

5: Create new individual program(s) by applying *genetic operations* with specified probabilities (Section 2.4).

6: **until** an acceptable solution is found or some other stopping condition is met (e.g., a maximum number of generations is reached).

7: **return** the best-so-far individual.

Algorithm 1.1: Genetic Programming

The best way to begin is *obviously* by reading this book, so you're off to a good start. We included a wide variety of references to help guide people through at least some of the literature. No single work, however, could claim to be completely comprehensive. Thus Appendix A reviews a whole host of books, videos, journals, conferences, and on-line sources (including several freely available GP systems) that should be of assistance.

We strongly encourage *doing* GP as well as reading about it; the dynamics of evolutionary algorithms are complex, and the experience of tracing through runs is invaluable. In Appendix B we provide the full Java implementation of Riccardo's TinyGP system.

1.3 Prerequisites

Although this book has been written with beginners in mind, unavoidably we had to make some assumptions about the typical background of our readers. The book assumes some working knowledge of computer science and computer programming; this is probably an essential prerequisite to get the most from the book.

We don't expect that readers will have been exposed to other flavours of evolutionary algorithms before, although a little background might be useful. The interested novice can easily find additional information on evolutionary computation thanks to the plethora of tutorials available on the Internet. Articles from Wikipedia and the genetic algorithm tutorial produced by Whitley (1994) should suffice.

1.4   Overview of this Field Guide

As we indicated in the section entitled "What's in this book" (page v), the book is divided up into four parts. In this section, we will have a closer look at their content.

Part I is mainly for the benefit of beginners, so notions are introduced at a relaxed pace. In the next chapter we provide a description of the key elements in GP. These include how programs are stored (Section 2.1), the initialisation of the population (Section 2.2), the selection of individuals (Section 2.3) and the genetic operations of crossover and mutation (Section 2.4). A discussion of the decisions that are needed before running GP is given in Chapter 3. These preparatory steps include the specification of the set of instructions that GP can use to construct programs (Sections 3.1 and 3.2), the definition of a fitness measure that can guide GP towards good solutions (Section 3.3), setting GP parameters (Section 3.4) and, finally, the rule used to decide when to stop a GP run (Section 3.5). To help the reader understand these, Chapter 4 presents a step-by-step application of the preparatory steps (Section 4.1) and a detailed explanation of a sample GP run (Section 4.2).

After these introductory chapters, we go up a gear in Part II where we describe a variety of more advanced GP techniques. Chapter 5 considers additional initialisation strategies and genetic operators for the main GP representation—syntax trees. In Chapter 6 we look at techniques for the evolution of structured and grammatically-constrained programs. In particular, we consider: modular and hierarchical structures including automatically defined functions and architecture-altering operations (Section 6.1), systems that constrain the syntax of evolved programs using grammars or type systems (Section 6.2), and developmental GP (Section 6.3). In Chapter 7 we discuss alternative program representations, namely linear GP (Section 7.1) and graph-based GP (Section 7.2).

In Chapter 8 we review systems where, instead of using mutation and recombination to create new programs, they are simply generated randomly according to a probability distribution which itself evolves. These are known as estimation of distribution algorithms, cf. Sections 8.1 and 8.2. Section 8.3 reviews hybrids between GP and probabilistic grammars, where probability distributions are associated with the elements of a grammar.

Many, if not most, real-world problems are multi-objective, in the sense that their solutions are required to satisfy more than one criterion at the same time. In Chapter 9, we review different techniques that allow GP to solve multi-objective problems. These include the aggregation of multiple objectives into a scalar fitness measure (Section 9.1), the use of the notion of Pareto dominance (Section 9.2), the definition of dynamic or staged fitness functions (Section 9.3), and the reliance on special biases on the genetic operators to aid the optimisation of multiple objectives (Section 9.4).

A variety of methods to speed up, parallelise and distribute genetic programming runs are described in Chapter 10. We start by looking at ways to reduce the number of fitness evaluations or increase their effectiveness (Section 10.1) and ways to speed up their execution (Section 10.2). We then point out (Section 10.3) that faster evaluation is not the only reason for running GP in parallel, as geographic distribution has advantages in its own right. In Section 10.4, we consider the first approach and describe master-slave parallel architectures (Section 10.4.1), running GP on graphics hardware (Section 10.4.2) and FPGAs (Section 10.4.3), and a fast method to exploit the parallelism available on every computer (Section 10.4.4). Finally, Section 10.5 looks at the second approach discussing the geographically distributed evolution of programs. We then give an overview of some of the considerable work that has been done on GP's theory and its practical uses (Chapter 11).

After this review of techniques, Part III provides information for people interested in using GP in practical applications. We survey the enormous variety of applications of GP in Chapter 12. We start with a discussion of the general kinds of problems where GP has proved successful (Section 12.1) and then describe a variety of GP applications, including: curve fitting, data modelling and symbolic regression (Section 12.2); human competitive results (Section 12.3); image analysis and signal processing (Section 12.4); financial trading, time series prediction and economic modelling (Section 12.5); industrial process control (Section 12.6); medicine, biology and bioinformatics (Section 12.7); the evolution of search algorithms and optimisers (Section 12.8); computer games and entertainment applications (Section 12.9); artistic applications (12.10); and GP-based data compression (Section 12.11). This is followed by a chapter providing a collection of troubleshooting techniques used by experienced GP practitioners (Chapter 13) and by our conclusions (Chapter 14).

In Part IV, we provide a resources appendix that reviews the many sources of further information on GP, on its applications, and on related problem solving systems (Appendix A). This is followed by a description and the source code for a simple GP system in Java (Appendix B). The results of a sample run with the system are also described in the appendix and further illustrated via a Flip-O-Rama animation[2] (see Section B.4).

The book ends with a large bibliography containing around 650 references. Of these, around 420 contain pointers to on-line versions of the corresponding papers. While this is very useful on its own, the users of the PDF version of this book will be able to do more if they use a PDF viewer that supports hyperlinks: they will be able to click on the URLs and retrieve the cited articles. Around 550 of the papers in the bibliography are included in

---

[2]This is in the footer of the odd-numbered pages in the bibliography and in the index.

the GP bibliography (Langdon, Gustafson, and Koza, 1995-2008).[3] We have linked those references to the corresponding B<small>IB</small>T_EXentries in the bibliography. Just click on the **GP**<small>BIB</small> symbols to retrieve them instantaneously. Entries in the bibliography typically include keywords, abstracts and often further URLs.

With a slight self-referential violation of bibliographic etiquette, we have also included in the bibliography the *excellent* (Poli et al., 2008) to clarify how to cite this book. L^AT_EX users can find the BibT_EX entry for this book at `http://www.cs.bham.ac.uk/~wbl/biblio/gp-html/poli08_fieldguide.html`.

---

[3] Available at `http://www.cs.bham.ac.uk/~wbl/biblio/`

Part I

Basics

Here Alice steps through the looking glass...

and the Jabberwock is slain.

Chapter 2

Representation, Initialisation and Operators in Tree-based GP

This chapter introduces the basic tools and terminology used in genetic programming. In particular, it looks at how trial solutions are represented in most GP systems (Section 2.1), how one might construct the initial random population (Section 2.2), and how selection (Section 2.3) as well as crossover and mutation (Section 2.4) are used to construct new programs.

2.1 Representation

In GP, programs are usually expressed as *syntax trees* rather than as lines of code. For example Figure 2.1 shows the tree representation of the program max(x+x,x+3*y). The variables and constants in the program (x, y and 3) are leaves of the tree. In GP they are called *terminals*, whilst the arithmetic operations (+, * and max) are internal nodes called *functions*. The sets of allowed functions and terminals together form the *primitive set* of a GP system.

In more advanced forms of GP, programs can be composed of multiple components (e.g., subroutines). In this case the representation used in GP is a set of trees (one for each component) grouped together under a special root node that acts as glue, as illustrated in Figure 2.2. We will call these (sub)trees *branches*. The number and type of the branches in a program, together with certain other features of their structure, form the *architecture* of the program. This is discussed in more detail in Section 6.1.

It is common in the GP literature to represent expressions in a *prefix* notation similar to that used in Lisp or Scheme. For example, `max(x+x,x+3*y)` becomes `(max (+ x x) (+ x (* 3 y)))`. This notation often makes it easier to see the relationship between (sub)expressions and their corresponding (sub)trees. Therefore, in the following, we will use trees and their corresponding prefix-notation expressions interchangeably.

How one implements GP trees will obviously depend a great deal on the programming languages and libraries being used. Languages that provide automatic garbage collection and dynamic lists as fundamental data types make it easier to implement expression trees and the necessary GP operations. Most traditional languages used in AI research (e.g., Lisp and Prolog), many recent languages (e.g., Ruby and Python), and the languages associated with several scientific programming tools (e.g., MATLAB[1] and Mathematica[2]) have these facilities. In other languages, one may have to implement lists/trees or use libraries that provide such data structures.

In high performance environments, the tree-based representation of programs may be too inefficient since it requires the storage and management of numerous pointers. In some cases, it may be desirable to use GP primitives which accept a variable number of arguments (a quantity we will call *arity*). An example is the sequencing instruction **progn**, which accepts any number of arguments, executes them one at a time and then returns the

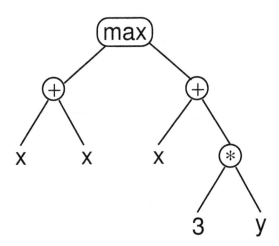

Figure 2.1: GP syntax tree representing `max(x+x,x+3*y)`.

[1]MATLAB is a registered trademark of The MathWorks, Inc
[2]Mathematica is a registered trademark of Wolfram Research, Inc.

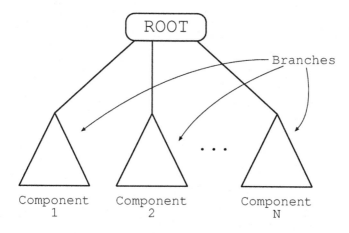

Figure 2.2: Multi-component program representation.

value returned by the last argument. However, fortunately, it is now extremely common in GP applications for all functions to have a fixed number of arguments. If this is the case, then, the brackets in prefix-notation expressions are redundant, and trees can efficiently be represented as simple linear sequences. In effect, the function's name gives its arity and from the arities the brackets can be inferred. For example, the expression (max (+ x x) (+ x (* 3 y))) could be written unambiguously as the sequence max + x x + x * 3 y.

The choice of whether to use such a linear representation or an explicit tree representation is typically guided by questions of convenience, efficiency, the genetic operations being used (some may be more easily or more efficiently implemented in one representation), and other data one may wish to collect during runs. (It is sometimes useful to attach additional information to nodes, which may be easier to implement if they are explicitly represented).

These tree representations are the most common in GP, e.g., numerous high-quality, freely available GP implementations use them (see the resources in Appendix A, page 148, for more information) and so does also the simple GP system described in Appendix B. However, there are other important representations, some of which are discussed in Chapter 7.

2.2   Initialising the Population

Like in other evolutionary algorithms, in GP the individuals in the initial population are typically randomly generated. There are a number of different approaches to generating this random initial population. Here we

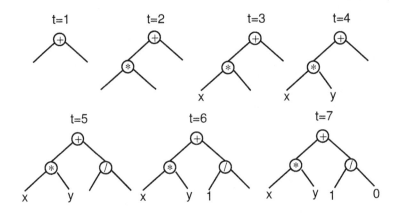

Figure 2.3: Creation of a full tree having maximum depth 2 using the `full` initialisation method (t = time).

will describe two of the simplest (and earliest) methods (the `full` and `grow` methods), and a widely used combination of the two known as *Ramped half-and-half*.

In both the `full` and `grow` methods, the initial individuals are generated so that they do not exceed a user specified maximum depth. The *depth* of a node is the number of edges that need to be traversed to reach the node starting from the tree's root node (which is assumed to be at depth 0). The depth of a tree is the depth of its deepest leaf (e.g., the tree in Figure 2.1 has a depth of 3). In the `full` method (so named because it generates full trees, i.e. all leaves are at the same depth) nodes are taken at random from the function set until the maximum tree depth is reached. (Beyond that depth, only terminals can be chosen.) Figure 2.3 shows a series of snapshots of the construction of a full tree of depth 2. The children of the * and / nodes must be leaves or otherwise the tree would be too deep. Thus, at both steps $t = 3$, $t = 4$, $t = 6$ and $t = 7$ a terminal must be chosen (x, y, 1 and 0, respectively).

Although, the `full` method generates trees where all the leaves are at the same depth, this does not necessarily mean that all initial trees will have an identical number of nodes (often referred to as the *size* of a tree) or the same shape. This only happens, in fact, when all the functions in the primitive set have an equal arity. Nonetheless, even when mixed-arity primitive sets are used, the range of program sizes and shapes produced by the `full` method may be rather limited. The `grow` method, on the contrary, allows for the creation of trees of more varied sizes and shapes. Nodes are selected from the whole primitive set (i.e., functions and terminals) until the depth limit is reached. Once the depth limit is reached only terminals

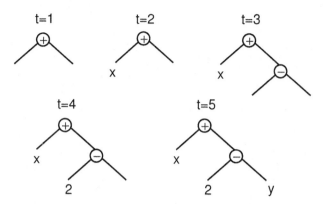

Figure 2.4: Creation of a five node tree using the `grow` initialisation method with a maximum depth of 2 (t = time). A terminal is chosen at $t = 2$, causing the left branch of the root to be closed at that point even though the maximum depth had not been reached.

may be chosen (just as in the `full` method). Figure 2.4 illustrates this process for the construction of a tree with depth limit 2. Here the first argument of the + root node happens to be a terminal. This closes off that branch preventing it from growing any more before it reached the depth limit. The other argument is a function (-), but its arguments are forced to be terminals to ensure that the resulting tree does not exceed the depth limit. Pseudocode for a recursive implementation of both the `full` and `grow` methods is given in Algorithm 2.1.

Because neither the `grow` or `full` method provide a very wide array of sizes or shapes on their own, Koza (1992) proposed a combination called *ramped half-and-half*. Half the initial population is constructed using `full` and half is constructed using `grow`. This is done using a range of depth limits (hence the term "ramped") to help ensure that we generate trees having a variety of sizes and shapes.

While these methods are easy to implement and use, they often make it difficult to control the statistical distributions of important properties such as the sizes and shapes of the generated trees. For example, the sizes and shapes of the trees generated via the `grow` method are highly sensitive to the sizes of the function and terminal sets. If, for example, one has significantly more terminals than functions, the `grow` method will almost always generate very short trees regardless of the depth limit. Similarly, if the number of functions is considerably greater than the number of terminals, then the `grow` method will behave quite similarly to the `full` method. The arities of the functions in the primitive set also influence the size and shape of the

---

procedure: gen_rnd_expr(func_set,term_set,max_d,method)

1: **if** max_d $= 0$ **or** $\left(\text{method} = \text{grow and rand}() < \frac{|\text{term\_set}|}{|\text{term\_set}|+|\text{func\_set}|} \right)$
   then
2:    expr = choose_random_element(term_set)
3: **else**
4:    func = choose_random_element(func_set)
5:    **for** i $= 1$ **to** arity(func) **do**
6:       arg_i = gen_rnd_expr(func_set, term_set, max_d - 1, method);
7:    **end for**
8:    expr = (func, arg_1, arg_2, ...);
9: **end if**
10: **return** expr

Notes: **func_set** is a function set, **term_set** is a terminal set, **max_d** is the maximum allowed depth for expressions, **method** is either `full` or `grow`, **expr** is the generated expression in prefix notation and `rand()` is a function that returns random numbers uniformly distributed between 0 and 1.

Algorithm 2.1: Pseudocode for recursive program generation with the `full` and `grow` methods.

---

trees produced by `grow`.[3] Section 5.1 (page 40) describes other initialisation mechanisms which address these issues.

The initial population need not be entirely random. If something is known about likely properties of the desired solution, trees having these properties can be used to seed the initial population. This, too, will be described in Section 5.1.

2.3   Selection

As with most evolutionary algorithms, genetic operators in GP are applied to individuals that are probabilistically selected based on fitness. That is, better individuals are more likely to have more child programs than inferior individuals. The most commonly employed method for selecting individuals in GP is tournament selection, which is discussed below, followed by fitness-proportionate selection, but any standard evolutionary algorithm selection mechanism can be used.

In *tournament selection* a number of individuals are chosen at random

---

[3]While these are particular problems for the `grow` method, they illustrate a general issue where small (and often apparently inconsequential) changes such as the addition or removal of a few functions from the function set can in fact have significant implications for the GP system, and potentially introduce important but unintended biases.

from the population. These are compared with each other and the best of them is chosen to be the parent. When doing crossover, two parents are needed and, so, two selection tournaments are made. Note that tournament selection only looks at which program is better than another. It does not need to know how much better. This effectively automatically rescales fitness, so that the selection pressure[4] on the population remains constant. Thus, a single extraordinarily good program cannot immediately swamp the next generation with its children; if it did, this would lead to a rapid loss of diversity with potentially disastrous consequences for a run. Conversely, tournament selection amplifies small differences in fitness to prefer the better program even if it is only marginally superior to the other individuals in a tournament.

An element of noise is inherent in tournament selection due to the random selection of candidates for tournaments. So, while preferring the best, tournament selection does ensure that even average-quality programs have some chance of having children. Since tournament selection is easy to implement and provides automatic fitness rescaling, it is commonly used in GP.

Considering that selection has been described many times in the evolutionary algorithms literature, we will not provide details of the numerous other mechanisms that have been proposed. (Goldberg, 1989), for example, describes fitness-proportionate selection, stochastic universal sampling and several others.

2.4 Recombination and Mutation

GP departs significantly from other evolutionary algorithms in the implementation of the operators of crossover and mutation. The most commonly used form of crossover is *subtree crossover*. Given two parents, subtree crossover randomly (and independently) selects a *crossover point* (a node) in each parent tree. Then, it creates the offspring by replacing the subtree rooted at the crossover point in a *copy* of the first parent with a *copy* of the subtree rooted at the crossover point in the second parent, as illustrated in Figure 2.5. Copies are used to avoid disrupting the original individuals. This way, if selected multiple times, they can take part in the creation of multiple offspring programs. Note that it is also possible to define a version of crossover that returns two offspring, but this is not commonly used.

Often crossover points are *not* selected with uniform probability. Typical GP primitive sets lead to trees with an average *branching factor* (the number of children of each node) of at least two, so the majority of the nodes will be leaves. Consequently the uniform selection of crossover points leads

---

[4]A key property of any selection mechanism is *selection pressure*. A system with a strong selection pressure very highly favours the more fit individuals, while a system with a weak selection pressure isn't so discriminating.

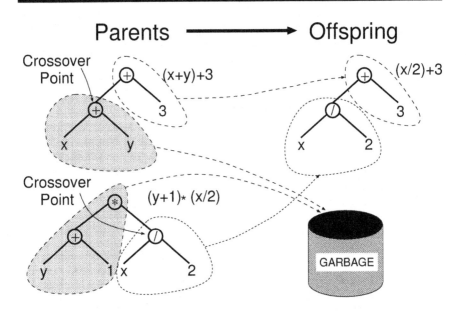

Figure 2.5: Example of subtree crossover. Note that the trees on the left are actually *copies* of the parents. So, their genetic material can freely be used without altering the original individuals.

to crossover operations frequently exchanging only very small amounts of genetic material (i.e., small subtrees); many crossovers may in fact reduce to simply swapping two leaves. To counter this, Koza (1992) suggested the widely used approach of choosing functions 90% of the time and leaves 10% of the time. Many other types of crossover and mutation of GP trees are possible. They will be described in Sections 5.2 and 5.3, pages 42–46.

The most commonly used form of mutation in GP (which we will call *subtree mutation*) randomly selects a mutation point in a tree and substitutes the subtree rooted there with a randomly generated subtree. This is illustrated in Figure 2.6. Subtree mutation is sometimes implemented as crossover between a program and a newly generated random program; this operation is also known as *"headless chicken"* crossover (Angeline, 1997).

Another common form of mutation is *point mutation*, which is GP's rough equivalent of the bit-flip mutation used in genetic algorithms (Goldberg, 1989). In point mutation, a random node is selected and the primitive stored there is replaced with a different random primitive of the same arity taken from the primitive set. If no other primitives with that arity exist, nothing happens to that node (but other nodes may still be mutated). When subtree mutation is applied, this involves the modification of exactly one subtree. Point mutation, on the other hand, is typically applied on a

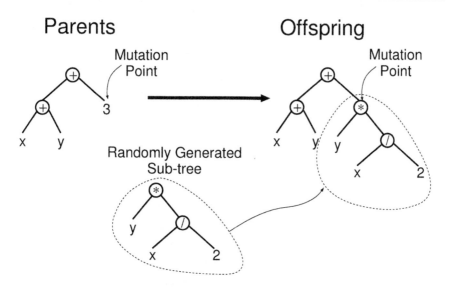

Figure 2.6: Example of subtree mutation.

per-node basis. That is, each node is considered in turn and, with a certain probability, it is altered as explained above. This allows multiple nodes to be mutated independently in one application of point mutation.

The choice of which of the operators described above should be used to create an offspring is probabilistic. Operators in GP are normally mutually exclusive (unlike other evolutionary algorithms where offspring are sometimes obtained via a *composition* of operators). Their probability of application are called *operator rates*. Typically, crossover is applied with the highest probability, the *crossover rate* often being 90% or higher. On the contrary, the *mutation rate* is much smaller, typically being in the region of 1%.

When the rates of crossover and mutation add up to a value p which is less than 100%, an operator called *reproduction* is also used, with a rate of $1 - p$. Reproduction simply involves the selection of an individual based on fitness and the insertion of a copy of it in the next generation.

Chapter 3

Getting Ready to Run Genetic Programming

To apply a GP system to a problem, several decisions need to be made; these are often termed the *preparatory steps*. The key choices are:

1. What it the *terminal set*?

2. What is the *function set*?

3. What is the *fitness measure*?

4. What *parameters* will be used for controlling the run?

5. What will be the *termination* criterion, and what will be designated the *result of the run*?

3.1 Step 1: Terminal Set

While it is common to describe GP as evolving *programs*, GP is not typically used to evolve programs in the familiar Turing-complete languages humans normally use for software development. It is instead more common to evolve programs (or expressions or formulae) in a more constrained and often domain-specific language. The first two preparatory steps, the definition of the terminal and function sets, specify such a language. That is, together they define the ingredients that are available to GP to create computer programs.

The terminal set may consist of:

- *the program's external inputs.* These typically take the form of named variables (e.g., x, y).

- *functions with no arguments.* These may be included because they return different values each time they are used, such as the function rand() which returns random numbers, or a function dist_to_wall() that returns the distance to an obstacle from a robot that GP is controlling. Another possible reason is because the function produces *side effects*. Functions with side effects do more than just return a value: they may change some global data structures, print or draw something on the screen, control the motors of a robot, etc.

- *constants.* These can be pre-specified, randomly generated as part of the tree creation process, or created by mutation.

Using a primitive such as rand can cause the behaviour of an individual program to vary every time it is called, even if it is given the same inputs. This is desirable in some applications. However, we more often want a set of fixed random constants that are generated as part of the process of initialising the population. This is typically accomplished by introducing a terminal that represents an *ephemeral random constant*. Every time this terminal is chosen in the construction of an initial tree (or a new subtree to use in an operation like mutation), a different random value is generated which is then used for that *particular* terminal, and which will remain fixed for the rest of the run. The use of ephemeral random constants is typically denoted by including the symbol ℜ in the terminal set; see Chapter 4 for an example.

3.2   Step 2: Function Set

The function set used in GP is typically driven by the nature of the problem domain. In a simple numeric problem, for example, the function set may consist of merely the arithmetic functions (+, -, *, /). However, all sorts of other functions and constructs typically encountered in computer programs can be used. Table 3.1 shows a sample of some of the functions one sees in the GP literature. Sometimes the primitive set includes specialised functions and terminals which are designed to solve problems in a specific problem domain. For example, if the goal is to program a robot to mop the floor, then the function set might include such actions as move, turn, and swish-the-mop.

Table 3.1: Examples of primitives in GP function and terminal sets.

Function Set	
Kind of Primitive	*Example(s)*
Arithmetic	+, *, /
Mathematical	sin, cos, exp
Boolean	AND, OR, NOT
Conditional	IF-THEN-ELSE
Looping	FOR, REPEAT
⋮	⋮

Terminal Set	
Kind of Primitive	*Example(s)*
Variables	x, y
Constant values	3, 0.45
0-arity functions	rand, go_left

3.2.1   Closure

For GP to work effectively, most function sets are required to have an important property known as *closure* (Koza, 1992), which can in turn be broken down into the properties of *type consistency* and *evaluation safety*.

Type consistency is required because subtree crossover (as described in Section 2.4) can mix and join nodes arbitrarily. As a result it is necessary that *any* subtree can be used in any of the argument positions for every function in the function set, because it is always possible that subtree crossover will generate that combination. It is thus common to require that all the functions be type consistent, i.e., they all return values of the same type, and that each of their arguments also have this type. For example +, -, *, and / can can be defined so that they each take two integer arguments and return an integer. Sometimes type consistency can be weakened somewhat by providing an automatic conversion mechanism between types. We can, for example, convert numbers to Booleans by treating all negative values as false, and non-negative values as true. However, conversion mechanisms can introduce unexpected biases into the search process, so they should be used with care.

The type consistency requirement can seem quite limiting but often simple restructuring of the functions can resolve apparent problems. For example, an `if` function is often defined as taking three arguments: the test, the value to return if the test evaluates to true and the value to return if the test evaluates to false. The first of these three arguments is clearly Boolean, which would suggest that `if` can't be used with numeric functions like +.

This, however, can easily be worked around by providing a mechanism to convert a numeric value into a Boolean automatically as discussed above. Alternatively, one can replace the 3-input if with a function of four (numeric) arguments a, b, c, d. The 4-input if implements "If $a < b$ then return value c otherwise return value d".

An alternative to requiring type consistency is to extend the GP system. Crossover and mutation might explicitly make use of type information so that the children they produce do not contain illegal type mismatches. When mutating a legal program, for example, mutation might be required to generate a subtree which returns the same type as the subtree it has just deleted. This is discussed further in Section 6.2.

The other component of closure is evaluation safety. Evaluation safety is required because many commonly used functions can fail at run time. An evolved expression might, for example, divide by 0, or call MOVE_FORWARD when facing a wall or precipice. This is typically dealt with by modifying the normal behaviour of primitives. It is common to use *protected* versions of numeric functions that can otherwise throw exceptions, such as division, logarithm, exponential and square root. The protected version of a function first tests for potential problems with its input(s) before executing the corresponding instruction; if a problem is spotted then some default value is returned. Protected division (often notated with %) checks to see if its second argument is 0. If so, % typically returns the value 1 (regardless of the value of the first argument).[1] Similarly, in a robotic application a MOVE_AHEAD instruction can be modified to do nothing if a forward move is illegal or if moving the robot might damage it.

An alternative to protected functions is to trap run-time exceptions and strongly reduce the fitness of programs that generate such errors. However, if the likelihood of generating invalid expressions is very high, this can lead to too many individuals in the population having nearly the same (very poor) fitness. This makes it hard for selection to choose which individuals might make good parents.

One type of run-time error that is more difficult to check for is numeric overflow. If the underlying implementation system throws some sort of exception, then this can be handled either by protection or by penalising as discussed above. However, it is common for implementation languages to ignore integer overflow quietly and simply wrap around. If this is unacceptable, then the GP implementation must include appropriate checks to catch and handle such overflows.

---

[1]The decision to return the value 1 provides the GP system with a simple way to generate the constant 1, via an expression of the form (% x x). This combined with a similar mechanism for generating 0 via (- x x) ensures that GP can easily construct these two important constants.

3.2.2 Sufficiency

There is one more property that primitives sets should have: *sufficiency*. Sufficiency means it is possible to express a solution to the problem at hand using the elements of the primitive set.[2] Unfortunately, sufficiency can be guaranteed only for those problems where theory, or experience with other methods, tells us that a solution can be obtained by combining the elements of the primitive set.

As an example of a sufficient primitive set consider {AND, OR, NOT, x1, x2, ..., xN}. It is always sufficient for Boolean induction problems, since it can produce all Boolean functions of the variables x1, x2, ..., xN. An example of insufficient set is {+, -, *, /, x, 0, 1, 2}, which is unable to represent transcendental functions. The function $\exp(x)$, for example, is transcendental and therefore cannot be expressed as a rational function (basically, a ratio of polynomials), and so cannot be represented exactly by any combination of {+, -, *, /, x, 0, 1, 2}. When a primitive set is insufficient, GP can only develop programs that approximate the desired one. However, in many cases such an approximation can be very close and good enough for the user's purpose. Adding a few unnecessary primitives in an attempt to ensure sufficiency does not tend to slow down GP overmuch, although there are cases where it can bias the system in unexpected ways.

3.2.3 Evolving Structures other than Programs

There are many problems where solutions cannot be directly cast as computer programs. For example, in many design problems the solution is an artifact of some type: a bridge, a circuit, an antenna, a lens, etc. GP has been applied to problems of this kind by using a trick: the primitive set is set up so that the evolved programs construct solutions to the problem. This is analogous to the process by which an egg grows into a chicken. For example, if the goal is the automatic creation of an electronic controller for a plant, the function set might include common components such as integrator, differentiator, lead, lag, and gain, and the terminal set might contain reference, signal, and plant output. Each of these primitives, when executed, inserts the corresponding device into the controller being built. If, on the other hand, the goal is to synthesise analogue electrical circuits, the function set might include components such as transistors, capacitors, resistors, etc. See Section 6.3 for more information on developmental GP systems.

---

[2]More formally, the primitive set is sufficient if the set of all the possible recursive compositions of primitives includes at least one solution.

3.3   Step 3: Fitness Function

The first two preparatory steps define the primitive set for GP, and therefore indirectly define the search space GP will explore. This includes all the programs that can be constructed by composing the primitives in all possible ways. However, at this stage, we still do not know which elements or regions of this search space are good. I.e., which regions of the search space include programs that solve, or approximately solve, the problem. This is the task of the fitness measure, which is our primary (and often sole) mechanism for giving a high-level statement of the problem's requirements to the GP system. For example, suppose the goal is to get GP to synthesise an amplifier automatically. Then the fitness function is the mechanism which tells GP to synthesise a circuit that amplifies an incoming signal. (As opposed to evolving a circuit that suppresses the low frequencies of an incoming signal, or computes its square root, etc. etc.)

Fitness can be measured in many ways. For example, in terms of: the amount of *error* between its output and the desired output; the amount of *time* (fuel, money, etc.) required to bring a system to a desired *target state*; the *accuracy* of the program in recognising patterns or classifying objects; the *payoff* that a game-playing program produces; the *compliance* of a structure with user-specified design criteria.

There is something unusual about the fitness functions used in GP that differentiates them from those used in most other evolutionary algorithms. Because the structures being evolved in GP are computer programs, fitness evaluation normally requires executing all the programs in the population, typically multiple times. While one can compile the GP programs that make up the population, the overhead of building a compiler is usually substantial, so it is much more common to use an interpreter to evaluate the evolved programs.

Interpreting a program tree means executing the nodes in the tree in an order that guarantees that nodes are not executed before the value of their arguments (if any) is known. This is usually done by traversing the tree recursively starting from the root node, and postponing the evaluation of each node until the values of its children (arguments) are known. Other orders, such as going from the leaves to the root, are possible. If none of the primitives have side effects, the two orders are equivalent.[3] This depth-first recursive process is illustrated in Figure 3.1. Algorithm 3.1 gives a pseudocode implementation of the interpretation procedure. The code assumes that programs are represented as prefix-notation expressions and that such expressions can be treated as lists of components.

---

[3] *Functional* operations like addition don't depend on the order in which their arguments are evaluated. The order of *side-effecting* operations such as moving or turning a robot, however, is obviously crucial.

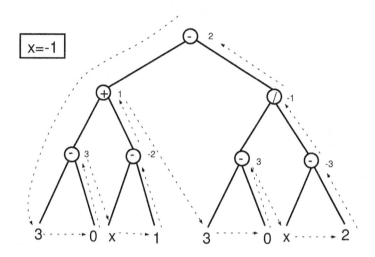

Figure 3.1: Example interpretation of a syntax tree (the terminal x is a variable and has a value of -1). The number to the right of each internal node represents the result of evaluating the subtree root at that node.

---

procedure: eval(expr)

1: **if** expr is a list **then**
2:     proc = expr(1) {Non-terminal: extract root}
3:     **if** proc is a function **then**
4:         value = proc(eval(expr(2)), eval(expr(3)), ...) {Function: evaluate arguments}
5:     **else**
6:         value = proc(expr(2), expr(3), ...) {Macro: don't evaluate arguments}
7:     **end if**
8: **else**
9:     **if** expr is a variable **or** expr is a constant **then**
10:         value = expr {Terminal variable or constant: just read the value}
11:     **else**
12:         value = expr() {Terminal 0-arity function: execute}
13:     **end if**
14: **end if**
15: **return** value

Notes: expr is an expression in prefix notation, expr(1) represents the primitive at the root of the expression, expr(2) represents the first argument of that primitive, expr(3) represents the second argument, etc.

Algorithm 3.1: Interpreter for genetic programming

In some problems we are interested in the *output* produced by a program, namely the value returned when we evaluate the tree starting at the root node. In other problems we are interested in the actions performed by a program composed of functions with side effects. In either case the fitness of a program typically depends on the results produced by its execution on many different inputs or under a variety of different conditions. For example the program might be tested on all possible combinations of inputs x1, x2, ..., xN. Alternatively, a robot control program might be tested with the robot in a number of starting locations. These different test cases typically contribute to the fitness value of a program incrementally, and for this reason are called *fitness cases.*

Another common feature of GP fitness measures is that, for many practical problems, they are *multi-objective*, i.e., they combine two or more different elements that are often in competition with one another. The area of multi-objective optimisation is a complex and active area of research in GP and machine learning in general. See Chapter 9 and also (Deb, 2001).

3.4   Step 4: GP Parameters

The fourth preparatory step specifies the control parameters for the run. The most important control parameter is the *population size*. Other control parameters include the *probabilities of performing the genetic operations*, the *maximum size* for programs and other details of the run.

It is impossible to make general recommendations for setting *optimal* parameter values, as these depend too much on the details of the application. However, genetic programming is in practice robust, and it is likely that many different parameter values will work. As a consequence, one need not typically spend a long time tuning GP for it to work adequately.

It is common to create the initial population randomly using ramped half-and-half (Section 2.2) with a depth range of 2–6. The initial tree sizes will depend upon the number of the functions, the number of terminals and the arities of the functions. However, evolution will quickly move the population away from its initial distribution.

Traditionally, 90% of children are created by subtree crossover. However, the use of a 50-50 mixture of crossover and a variety of mutations (cf. Chapter 5) also appears to work well.

In many cases, the main limitation on the population size is the time taken to evaluate the fitnesses, not the space required to store the individuals. As a rule one prefers to have the largest population size that your system can handle gracefully; normally, the population size should be at least 500, and people often use much larger populations.[4] Often, to a first

---

[4]There are, however, GP systems that frequently use much smaller populations. These

approximation, GP runtime can be estimated by the product of: the number of runs R, the number of generations G, the size of the population P, the average size of the programs s and the number of fitness cases F.

Typically, the number of generations is limited to between ten and fifty; the most productive search is usually performed in those early generations, and if a solution hasn't been found then, it's unlikely to be found in a reasonable amount of time. The folk wisdom on population size is to make it as large as possible, but there are those who suggest using many runs with much smaller populations instead. Some implementations do not require arbitrary limits of tree size. Even so, because of bloat (the uncontrolled growth of program sizes during GP runs; see Section 11.3), it is common to impose either a size or a depth limit or both (see Section 11.3.2).

Sometimes the number of fitness cases is limited by the amount of training data[5] available. In this case, the fitness function should use all of it. (One does not necessarily need to use verification or holdout data, since over-fitting can be avoided by other means, as discussed in Section 13.12, page 140.) In other cases, e.g. 22-bit even parity, there can almost be too much training data. Then the fitness function may be reduced to use just a subset of the training data. This does not necessarily have to be done manually as there are a number of algorithms that dynamically change the test set as the GP runs. (These and other speedup techniques will be discussed in Chapter 13, particularly Section 10.1, page 83.)

It is common to record these details in a tableau, such as Table 4.1 on page 31.

3.5 Step 5: Termination and solution designation

The fifth preparatory step consists of specifying the *termination criterion* and the method of *designating the result* of the run. The termination criterion may include a maximum number of generations to be run as well as a problem-specific success predicate. Typically, the single best-so-far individual is then harvested and designated as the result of the run, although one might wish to return additional individuals and data as necessary or appropriate for the problem domain.

---

typically rely more on mutation than crossover for their primary search mechanism.

[5] *Training data* refers to the test cases used to evaluate the fitness of the evolved individuals.

Chapter 4

Example Genetic Programming Run

This chapter provides an illustrative run of GP in which the goal is to automatically create a program with a target input/output behaviour. In particular, we want to evolve an expression whose values match those of the quadratic polynomial $x^2 + x + 1$ in the range $[-1, +1]$. The process of mechanically creating a computer program that fit certain numerical data is sometimes called *system identification* or *symbolic regression* (see Section 12.2 for more).

We begin with the five preparatory steps from the previous chapter and then describe in detail the events in one run.

4.1 Preparatory Steps

The purpose of the first two preparatory steps is to specify the ingredients the evolutionary process can use to construct potential solutions. Because the problem is to find a mathematical function of one independent variable, x, the terminal set (the inputs of the to-be-evolved programs) must include this variable. The terminal set also includes ephemeral random constants drawn from some reasonable range,[1] say from -5.0 to $+5.0$, as described in

---

[1]What is a "reasonable" range is likely to be *extremely* problem dependent. While in theory you can build up large constants using small constants and arithmetic operators, the performance of your system is likely to improve considerably if you provide constants of roughly the right magnitude from the beginning. Your choice of genetic operators can also be important here. If you're finding that your system is struggling to evolve the right constants, it may be helpful to introduce mutation operators specifically designed to search of the space of constants.

Section 3.1. Thus the terminal set, T, is

$$T = \{x, \Re\}.$$

The statement of the problem does not specify which functions may be employed in the to-be-evolved program. One simple choice for the function set is the four ordinary arithmetic functions: addition, subtraction, multiplication and division. Most numeric regression problems will require at least these operations, sometimes with additional functions such as sin() and log(). We will use the simple function set

$$F = \{+, -, *, \%\},$$

where % is protected division as discussed in Section 3.2.1. Note that the target polynomial can be expressed exactly using the terminal and function sets we have chosen, so these primitives are sufficient (cf. page 23) for the quadratic polynomial problem.

The third preparatory step involves constructing the fitness measure that specifies what the user wants. The high-level goal of this problem is to find a program whose output is equal to the values of the quadratic polynomial x^2+x+1. Therefore, the fitness assigned to a particular individual in the population must reflect how closely the output of an individual program comes to the target polynomial $x^2 + x + 1$.

In principle, the fitness measure could be defined in terms of the mathematical integral of the difference between the evolved function and the target function. However, for most symbolic regression problems, it is not practical or even possible to compute the value of the integral analytically. Thus, it is common to define the fitness to be the *sum of absolute errors* measured at different values of the independent variable x in the range $[-1.0, +1.0]$. In particular, we will measure the errors for $x \in \{-1.0, -0.9, \cdots, 0.9, 1.0\}$. A smaller value of fitness (error) is better; a fitness (error) of zero would indicate a perfect fit. With this definition, our fitness is (approximately) proportional to the area between the parabola $x^2 + x + 1$ and the curve representing the candidate individual (see Figure 4.2 for examples).

The fourth step is where we set our run parameters. The population size in this small illustrative example will be just four. The population size for a run of GP typically consists of thousands of individuals, but we will use this tiny population size to keep the example manageable. The crossover operation is commonly used to generate about 90% of the individuals in the population; the reproduction operation (where a fit individual is simply copied from one generation to the next) is used to generate about 8% of the population; the mutation operation is used to generate about 1% of the population; and the architecture-altering operations (see Section 6.1.2) are used to generate perhaps 1% of the population. However, because this example involves an abnormally small population of only four individuals,

Table 4.1: Parameters for example genetic programming run

Objective:	Find program whose output matches $x^2 + x + 1$ over the range $-1 \leq x \leq +1$.
Function set:	$+$, $-$, $\%$ (protected division), and $\times$; all operating on floats
Terminal set:	x, and constants chosen randomly between -5 and $+5$
Fitness:	sum of absolute errors for $x \in \{-1.0, -0.9, \ldots 0.9, 1.0\}$
Selection:	fitness proportionate (roulette wheel) non elitist
Initial pop:	ramped half-and-half (depth 1 to 2. 50% of terminals are constants)
Parameters:	population size 4, 50% subtree crossover, 25% reproduction, 25% subtree mutation, no tree size limits
Termination:	Individual with fitness better than 0.1 found

the crossover operation will be used twice (each time generating one individual), which corresponds to a crossover rate of 50%, while the mutation and reproduction operations will each be used to generate one individual. These are therefore applied with a rate of 25% each. For simplicity, the architecture-altering operations are not used for this problem.

In the fifth and final step we need to specify a termination condition. A reasonable termination criterion for this problem is that the run will continue from generation to generation until the fitness (or error) of some individual is less than 0.1. In this contrived example, our example run will (atypically) yield an algebraically perfect solution with a fitness of zero after just one generation.

4.2 Step-by-Step Sample Run

Now that we have performed the five preparatory steps, the run of GP can be launched. The GP setup is summarised in Table 4.1.

4.2.1 Initialisation

GP starts by randomly creating a population of four individual computer programs. The four programs are shown in Figure 4.1 in the form of trees.

The first randomly constructed program tree (Figure 4.1a) is equivalent to the expression $x+1$. The second program (Figure 4.1b) adds the constant terminal 1 to the result of multiplying x by x and is equivalent to x^2+1. The third program (Figure 4.1c) adds the constant terminal 2 to the constant terminal 0 and is equivalent to the constant value 2. The fourth program (Figure 4.1d) is equivalent to x.

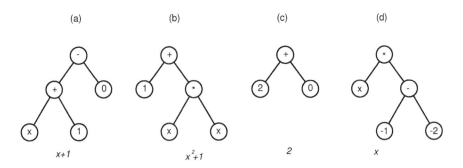

Figure 4.1: Initial population of four randomly created individuals of generation 0.

4.2.2 Fitness Evaluation

Randomly created computer programs will typically be very poor at solving any problem. However, even in a population of randomly created programs, some programs are better than others. The four random individuals from generation 0 in Figure 4.1 produce outputs that deviate by different amounts from the target function $x^2 + x + 1$. Figure 4.2 compares the plots of each of the four individuals in Figure 4.1 and the target quadratic function $x^2 + x + 1$. The sum of absolute errors for the straight line $x + 1$ (the first individual) is 7.7 (Figure 4.2a). The sum of absolute errors for the parabola $x^2 + 1$ (the second individual) is 11.0 (Figure 4.2b). The sums of the absolute errors for the remaining two individuals are 17.98 (Figure 4.2c) and 28.7 (Figure 4.2d).

As can be seen in Figure 4.2, the straight line $x + 1$ (Figure 4.2a) is closer to the parabola $x^2 + x + 1$ in the range from -1 to $+1$ than any of three other programs in the population. This straight line is, of course, not equivalent to the parabola $x^2 + x + 1$; it is not even a quadratic function. It is merely the best candidate that happened to emerge from the blind (and very limited) random search of generation 0.

> *In the valley of the blind,*
> *the one-eyed man is king.*

4.2.3 Selection, Crossover and Mutation

After the fitness of each individual in the population is found, GP then probabilistically selects the fitter programs from the population to act as the parents of the next generation. The genetic operations are applied to the selected individuals to create offspring programs. The important point is that our selection process is not greedy. Individuals that are known to be inferior still have some chance of being selected. The best individual in the population is not guaranteed to be selected and the worst individual in the

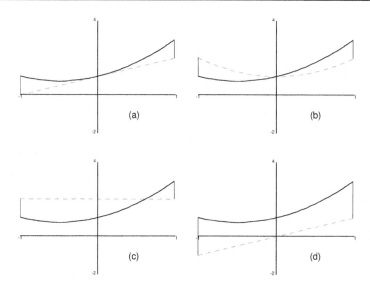

Figure 4.2: Graphs of the evolved functions from generation 0. The solid line in each plot is the target function $x^2 + x + 1$, with the dashed line being the evolved functions from the first generation (see Figure 4.1). The fitness of each of the four randomly created individuals of generation 0 is approximately proportional to the area between two curves, with the actual fitness values being 7.7, 11.0, 17.98 and 28.7 for individuals (a) through (d), respectively.

population will not necessarily be excluded.

In this example we will start with the reproduction operation. Because the first individual (Figure 4.1a) is the most fit individual in the population, it is very likely to be selected to participate in a genetic operation. Let us suppose that this particular individual is, in fact, selected for reproduction. If so, it is copied, without alteration, into the next generation (generation 1). It is shown in Figure 4.3a as part of the population of the new generation.

We next perform the mutation operation. Because selection is probabilistic, it is possible that the third best individual in the population (Figure 4.1c) is selected. One of the three nodes of this individual is then randomly picked as the site for the mutation. In this example, the constant terminal 2 is picked as the mutation site. This program is then randomly mutated by deleting the entire subtree rooted at the picked point (in this case, just the constant terminal 2) and inserting a subtree that is randomly constructed in the same way that the individuals of the initial random population were originally created. In this particular instance, the randomly grown subtree computes x divided by x using the protected division oper-

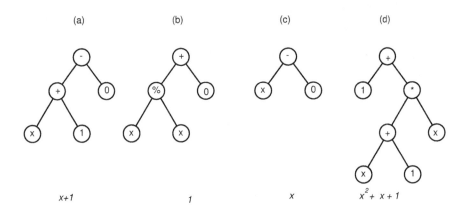

Figure 4.3: Population of generation 1 (after one reproduction, one mutation, and two one-offspring crossover operations).

ation %. The resulting individual is shown in Figure 4.3b. This particular
mutation changes the original individual from one having a constant value
of 2 into one having a constant value of 1, improving its fitness from 17.98
to 11.0.

Finally, we use the crossover operation to generate our final two individuals for the next generation. Because the first and second individuals in
generation 0 are both relatively fit, they are likely to be selected to participate in crossover. However, selection can always pick suboptimal individuals. So, let us assume that in our first application of crossover the pair of
selected parents is composed of the above-average tree in Figures 4.1a and
the below-average tree in Figure 4.1d. One point of the first parent, namely
the + function in Figure 4.1a, is randomly picked as the crossover point for
the first parent. One point of the second parent, namely the leftmost terminal x in Figure 4.1d, is randomly picked as the crossover point for the second
parent. The crossover operation is then performed on the two parents. The
offspring (Figure 4.3c) is equivalent to x and is not particularly noteworthy.

Let us now assume, that in our second application of crossover, selection
chooses the two most fit individuals as parents: the individual in Figure 4.1b
as the first parent, and the individual in Figure 4.1a as the second. Let us
further imagine that crossover picks the leftmost terminal x in Figure 4.1b
as a crossover point for the first parent, and the + function in Figure 4.1a as
the crossover point for the second parent. Now the offspring (Figure 4.3d)
is equivalent to $x^2 + x + 1$ and has a fitness (sum of absolute errors) of zero.

4.2.4   Termination and Solution Designation

Because the fitness of the individual in Figure 4.3d is below 0.1, the termination criterion for the run is satisfied and the run is automatically terminated. This best-so-far individual (Figure 4.3d) is then designated as the result of the run.

Note that the best-of-run individual (Figure 4.3d) incorporates a good trait (the quadratic term x^2) from the first parent (Figure 4.1b) with two other good traits (the linear term x and constant term of 1) from the second parent (Figure 4.1a). The crossover operation thus produced a solution to this problem by recombining good traits from these two relatively fit parents into a superior (indeed, perfect) offspring.

This is, obviously, a highly simplified example, and the dynamics of a real GP run are typically far more complex than what is presented here. Also, in general, there is no guarantee that an exact solution like this will be found by GP.

Part II

Advanced Genetic Programming

In which a search is organdized ...

and Piglet encounters the Heffalump of Bloat.

Chapter 5

Alternative Initialisations and Operators in Tree-based GP

The genetic programming system described in the preceding chapters is just the beginning; in many ways it is the simplest thing that could possibly work. Most of the techniques described in Part I date back to the late 1980's and early 1990's, a wide array of alternatives and extensions have been explored since. A full catalogue of these would be far beyond the scope of this book. The chapters in Part II survey a number of the more prominent or historically important extensions to GP, particularly (but not exclusively) in relation to the tree-based representation for programs.

We start, in this chapter, by reviewing a variety of initialisation strategies (Section 5.1) and genetic operators (Sections 5.2 and 5.3) for tree-based GP not covered in Part I. We also briefly look at some hybridisations of GP with other techniques (Section 5.4).

5.1   Constructing the Initial Population

Koza's ramped half-and-half method is the most common way of creating the initial GP population (cf. Section 2.2, page 11). However, there are several other ways of constructing a collection of random trees. In Section 5.1.2 we will briefly consider an unexpected impact of population initialisation. There has also been some work with non-random or informed starting points (cf. Section 5.1.3).

5.1.1   Uniform Initialisation

The shape of the initial trees can be lost within a few generations (more on this below). However, a good start given by the initial population can still be crucial to the success of a GP run. In general, there are an infinite number of possible computer programs. This means that it is impossible to search them uniformly. Therefore, any method used to create the initial population will have a bias. For example, ramped half-and-half tends to create bushy trees. Such trees have a higher proportion of solutions to symmetric problems, such as parity. Conversely, the smallest solution to the Sante Fe ant trail-following problem is more randomly shaped (Langdon and Poli, 1998a). This is partly why ramped half-and-half is very poor at finding programs which can navigate the Sante Fe trail. Another reason is that many of the programs generated by ramped half-and-half (with standard parameters) are simply too small. Chellapilla (1997a) claims good results when the size of the initial trees was more tightly controlled.

Iba (1996a) and Bohm and Geyer-Schulz (1996) report methods to precisely sample trees uniformly based on Alonso's bijective algorithm (Alonso and Schott, 1995). Although this algorithm has been criticised (Luke, 2000) for being computationally expensive, it can be readily used in practice. Langdon (2000) introduced the *ramped uniform initialisation* which extends Alonso's bijective algorithm by allowing the user to specify a range of initial tree sizes. It then generates equal numbers of random trees for each length in the chosen range. (C++ code can be obtained from ftp://cs.ucl.ac.uk/genetic/gp-code/rand_tree.cc.)

With these more "uniform" initialisations, most trees are asymmetric with some leaves very close to the root of the tree. This is quite different from the trees generated by ramped half-and-half which are on average some distance from the root. Uniform sampling may be better in problems where the desired solutions are asymmetric with some leaves being much more important than others. For example, in data mining it is common to look for solutions with a few dominant variables (which may be close to the root node) whilst other variables are of little or no interest and may be some distance from the root (or indeed not present in the tree). On the other hand, problems like multiplexer or parity require all the inputs to be used and are of similar importance. Bushier trees may be better at solving such problems.

5.1.2   Initialisation may Affect Bloat

Crossover has a strong preference for creating a very non-uniform distributions of tree sizes (Poli, Langdon, and Dignum, 2007). Crossover generates very short programs much more often than longer ones. Selection can only partially combat this tendency. Typically, crossover will totally rearrange the size and shape of the initial trees within a few generations. As discussed in Section 11.3.1 (page 101), the excessive sampling of short programs appears to be an important cause of bloat (the uncontrolled growth of programs during GP runs, which will be described in more detail in Section 11.3, page 101 onwards). It has been shown (Dignum and Poli, 2007) that when the initial population is created with the size distribution preferred by crossover (see Section 11.3.1), bloat is more marked. The distribution has a known mathematical formula (it is a Lagrange distribution of the second kind), but in practice it can be created by simply performing multiple rounds of crossover on a population created in the traditional way before the GP run starts. This is known as *Lagrange initialisation*. These findings suggest that initialisation methods which tend to produce many short programs may in fact induce bloat sooner than methods that produce distributions more skewed towards larger programs.

5.1.3   Seeding

The most common way of starting a GP run from an informed non-random point is *seeding* the initial population with an individual which, albeit not a solution, is thought to be a good starting point. Such a seed may have been produced by an earlier GP run or perhaps constructed by the user (Aler, Borrajo, and Isasi, 2002; Holmes, 1995; Hsu and Gustafson, 2001; Langdon and Nordin, 2000; Langdon and Treleaven, 1997; Westerberg and Levine, 2001). However, Marek, Smart, and Martin (2002) reported that hand written programs may not be robust enough to prosper in an evolving population.

One point to be careful of is that such a seed individual is liable to be much better than randomly created trees. Thus, its descendants may take over the population within a few generations. So, under evolution the seeded population is initially liable to lose diversity rapidly. Furthermore, depending upon the details of the selection scheme used, a single seed individual may have some chance of being removed from the population. Both problems are normally dealt with by filling the whole population with either identical or mutated copies of the seed. This method creates a low diversity initial population in a controlled way, thereby avoiding the initial uncontrolled loss of diversity associated with single seeds. Furthermore, with many copies of the seed, few selection methods will have much chance of removing all copies of the seed before they are able to create children. Diversity preserving techniques, such as multi-objective GP (e.g., (Parrott, Li, and Ciesielski, 2005), (Setzkorn, 2005) and Chapter 9), demes (Langdon, 1998) (see Section 10.3), fitness sharing (Goldberg, 1989) and the use of multiple seed trees, might also be good cures for the problems associated with the use of a single seed. In any case, the diversity of the population should be monitored to ensure that there is significant mixing of different initial trees.

5.2 GP Mutation

5.2.1 Is Mutation Necessary?

Mutation was used in early experiments in the evolution of programs, e.g., in (Bickel and Bickel, 1987; Cramer, 1985; Fujiki and Dickinson, 1987). It was not, however, used in (Koza, 1992) and (Koza, 1994), as Koza wished to demonstrate that mutation was not necessary and that GP was not performing a simple random search. This has significantly influenced the field, and mutation is often omitted from GP runs. While mutation is not necessary for GP to solve many problems, O'Reilly (1995) argued that mutation — in combination with simulated annealing or stochastic iterated hill climbing — can perform as well as crossover-based GP in some cases. Nowadays, mutation is widely used in GP, especially in modelling applications. Koza also advises to use of a low level of mutation; see, for example, (Koza, Bennett, Andre, and Keane, 1996b).

Comparisons of crossover and mutation suggest that including mutation can be advantageous. Chellapilla (1997b) found that a combination of six mutation operators performed better than previously published GP work on four simple problems. Harries and Smith (1997) also found that mutation based hill climbers outperformed crossover-based GP systems on similar problems. Luke and Spector (1997) suggested that the situation is complex, and that the relative performance of crossover and mutation depends on both the problem and the details of the GP system.

5.2.2 Mutation Cookbook

With linear bit string GAs, mutation usually consists of random changes in bit values. In contrast, in GP there are many mutation operators in use. Often multiple types of mutation are beneficially used simultaneously (e.g., see (Kraft, Petry, Buckles, and Sadasivan, 1994) and (Angeline, 1996)). We describe a selection of mutation operators below:

Subtree mutation replaces a randomly selected subtree with another randomly created subtree (Koza, 1992, page 106). Kinnear (1993) defined a similar mutation operator, but with a restriction that prevents the offspring from being more than 15% deeper than its parent.

Size-fair subtree mutation was proposed in two forms by Langdon (1998). In both cases, the new random subtree is, on average, the same size as the code it replaces. The size of the random code is given either by the size of another random subtree in the program or chosen at random in the range $[l/2, 3l/2]$ (where l is the size of the subtree being replaced). The first of these methods samples uniformly in the space of possible programs, whereas the second samples uniformly in the space of program lengths. Experiments suggested that there was far more bloat (cf. Section 11.3.1 page 101) with the first mutation operator.

Node replacement mutation (also known as *point mutation*) is similar to bit string mutation in that it randomly changes a point in the individual. In linear GAs the change would be a bit flip. In GP, instead, a node in the tree is randomly selected and randomly changed. To ensure the tree remains legal, the replacement node has the same number of arguments as the node it is replacing, e.g. (McKay, Willis, and Barton, 1995, page 488).

Hoist mutation creates a new offspring individual which is copy of a randomly chosen subtree of the parent. Thus, the offspring will be smaller than the parent and will have a different root node (Kinnear, 1994a).

Shrink mutation replaces a randomly chosen subtree with a randomly created terminal (Angeline, 1996). This is a special case of subtree mutation where the replacement tree is a terminal. As with hoist mutation, it is motivated by the desire to reduce program size.

Permutation mutation selects a random function node in a tree and then randomly permuting its arguments (subtrees). Koza (1992) used permutation in one experiment [page 600] where it was shown to have little effect. In contrast, Maxwell (1996) had more success with a mutation operator called *swap*, which is simply a permutation mutation restricted to binary non-commutative functions.

Mutating constants at random Schoenauer, Sebag, Jouve, Lamy, and Maitournam (1996) mutated constants by adding random noise from a Gaussian distribution. Each change to a constant was considered a separate mutation.

Mutating constants systematically A variety of potentially expensive optimisation tools have been applied to try and fine-tune an existing program by finding the "best" value for the constants within it. Indeed *STROGANOFF* (Iba, Sato, and de Garis, 1995b; Nikolaev and Iba, 2006) optimises each tree modified by crossover. Clever mechanisms are employed to minimise the computation required.

(McKay et al., 1995, page 489) is more in keeping with traditional GP and uses a mutation operator that operates on terminals, replacing input variables by constants and *vice versa*. In this approach "whenever a new constant is introduced [...] a non-linear least squares optimisation is performed to obtain the 'best' value of the constant(s)". Schoenauer, Lamy, and Jouve (1995) also used a mutation operator that affects all constants in an individual where "a numerical partial gradient ascent is achieved to reach the nearest local optimum". Finally, Sharman, Esparcia Alcazar, and Li (1995) used simulated annealing to update numerical values (which represented signal amplification gains) within individuals.

5.3   GP Crossover

During biological sexual reproduction, the genetic material from both mother and father is combined in such a way that genes in the child are in approximately the same position as they were in its parents. This is quite different from traditional tree-based GP crossover, which can move a subtree to a totally different position in the tree structure.

Crossover operators that tend to preserve the position of genetic material are called *homologous*, and several notions of homologous crossover have been proposed for GP. It is fairly straightforward to realise homologous crossover when using linear representations, and homologous operators are widely used in linear GP (cf. Figure 7.4, page 65) (Defoin Platel, Clergue, and Collard, 2003; Francone, Conrads, Banzhaf, and Nordin, 1999; Hansen, 2003; Hansen, Lowry, Meservy, and McDonald, 2007; Nordin, Banzhaf, and Francone, 1999; O'Neill, Ryan, Keijzer, and Cattolico, 2003). Various forms of homologous crossover have also been proposed for tree-based GP (Collet, 2007; Langdon, 2000; Lones, 2003; MacCallum, 2003; Yamamoto and Tschudin, 2005).

The oldest homologous crossover in tree-based GP is *one-point crossover* (Langdon and Poli, 2002; Poli and Langdon, 1997, 1998a). This works by selecting a *common* crossover point in the parent programs and then swapping the corresponding subtrees. To allow for the two parents having different shapes, one-point crossover analyses the two trees from the root nodes and selects the crossover point only from the parts of the two trees in the *common region* (see Figure 5.1). In the common region, the parents have the same shape.[1] The common region is related to homology, in the sense that the common region represents the result of a matching process between parent trees. Within the common region between two parent trees, the transfer of homologous primitives can happen like it does in a linear bit string genetic algorithm.

Uniform crossover for trees (Poli and Langdon, 1998b) works (in the common region) like uniform crossover in GAs. That is, the offspring are created by visiting the nodes in the common region and flipping a coin at

---

[1] Nodes in the common region need not be identical but they must have the same arity. That is, they must both be leaves or both be functions with the same number of inputs.

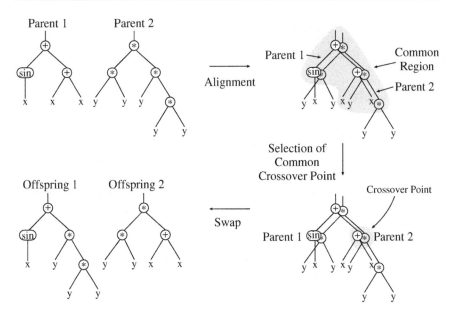

Figure 5.1: Example of one-point crossover between parents of different sizes and shapes.

each locus to decide whether the corresponding offspring node should be picked from the first or the second parent. If a node to be inherited belongs to the base of the common region and is a function, then the subtree rooted there is inherited as well. With this form of crossover, there can be a greater mixing of the code near the root than with other operators.

In *context-preserving crossover* (D'haeseleer, 1994), the crossover points are constrained to have the same coordinates, like in one-point crossover. Note that the crossover points are not limited to the common region.

In *size-fair crossover* (Langdon, 1999a, 2000) the first crossover point is selected randomly, as with standard crossover. Then the size of the subtree to be removed from the first parent is calculated. This is used to constrain the choice of the second crossover point so as to guarantee that the subtree excised from the second parent will not be "unfairly" big.

Harries and Smith (1997) suggested five new crossover operators that are like standard crossover but with probabilistic restrictions on the depth of crossover points within the parent trees.

Since crossover and mutation are specific to the representation used in GP, each new representation tends to need new crossover and mutation operators. For example "ripple crossover" (O'Neill et al., 2003) is a way of looking at crossover in grammatical evolution (Section 6.2.3 page 55).

As we shall see in Chapter 7, specific crossover operators exist for linear GP (Section 7.1) and graph based GP systems (Section 7.2), such as PDGP (page 65), PADO (page 67) and Cartesian GP (page 67).

5.4   Other Techniques

GP can be hybridised with other techniques. For example, Iba, de Garis, and Sato (1994), Nikolaev and Iba (2006), and Zhang and Mühlenbein (1995) have incorporated information theoretic and minimum description length ideas into GP fitness functions to provide a degree of regularisation and so avoid over-fitting (and bloat, see Section 11.3). As mentioned in Section 6.2.3, computer language grammars can be incorporated into GP.

Whereas genetic programming typically uses an evolutionary algorithm to search the space of computer programs, various other heuristic search methods can also be applied to program search, including: enumeration (Olsson, 1995), hill climbing (O'Reilly and Oppacher, 1994a), and simulated annealing (O'Reilly, 1996; Tsoulos and Lagaris, 2006). As discussed in Chapter 8, it is also possible to extend Estimation of Distribution Algorithms (EDAs) to the variable size representations used in GP.

Another alternative is to use *co-evolution* with multiple populations, where the fitness of individuals in one population depends on the behaviour of individuals in other populations. There have been many successful applications of co-evolution in GP, including (Azaria and Sipper, 2005a; Brameier, Haan, Krings, and MacCallum, 2006; Buason, Bergfeldt, and Ziemke, 2005; Channon, 2006; Dolinsky, Jenkinson, and Colquhoun, 2007; Funes, Sklar, Juille, and Pollack, 1998a; Gagné and Parizeau, 2007; Hillis, 1992; Hornby and Pollack, 2001; Mendes, de B. Voznika, Nievola, and Freitas, 2001; Piaseczny, Suzuki, and Sawai, 2004; Schmidt and Lipson, 2006; Sharabi and Sipper, 2006; Soule, 2003; Soule and Komireddy, 2006; Spector, 2002; Spector and Klein, 2006; Spector, Klein, Perry, and Feinstein, 2005b; Wilson and Heywood, 2007; Zhang and Cho, 1999).

Finally, it is worth mentioning that program trees can be manipulated with *editing* operations (Koza, 1992). For example, if the root node of a subtree is × but one of its arguments is always guaranteed to evaluate to 0, then we can replace the subtree rooted there with the terminal 0. If the root node of a subtree is + and one argument evaluates to 0, we can replace the subtree with the other argument of the +. Editing can reduce the complexity of evolved solutions and can make them easier to understand. However, it may also lead to GP getting stuck in local optima, so editing operations should probably be used sparingly at run time. Other *reorganisation operations* of various types are also possible. For example, after trees are generated by GP, (Garcia-Almanza and Tsang, 2006, 2007) prune branches and combine branches from different trees.

Chapter 6

Modular, Grammatical and Developmental Tree-based GP

This chapter discusses advanced techniques that are primarily focused on two important issues in genetic programming: modularity and constraint. In Section 6.1 we explore the evolution of modular, hierarchical structures, and in Section 6.2 we looks at ways of constraining the evolutionary process, typically based on some sort of domain knowledge. We also look at using GP to evolve programs which themselves develop solutions (Section 6.3) or even construct other programs (Section 6.4).

6.1 Evolving Modular and Hierarchical Structures

The construction of any highly complex object or individual, whether an oak tree or an airliner, typically uses hierarchical, modular structures to manage and organise that complexity. Animals develop in a highly regular way that yields a hierarchical structure of components ranging from systems and organs down to cells and organelles. GP, as described so far, is typically used to evolve expressions that, while being suitable solutions to many problems, rarely exhibit any large-scale modular structure.

Given the pervasiveness of hierarchical structure as an organisational tool in both biology and engineering, it seems likely that such modular structure could be valuable in genetic programming as well. Consequently, this has been a subject of study from the early days of genetic programming. For example, Angeline and Pollack (1992) created dynamic libraries of subtrees

47

taken from parts of fit GP trees. Special mutation operations allowed the GP population to share code by referring to the same code within the library. Subsequently, Angeline suggested that the scheme's advantages lay in allowing GP individuals to access far more code than they actually "held" within themselves, rather than principally in developing more modular code. Rosca and Ballard (1996a) used a similar scheme, but were able to use much more information from the fitness function to guide the selection of the code to be inserted into the library and its subsequent use by members of the GP population. Olsson (1999, 1995) later developed an abstraction operator for use in his ADATE system, where sub-functions (anonymous lambda expressions) were automatically extracted. Unlike Angeline's library approach, Olsson's modules remained attached to the individual they were extracted from.

Koza's *automatically defined functions* (ADFs) (Koza, 1994) remain the most widely used method of evolving reusable components and have been used successfully in a variety of settings. Basic ADFs (covered in Section 6.1.1) use a fixed architecture specified in advance by the user. Koza later extended this using *architecture altering operations* (Section 6.1.2), which allow the architecture to evolve along with the programs.

6.1.1   Automatically Defined Functions

Human programmers organise sequences of repeated steps into reusable components such as subroutines, functions and classes. They then repeatedly invoke these components, typically with different inputs. Reuse eliminates the need to "reinvent the wheel" every time a particular sequence of steps is needed. Reuse also makes it possible to exploit a problem's modularities, symmetries and regularities (thereby potentially accelerate the problem-solving process). This can be taken further, as programmers typically organise these components into hierarchies in which top level components call lower level ones, which call still lower levels, etc. Koza's ADFs provide a mechanism by which the evolutionary process can evolve these kinds of potentially reusable components. We will review the basic concepts here, but ADFs are discussed in great detail in (Koza, 1994).

When ADFs are used, a program consists of multiple components. These typically consist of one or more function-defining branches (i.e., ADFs), as well as one or more main result-producing branches (the *RPB*), as illustrated in the example in Figure 6.1. The RPB is the "main" program that is executed when the individual is evaluated. It can, however, call the ADFs, which can in turn potentially call each other. A single ADF may be called multiple times by the same RPB, or by a combination of the RPB and other ADFs, allowing the logic that evolution has assembled in that ADF to be re-used in different contexts.

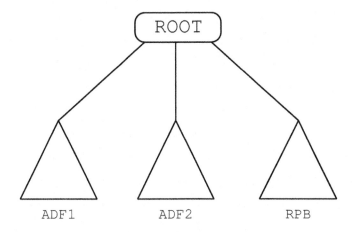

Figure 6.1: Example of program structure with two automatically-defined functions (`ADF1` and `ADF2`) and one result-producing branch (RPB).

Consider, for example, the following individual consisting of a result-producing branch and a single ADF:

$$\text{RPB} : \text{ADF}(\text{ADF}(\text{ADF}(x))) \tag{6.1}$$

$$\text{ADF} : \text{arg0} \times \text{arg0} \tag{6.2}$$

The ADF (Equation 6.2) is simply the squaring function, but by combining this multiple times in the RPB (Equation 6.1) this individual computes x^8 in a highly compact fashion.

It is important to not be fooled by a tidy example like this. ADFs evolved in real applications are typically complex and can be very difficult to understand. Further, simply including ADFs provides no guarantee of modular re-use. As is discussed in Chapter 13, there are no silver bullets. It may be that the RPB never calls an ADF or only calls it once. It is also common for an ADF to not actually encapsulate any significant logic. For example, an ADF might be as simple as a single terminal, in which case it is essentially just providing a new name for that terminal.

In Koza's approach, each ADF is attached (as a branch) to a *specific* individual in the population. This is in contrast to both Angeline's and Rosca's systems mentioned above, both of which have general pools of modules or components which are shared across the population. Sometimes recursion is allowed in ADFs, but this frequently leads to infinite computations. Typically, recursion is prevented by imposing an order on the ADFs within an individual and by restricting calls so that ADF_i can only call ADF_j if $i < j$.

In the presence of ADFs, recombination operators are typically constrained to respect the larger structure. That is, during crossover, a subtree from ADF_i can only be swapped with a subtree from another individual's ADF_i.

The program's result-producing branch and its ADFs typically have different function and terminal sets. For example, the terminal set for ADFs usually include arguments, such as arg0, arg1. Typically the user must decide in advance the primitive sets, the number of ADFs and any call restrictions to prevent recursion. However, these choices can be evolved using the architecture-altering operations described in Section 6.1.2.

Koza also proposed other types of automatically evolved program components (Koza, Andre, Bennet, and Keane, 1999). Automatically defined iterations (ADIs), automatically defined loops (ADLs) and automatically defined recursions (ADRs) provide means to reuse code. Automatically defined stores (ADSs) provide means to reuse the result of executing code.

6.1.2   Program Architecture and Architecture-Altering Operations

Koza (1994) defined the *architecture* of a program to be the total number of trees, the type of each tree (e.g., RPB, ADF, ADI, ADL, ADR, or ADS), the number of arguments (if any) possessed by each tree, and, finally, if there is more than one tree, the nature of the hierarchical references (if any) allowed among the trees (e.g., whether ADF1 can call ADF2).

There are three ways to determine the architecture of the computer programs that will be evolved:

1. The user may specify in advance the architecture of the overall program, i.e., perform an *architecture-defining preparatory step* in addition to the five steps itemised in Chapter 3.

2. A run of genetic programming may employ the *evolutionary design of the architecture* (as described in (Koza, 1994)), thereby enabling the architecture of the overall program to emerge from a competitive process during the run.

3. The run may employ a set of *architecture-altering operations* (Koza, 1994, 1995; Koza, Bennett, Andre, and Keane, 1999) which can create new ADFs, remove ADFs, and increase or decrease the number of inputs an ADF has. Note that many architecture changes (such as those defined in (Koza, 1994)) are designed not to initially change the semantics of the program and, so, the altered program often has exactly the same fitness as its parent. Nevertheless, the new arrangement of ADFs may make it easier for subsequent changes to evolve better programs later.

Koza and his colleagues have used these architecture altering operations quite widely in their genetic design work, where they evolve GP trees that encode a collection of developmental operations that, when interpreted, generate a complex structure like a circuit or an optical system (see, for example, Section 12.3, page 118).

The idea of architecture altering operations was extended to the extremely general *Genetic Programming Problem Solver* (GPPS), which is described in detail in (Koza et al., 1999, part 4). This is an open ended system which combines a small set of basic vector-based primitives with the architecture altering operations in a way that can, in theory, solve a wide range of problems with almost no input required from the user other than the fitness function. The problem is that this open-ended system needs a very carefully constructed fitness function to guide it to a viable solution, an enormous amount of computational effort, or both. As a result it is currently an idea of more conceptual than practical value.

6.2   Constraining Structures

As discussed in Section 3.2.1, most GP systems require *type consistency* where all subtrees return data of the same type. This ensures that the output of any subtree can be used as one of the inputs to any node. The basic subtree crossover operator shuffles tree components entirely randomly. Universal type compatibility ensures that crossover cannot lead to incompatible connections between nodes. This is also required to stop mutation from producing illegal programs.

An implicit assumption underlying this approach is that all combinations of structures are equally likely to be useful. In many cases, however, we know in advance that there are constraints on the structure of the solution, or we have strong suspicions about the likely form solutions will take. In this section, we will look at several different systems that use tools such as types and grammars to bias or constrain search with the primary aim of increasing the chance of finding a suitable program.

A problem domain might be naturally represented with multiple types. This suggests that the functions used by GP and their arguments will not necessarily be all of the same type. This can often be addressed through creative definitions of functions and implicit type conversion. For example, the Odin system (Holmes and Barclay, 1996) defines operations on inappropriate types to return a new *fail* object. These are handled by introducing a binary *fatbar* that returns its first argument unless it is *fail*, in which case it returns its second argument.

This sort of approach may not always be desirable. For example, if a key goal is to evolve solutions that can be easily understood or analysed, then one might prefer a GP system that is constrained structurally or via a type system, since these often generate results that are more comprehensible (Haynes, Wainwright, Sen, and Schoenefeld, 1995), (Langdon, 1998, page 126). Similarly, if there is domain knowledge that strongly suggests a particular syntactic constraint on the solution, then ignoring that constraint may make it much harder to find a solution.

We will focus here on three different approaches to constraining the syntax of the evolved expression trees in GP: simple structure enforcement (Section 6.2.1), strongly typed GP (Section 6.2.2) and grammar-based constraints (Section 6.2.3). Finally, we consider the advantages and disadvantages of syntactic and type constraints and their biases (Section 6.2.4).

6.2.1   Enforcing Particular Structures

If a particular structure is believed or known to be important then one can modify the GP system to require that all individuals have that structure (Koza, 1992). For example, if a problem is believed to have (or require) a periodic solution, one might want to consider constraining the search to solutions of the form $a \times \sin(b \times t)$. By allowing a and b to evolve freely but keeping the rest of the structure fixed, one could restrict GP to evolving expressions that are periodic. Syntax restrictions can also be used to make GP follow sensible engineering practices. For example, we might want to ensure that loop control variables appear in the correct parts of for loops and nowhere else (Langdon, 1998, page 126).

Enforcing a user specified structure on the evolved solutions can be implemented in a number of ways. One could ensure that all the initial individuals have the structure of interest (for example, generating random subtrees for a and b while fixing the rest) and then constrain crossover and mutation so that they do not alter any of the fixed regions of a tree. An alternative approach would be to evolve the various (sub)components separately. One could evolve pairs of trees (a, b) (like ADFs). Alternatively, one could have two separate populations, one of which is used to evolve candidates for a while the other is evolving candidates for b.

A form of constraint-directed search in GP was also proposed in (Tsang and Jin, 2006; Tsang and Li, 2002) to help GP to focus on more promising areas of the space.

6.2.2   Strongly Typed GP

Since constraints are often driven by or expressed using a type system, a natural approach is to incorporate types and their constraints into the GP system (Montana, 1995). In *strongly typed GP*, every terminal has a type, and every function has types for each of its arguments and a type for its return value. The process that generates the initial, random expressions, and all the genetic operators are implemented so as to ensure that they do not violate the type system's constraints.

Returning to the if example from Section 3.2.1 (page 21), we might have an application with both numeric and Boolean terminals (e.g., get_speed and is_food_ahead). We might then have an if function that takes three arguments: a test (Boolean), the value to return if the test is *true*, and the value to return if the test is *false*. Assuming that the second and third values are numbers, then the output of the if is also going to be numeric. If we choose the test argument as a crossover point in the first parent, then the subtree (excised from the second parent) to insert must have a Boolean output. That is, we must find either a function which returns a Boolean or a Boolean terminal in the other parent tree to be the root of the subtree which we will insert into the new child. Conversely if we choose either the second or third argument as a crossover point in the first parent, then the inserted subtree must be numeric. In all three cases, given that both parents are type correct, restricting the second crossover point in this way ensures the child will also be type correct.

This basic approach to types can be extended to more complex type systems including simple generics (Montana, 1995), multi-level type systems (Haynes, Schoenefeld, and Wainwright, 1996), fully polymorphic types (Olsson, 1994), and polymorphic higher-order type systems (Yu, 2001).

6.2.3 Grammar-based Constraints

Another natural way to express constraints is via *grammars*, and these have been used in GP in a variety of ways (Gruau, 1996; Hoai, McKay, and Abbass, 2003; O'Neill and Ryan, 2003; Whigham, 1996; Wong and Leung, 1996). Many of these simply use a grammar as a means of expressing the kinds of constraints discussed above in Section 6.2.1. For example, one could enforce the structure for the period function using a grammar such as the following:

$$
\begin{aligned}
tree &\ ::=\ E \times \sin(E \times t) &\quad (6.3)\\
E &\ ::=\ \texttt{var}\ \mid\ (E\ \texttt{op}\ E)\\
\texttt{op} &\ ::=\ +\ \mid\ -\ \mid\ \times\ \mid\ \div\\
\texttt{var} &\ ::=\ x\ \mid\ y\ \mid\ z
\end{aligned}
$$

Each line in this grammar is known as a *rewrite rule* or a *production rule*. Elements that cannot be rewritten are known as the *terminals of the grammar*[1] while symbols that appear on the left-hand-side of a rule are known as *non-terminal symbols*.

---

[1]Not to be confused with the terminals in the primitive set of a GP system.

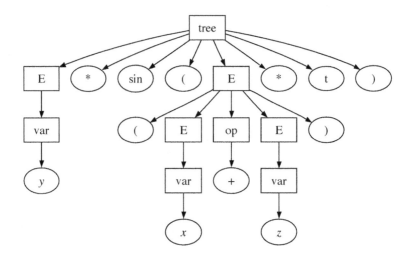

Figure 6.2: Example individual (a derivation tree) that might be evolved in Whigham's grammar-based GP system (Whigham, 1996) if the grammar in Equation (6.3) was used. Rectangles represent non-terminal symbols of the grammar.

In this sort of system, the grammar is typically used to ensure the initial population is made up of legal "grammatical" programs. The grammar is also used to guide the operations of the genetic operators. Thus we need to keep track not only of the program itself, but also the syntax rules used to derive it.

What actually is evolved in a grammar-based GP system depends on the particular system. Whigham (1996), for example, evolved *derivation trees*, which effectively are a hierarchical representation of which rewrite rules must be applied, and in which order, to obtain a particular program. Figure 6.2 shows an example of a derivation tree representing a grammatical program with respect to the grammar in Equation (6.3). In this system, crossover is restricted to only swapping subtrees deriving from a common non-terminal symbol in the grammar. So, for example, a subtree rooted by an E node could be replaced by another also rooted by an E, while an E-rooted subtree could not be replaced by an op-rooted one.

The actual program represented by a derivation tree can be obtained by reading out the leaves of the tree one by one from left to right. For the derivation tree in Figure 6.2, for example, this produces the program

$$y \times \sin((x + z) \times t).$$

However, for efficiency reasons, in an actual implementation it is not convenient to extract the program represented by a derivation tree is this way.

This is because programs need to be executed in order to evaluate their fitness, and this flat program representation often requires further transformations before execution. It is, therefore, common to directly convert a derivation tree into a standard GP tree.

Grammar-based GP approaches can be extended by incorporating concepts from computational linguistics. For example, McKay and colleagues used *tree adjoining grammars* (TAGs) (Joshi and Schabes, 1997) to design new genetic representations and operators that respect grammatical constraints while allowing new types of structural modifications (Hoai and McKay, 2004; Hoai et al., 2003; Hoai, McKay, Essam, and Hao, 2005).

Another major grammar-based approach is *grammatical evolution* (GE) (O'Neill and Ryan, 2003; Ryan, Collins, and O'Neill, 1998). GE does not use trees, instead it represents individuals as variable-length sequences of integers (cf. Equation 6.4) which are interpreted in the context of a user supplied grammar.

For each rule in the grammar, the set of alternatives on the right hand side are numbered from 0 upwards. In the example grammar in Equation (6.3) above, the first rule only has one option on the right hand side; so this would be numbered 0. The second rule has two options, which would be numbered 0 and 1. The third rule has four options which would be numbered 0 to 3. Finally the fourth rule has three options numbered 0 to 2. To create a program from a GE individual one uses the values in the individual to "choose" which alternative to take in the production rules. For example, suppose a GE individual is represented by the sequence

$$39, 7, 2, 83, 66, 92, 57, 80, 47, 94 \qquad (6.4)$$

then we start with 39 and the first syntax rule, *tree*. However *tree* has no alternatives, so we move to 7 and rule E. Now E has two alternatives and 7 is used (via modulus) to chose between them. More of the translation process is given in Figure 6.3.

In this example we did not need to use all the numbers in the sequence to generate a complete program. Indeed the last integer, 94, was not used. In general, "extra" genetic material is simply ignored. More problematic is when a sequence is "too short" in the sense that the end of the sequence is reached before the translation process is complete. There are a variety of options in this case, including failure (assigning this individual the worst possible fitness) and wrapping (continuing the translation process, moving back to the front of the numeric sequence). Grammatical evolution has been very successful and is widely used.

6.2.4 Constraints and Bias

One of the common arguments in favour of constraint systems like types and grammars is that they limit the search space by restricting the kind

$\underline{tree}$

$\rightarrow$ $\langle$ 39 mod 1 = 0, i.e., there is only one option $\rangle$
$\underline{E} \times \sin(E \times t)$

$\rightarrow$ $\langle$ 7 mod 2 = 1, i.e., choose second option $\rangle$
$(\underline{E} \text{ op } E) \times \sin(E \times t)$

$\rightarrow$ $\langle$ 2 mod 2 = 0, i.e., take the first option $\rangle$
$(\underline{\text{var}} \text{ op } E) \times \sin(E \times t)$

$\rightarrow$ $\langle$ 83 mod 3 = 2, pick the third variable, $\rangle$
$(z \text{ } \underline{\text{op}} \text{ } E) \times \sin(E \times t)$

$\rightarrow$ $\langle$ 66 mod 4 = 2, take the third operator $\rangle$
$(z \times \underline{E}) \times \sin(E \times t)$

...

$(z \times x) \times \sin(z \times t)$

Figure 6.3: Sample grammatical evolution derivation using the grammar in Equation (6.3) and the integer sequence in Equation (6.4). The non-terminal to be rewritten is underlined in each case.

of structures that can be constructed. While this is true, it can come at a price.

An expressive type system typically requires more complex machinery to support it. It often makes it more difficult to generate type-correct individuals in the initial population or during mutation and it is more difficult to find crossover points that do not violate the type system. In an extreme case like, constructive type theory (Thompson, 1991), the type system is so powerful that it can completely express the formal specification of the program. Thus, any program/expression having this type is guaranteed to meet that specification. In GP this would mean that all the members of the initial population would need to be solutions to the problem, thus putting all the problem solving burden on the initialisation phase and removing the need for any evolution at all! Even without such extreme constraints, it has often been found necessary to develop additional machinery in order to efficiently generate an initial population that satisfies the constraints (Montana, 1995; Ratle and Sebag, 2000; Schoenauer and Sebag, 2001; Yu, 2001).

As a rule, systems that focus on *syntactic constraints* (such as grammar-based systems) require less machinery than those that focus on *semantic* constraints (such as type systems), since it is typically easier to satisfy the syntactic constraints in a mechanistic fashion. For example, grammar-based systems, such as grammatical evolution and the various TAG-based systems, are typically simple to initialise, and mutation and crossover need to enforce few, if any, constraints on the new child. The work (and the bias) in these systems is much more in the choice of the grammar, and once it has been designed, there is often little additional work required of the practitioner or the GP system to enforce the implied constraints.

While a constraint system may limit the search space in valuable ways (Ratle and Sebag, 2000) and can improve performance on interesting problems (Hoai, McKay, and Essam, 2006), there is no general guarantee that constraint systems will make the evolutionary search process easier. There is no broad assurance that a constraint will increase the *density of solutions* or (perhaps more importantly) approximate solutions.[2] Also, while there are cases where constraint systems smooth the search landscape (Hoai et al., 2006), it is also possible for constraint systems to make the search landscape more rugged by preventing genetic operations from creating intermediate forms on potentially valuable evolutionary paths. In the future, it might be useful to extend solution density studies such as those summarised in (Langdon and Poli, 2002) to the landscapes generated by constraint systems in order to better understand the impact of these constraints on the underlying search spaces.

In summary, while types, grammars, and other constraint systems can be powerful tools, all such systems carry biases. One therefore needs to be careful to explore the biases introduced by the constraints and not simply assume that they are beneficial.

6.3   Developmental Genetic Programming

By using appropriate terminals, functions and/or interpreters, GP can go beyond the production of computer programs. In *cellular encoding* (Gruau, 1994; Gruau and Whitley, 1993; Gruau, 1994), programs are interpreted as sequences of instructions which modify (grow) a simple initial structure (embryo). Figure 6.4 shows part of the development of an electronic circuit.[3] Once the program has finished, the quality of the structure it has produced is measured and this is taken to be the fitness of the program.

Naturally, for cellular encoding to work the primitives of the language must be able to grow structures appropriate to the problem domain. Typical instructions involve the insertion and/or sizing of components, topological

---

[2]By "solution density" we refer to the ratio between the number of acceptable solutions in a program search space and the size of the search space itself. This is a rough assessment of how hard a problem is, since it gives an indication of how long random search would take to explore the program space before finding an acceptable solution.

[3]The process is easier to explain with a movie. This can be downloaded from http://www.genetic-programming.com/gpdevelopment.html.

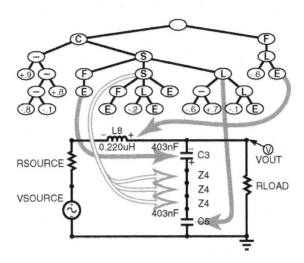

Figure 6.4: Screen shot of an animated gif showing the development of the topology and the sizing of an electrical circuit (from `http://www.genetic-programming.com/gpdevelopment.html`).The program is interpreted in parallel. Solid arrows link the active code to the parts of the electronic circuit (lower half) that are being modified. The three-headed arrow from S shows that three new components (Z4) have just been created in series. Their types (e.g., capacitor, inductor or resistor) and values will be determined by the three arguments of the S "function".

modifications of the structure, etc. Cellular encoding GP has successfully been used to evolve neural networks (Gruau, 1994; Gruau and Whitley, 1993; Gruau, 1994) and electronic circuits (Koza et al., 1999; Koza, Andre, Bennett, and Keane, 1996a; Koza, Bennett, Andre, and Keane, 1996c), as well as in numerous other domains. A related approach proposed by Hoang, Essam, McKay, and Nguyen (2007) combines tree adjoining grammars (Section 6.2.3) with L-systems (Lindenmayer, 1968) to create a system where each stage in the developmental process is a working program that respects the grammatical constraints.

One of the advantages of indirect representations such as cellular encoding is that the standard GP operators can be used to evolve structures (such as circuits) which may have nothing in common with standard GP trees. In many of these systems, the structures being "grown" are also still meaningful (and evaluable) at each point in their development. This allows fitness evaluation. Another important advantage is that structures resulting from developmental processes often have some regularity, which other methods obtain through the use of ADFs, constraints, types, etc. A disadvantage is that, with cellular encoding, individuals require an additional genotype-to-phenotype decoding step. However, when the fitness function involves complex calculations with many fitness cases, the relative cost of the decoding step is often small compared with the rest of the fitness function.

6.4 Strongly Typed Autoconstructive GP with PushGP

While types are often used to constrain evolution, Spector's *PushGP* (Klein and Spector, 2007; Robinson and Spector, 2002; Spector, 2001; Spector, Klein, and Keijzer, 2005a) is a move away from constraining evolution.

Essentially PushGP uses genetic programming to automatically create programs written in the Push programming language. *Push* is a strongly typed tree based language which does not enforce syntactic constraints. Each of Push's types has its own stack. In addition to stacks for integers, floats, Booleans and so on, there is a stack for objects of type program. Using this code stack, Push naturally supports both recursion and program modules (see Section 6.1.1) without human pre-specification. The code stack allows an evolved program to push itself or fragments of itself onto the stack for subsequent manipulation.

PushGP can use the code stack and other operations to allow programs to construct their own crossover and other genetic operations and create their own offspring. Programs are prevented from simply duplicating themselves to deflect catastrophic loss of population diversity.

Chapter 7

Linear and Graph Genetic Programming

Until now we have been talking about the evolution of programs expressed as one or more trees which are evaluated by a suitable interpreter. This is the original and most widespread type of GP, but there are other types of GP where programs are represented in different ways. This chapter will look at linear programs and graph-like (parallel) programs.

7.1 Linear Genetic Programming

In linear GP programs are linear sequences of instructions, such as the one in Figure 7.1. The number of instructions can be fixed, meaning that every program in the population has the same length, or variable, meaning that different individuals can be of different sizes. In the following sections we discuss reasons for using linear GP (Section 7.1.1). We then provide more details on the different flavours of linear GP (Section 7.1.2). Finally, we describe briefly the main genetic operations for linear GP (Section 7.1.3).

7.1.1 Motivations

There are two different reasons for trying linear GP. Firstly, almost all computer architectures represent computer programs in a linear fashion with

Instruction 1	Instruction 2	· · · ·	Instruction N

Figure 7.1: Typical linear GP representation for programs.

Output RO..R7	Arg 1 RO..R7	Opcode + − * /	Arg 2 0...127 or RO..R7

Figure 7.2: Format of a linear GP engine instruction. RO to R7 refer to CPU's registers.

neighbouring instructions being normally executed in consecutive time steps (albeit control structures, jumps and loops may change the execution order). So, why not evolve linear programs? This led Banzhaf (1993), Perkis (1994) as well as Openshaw and Turton (1994) to try linear GP.

Secondly, computers do not naturally run tree-shaped programs, so interpreters or compilers have to be used as part of tree-based GP. On the contrary, by evolving the binary bit patterns actually obeyed by the computer, linear GP can avoid the use of this computationally expensive machinery and GP can run several orders of magnitude faster. This desire for speed drove Nordin (1994), Nordin et al. (1999), Crepeau (1995) and Eklund (2002).

7.1.2   Linear GP Representations

As discussed in Section 2.1, it is possible to use a linear representation in tree-based GP. When doing so, however, the linear structures are simply flattened representations of the trees. Thus, in the linear structure one can still identify the root node, its children, and the rest of the tree structure. In such a system, instructions typically communicate via their arguments.

The semantics of linear GP are quite different, however. In linear GP, instructions typically read their input(s) from one or more registers or memory locations and store the results of their calculations in a register. For example, they might take the form shown in Figure 7.2. This means instructions in linear GP all have equivalent roles and communicate only via registers or memory. In linear GP there is no equivalent of the distinction between functions and terminals inherent in tree-based GP. Also, in the absence of loops or branches, the position of the instructions determines the order of their execution. Typically, this not the case for the structures representing trees.[1]

The instructions in linear GP may or may not represent executable machine code. That is, there are essentially two flavour of linear GP: *machine code GP*, where each instruction is directly executable by the CPU, and

---

[1] Typically, in tree-based-GP the nodes are *visited* (but not *executed*) from left to right in depth-first order. Primitives are only executed, however, when their arguments have been evaluated. So, the root node is the first node visited but the last executed.

interpreted linear GP, where each instruction is executable by some higher-level virtual machine (typically written in an efficient language such as C or C++). When the instructions are actual machine code, then the order of the elements of the representation shown in Figure 7.2 is determined by the particular computer architecture used, and the corresponding data must be packed into bit fields of appropriate sizes. The overhead of packing and unpacking data can be avoided, however, when one is using virtual machine instructions since then the designer of a GP system has complete freedom as to how the virtual machine will interpret its instructions.

If the goal is execution speed, then the evolved code should be machine code for a real computer rather than some higher level language or virtual-machine code. This is why Nordin (1994) started by evolving machine code for SUN computers and Crepeau (1995) targeted the Z80. The linear GP of Leung, Lee, and Cheang (2002) was designed for novel hardware, but much of the GP development had to be run in simulation whilst the hardware itself was under development.

The Sun SPARC has a simple 32-bit RISC architecture which eases designing genetic operations which manipulate its machine code. Nordin (1997) wrapped each machine code GP individual (which was a sequence of machine instructions) inside a C function. Each of the GP program's inputs was copied from one of the C function's arguments into one of the machine registers. As well as the registers used for inputs,[2] a small number (e.g., 2–4) of other registers are used for scratch memory to store partial results of intermediate calculations. Finally, the GP simply leaves its answer in one of the registers. The external framework uses this as the C function's `return` value.

Since Unix was ported onto the x86, Intel's complex instruction set, which was already standard with Windows-based PCs, has had almost complete dominance. Seeing this, Nordin ported his Sun RISC linear GP system onto Intel's CISC. Various changes were made to the genetic operations which ensure that the initial random programs are made only of legal Intel machine code and that mutation operations, which act inside the x86's 32-bit word, respect the x86's complex sub-fields. Since the x86 has instructions of different lengths, special care has to be taken when altering them. Typically, several short instructions are packed into each 4-byte word. If there are any bytes left over, they are filled with no-operation codes. In this way, best use is made of the available space, without instructions crossing 32-bit boundaries. Nordin's work led to `Discipulus` (Foster, 2001), which has been used in applications ranging from bioinformatics (Vukusic, Grellscheid, and Wiehe, 2007) to robotics (Langdon and Nordin, 2001) and

---

[2]Anyone using a register-based GP (linear or tree-based) should consider write-protecting the input registers to prevent the inputs from being overwritten. Otherwise evolved programs (especially in the early generations) are prone to writing over their inputs before they've had a chance to use them in any constructive way.

bomb disposal (Deschaine, Hoover, Skibinski, Patel, Francone, Nordin, and Ades, 2002).

Note that execution speed is not the only reason for using linear GP. Although interpreted linear programs are slower than machine-code programs, an interpreted linear GP system can be more efficient than an interpreted tree-based systems. Also, a simple linear structure lends itself to rapid analysis. Brameier and Banzhaf (2001) showed a linear program can be easily scanned and any "dead code" it contains can be removed. In some ways the search space of linear GP is also easier to analyse than that of trees (Langdon, 1999b, 2002a,b, 2003a; Langdon and Banzhaf, 2005). For example, Langdon (2006); Langdon and Poli (2006,?, 2008) have used (in simulation) two simple architectures, called *T7* and *T8*), for several large scale experiments and for the mathematical analysis of Turing complete GP. For these reasons, it makes sense to consider linear virtual-machine code GP even when using languages like Java that are typically run on virtual machines; one can in fact use a virtual machine (like (Leung et al., 2002)) to interpret the evolved byte code (Harvey, Foster, and Frincke, 1999; Lukschandl, Borgvall, Nohle, Nordahl, and Nordin, 2000).

7.1.3 Linear GP Operators

The typical crossover and mutation operators for linear GP ignore the details of the machine code of the computer being used. For example, crossover may choose randomly two crossover points in each parent and swaps the code between them. Since the crossed over fragments are typically of different lengths, such a crossover may change the programs' lengths, cf. Figure 7.3. Since computer machine code is organised into 32- or 64-bit words, the crossover points occur only at the boundaries between words. Therefore, a whole number of words, containing a whole number of instructions are typically swapped over. Similarly, mutation operations normally respect word boundaries and generate legal machine code. However, linear GP lends itself to a variety of other genetic operations. For example, Figure 7.4 shows homologous crossover. Many other crossover and mutation operations are possible (Langdon and Banzhaf, 2005).

In a compiling genetic programming system (Banzhaf, Francone, and Nordin, 1996) the mutation operator acts on machine code instructions and is constrained to "ensure that only instructions in the function set are generated and that the register and constant values are within predefined ranges allowed in the experimental set up". On some classification problems Banzhaf et al. (1996) reported that performance was best when using crossover and mutation in equal proportions. They suggested that this was due to the GP population creating "introns" (blocks of code that does not affect fitness) in response to the crossover operator, and that these were subsequently converted into useful genetic material by their mutation operator.

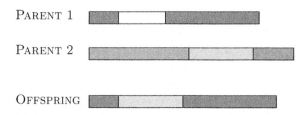

Figure 7.3: Typical linear GP crossover. Two instructions are randomly chosen in each parent (top two genomes) as cut points. The code fragment excised from the first parent is then replaced with the code fragment excised from the second to generate the child (lower chromosome).

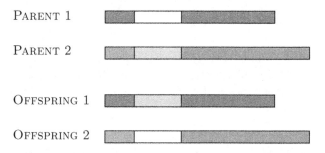

Figure 7.4: Discipulus's "homologous" crossover (Foster, 2001; Francone et al., 1999; Nordin et al., 1999). Crossover is performed on two parents (top two programs) to yield two offspring (bottom). The two crossover points are the same in both parents, so the exised code does not change its position relative to the start of the program (left edge), and the child programs have the same lengths as their parents. Homologous crossover is often combined with a small amount of normal two point crossover (Figure 7.3) to introduce length changes into the GP population.

7.2 Graph-Based Genetic Programming

Trees are special types of graphs. So it is natural to ask what would happen if one extended GP so as to be able to evolve graph-like programs. Starting from the mid 1990s, researchers have proposed several extensions of GP that do just that, albeit in different ways.

7.2.1 Parallel Distributed GP

Poli (1996a, 1999a) proposed *parallel distributed GP* (PDGP), a form of GP that is suitable for the evolution of highly parallel programs which effectively reuse partial results. Programs are represented in PDGP as graphs

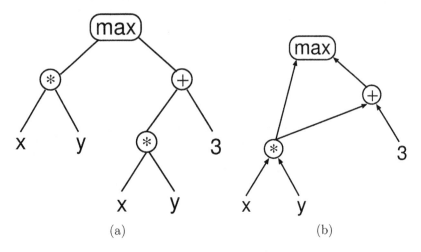

(a)   (b)

Figure 7.5: A sample tree where the same subtree is used twice (a) and the corresponding graph-based representation of the same program (b). The graph representation may be more efficient since it makes it possible to avoid the repeated evaluation of the same subtree.

with nodes representing functions and terminals. Edges represent both control flow and data flow. The possible efficiency gains obtained by a graph representation are illustrated in Figure 7.5.

In the simplest form of PDGP edges are directed and unlabelled, in which case PDGP is a generalisation of standard GP. However, more complex representations can be used, which allow the evolution of: programs, including standard tree-like programs, logic networks, neural networks, recurrent transition networks and finite state automata. This can be achieved by extending the representation by associating labels with the edges of the program graph. In addition to the function and terminal sets, this form of PDGP requires the definition of a *link set*. The labels on the links depend on what is to be evolved. For example, in neural networks, the link labels are numerical constants for the neural network weights. In a finite state automaton, the edges are labelled with the input symbols that determine the FSA's state transitions. It is even possible for the labels to be *automatically defined edges*, which play a role similar to ADFs (Section 6.1.1) by invoking other PDGP graphs.

In PDGP, programs are manipulated by special crossover and mutation operators which guarantee the syntactic correctness of the offspring. Each node occupies a position in a regular grid. The genetic operators act by moving, copying or randomly generating sub-regions of the grid. For this reason PDGP search operators are very efficient.

PDGP programs can be executed according to different policies depending on whether instructions with side effects are used or not. If there are no side effects, running a PDGP program can be seen as a propagation of the input values from the bottom to the top of the program's graph (as in a feed-forward artificial neural network or data flow parallel computer).

7.2.2 Parallel Algorithm Discovery and Orchestration

In a system called *parallel algorithm discovery and orchestration* (PADO), Teller (1996) used a combination of GP and linear discrimination to obtain parallel classification programs for signals and images.

PADO programs include three parts: a main loop, some ADFs and an indexed memory. The main loop is repeatedly executed for a fixed amount of time. When the time is up, PADO programs are forced to halt by some external control structure. The output of a program is the weighted average of the outputs produced at each iteration of the loop. The weights are proportional to the iteration count, so that more recent outputs count more.

The main loop and the ADFs in PADO are structured as arbitrary directed graphs of nodes. Each node can have multiple outgoing arcs that indicate possible flows of control. Each node has two main parts: an action and a branch-decision. Each program has an argument stack and all PADO actions pop their inputs from this argument stack and push their result back onto the argument stack. The actions are drawn from a primitive set including the standard algebraic operations, minimum, maximum, negation, read from indexed memory, write to indexed memory, deterministic and non-deterministic branching instructions, and primitives related to the task of classifying images. The evaluation of PADO programs starts from a designated node. After the execution of each node, control is passed to the node chosen by the branch-decision function of the current node.

7.2.3 Cartesian GP

In Miller's *Cartesian GP* (Miller, 1999; Miller and Smith, 2006), programs are represented by linear chromosomes containing integers. These are divided into groups of three or four. Each group corresponds to a position in a 2-D array. One integer in each group defines the primitive (e.g., an AND gate) at that location in the array. Other integers in the group define the locations (coordinates) in the genome from which the inputs for that primitive should be drawn. Each primitive does not itself define where its output is used; this is done by later primitives. A primitive's output may be used more than once, or indeed not used at all, depending on the way in which the other functions' inputs are specified. Thus, Cartesian GP's chromosomes represent graph-like programs, which is very similar to PDGP. The main difference between the two systems is that Cartesian GP operators act at the level of the linear chromosome, while in PDGP they act directly on the graph. Also, traditionally Cartesian GP has always used mutation as its main search operation, while PDGP used both crossover and mutation. However, recently a new crossover has been proposed for Cartesian GP that provides faster convergence (Clegg, Walker, and Miller, 2007).

7.2.4 Evolving Parallel Programs using Indirect Encodings

The graph-based systems discussed above use representations which directly encode parallel programs. However, it is also possible to use non-graph-based GP to evolve parallel programs. For example, Bennett (1996) used a parallel virtual machine in which several standard tree-like programs (called "agents") would have their nodes executed in parallel. He included a two-stage mechanism which simulated parallelism of sensing actions and simple conflict resolution (prioritisation) for actions with side effects. Andre, Bennett, and Koza (1996) used GP to discover rules for cellular automata, a highly parallel computational architecture, which could solve large majority-classification problems. In conjunction with an interpreter implementing a parallel virtual machine, GP can also be used to translate sequential programs into parallel ones (Walsh and Ryan, 1996), or to develop parallel programs.

Chapter 8

Probabilistic Genetic Programming

Genetic programming typically uses an evolutionary algorithm as its main search engine. However, this is not the only option. The use of simulated annealing and hill climbing to search the space of computer programs was mentioned in Section 5.4. This chapter considers recent work where the exploration is performed by population-based search algorithms which adapt and sample probability distributions instead of using traditional genetic operators.

Sampling from a probability distribution means generating random values whose statistical properties match those of the given distribution. For example, if one sampled a univariate Gaussian distribution, one would expect the resulting values to tend to have mean and standard deviation similar to the mean and standard deviation of the Gaussian. The notion of sampling can be extended to much more complex distributions involving multiple variables. Furthermore, discrete as well as continuous variables are possible.

8.1 Estimation of Distribution Algorithms

Estimation of distribution algorithms (EDAs) are powerful population-based searchers where the variation operations traditionally implemented via crossover and mutation in EAs are replaced by the process of random sampling from a probability distribution. The distribution is modified generation after generation, using information obtained from the fitter individuals in the population. The objective of these changes in the distribution is to increase the probability of generating individuals with high fitness.

Different EDAs use different models for the probability distribution that controls the sampling (see (Larrañaga, 2002; Larrañaga and Lozano, 2002) for more information). For example, *population-based incremental learning* (PBIL) (Baluja and Caruana, 1995) and the *uniform multivariate distribution algorithm* (UMDA) (Mühlenbein and Mahnig, 1999a,b) assume that each variable is independent of the other variables. Consequently, these algorithms need to store and adjust only a linear array of probabilities, one for each variable. This works well for problems with weak interactions between variables. Since no relationship between the variables is stored or learned, however, PBIL and UMDA may have difficulties solving problems where the interactions between variables are significant.

Naturally, higher order models are possible. For example, the *MIMIC* algorithm of de Bonet, Isbell, and Viola (1997) uses second-order statistics. It is also possible to use flexible models where interactions of different orders are captured. The *Bayesian optimisation algorithm* (BOA) (Pelikan, Goldberg, and Cantú-Paz, 1999) uses baysian networks to represent generic sampling distributions, while the *extended compact genetic algorithm* (eCGA) (Harik, 1999) clusters genes into groups where the genes in each group are assumed to be linked but groups are considered independent. The sampling distribution is then taken to be the product of the distributions modelling the groups.

EDAs have been very successful. However, they are often unable to represent both the overall structure of the distribution and its local details, typically being more successful at the former. This is because EDAs represent the sampling distribution using models with an, inevitably, limited number of degrees of freedom. For example, suppose the optimal sampling distribution has multiple peaks, corresponding to different local optima, separated by large unfit areas. Then, an EDA can either decide to represent only one peak, or to represent all of them together with the unfit areas. If the EDA chooses the wrong local peak this may lead to it getting stuck and not finding the global optimum. Conversely if it takes a wider view, this leads to wasting many trials sampling irrelevant poor solutions.

Consider, for example, a scenario where there are five binary variables, x_1, x_2, x_3, x_4 and x_5, and two promising regions: one near the string of all zeros, i.e., $(x_1, x_2, x_3, x_4, x_5) = (0, 0, 0, 0, 0)$, and the other near the string of all ones, i.e., $(x_1, x_2, x_3, x_4, x_5) = (1, 1, 1, 1, 1)$. One option for a (simple) EDA is to focus on one of the two regions, e.g., setting the variables x_i to 0 with high probability (say, 90%). This, however, fails to explore the other region, and risks missing the global optimum. The other option is to maintain both regions as possibilities by setting all the probabilities to 50%, i.e., each of the variables x_i is as likely to be 0 as 1. These probabilities will generate samples in both of the promising regions. For example, the strings $(0, 0, 0, 0, 0)$ and $(1, 1, 1, 1, 1)$ will each be generated with a 3.125% proba-

bility. Also, simple calculations show that 31.25% of individuals generated
by this distribution will be at Hamming distance 1 from either $(0, 0, 0, 0, 0)$
or $(1, 1, 1, 1, 1)$.[1] So, both optimal regions are sampled reasonably often.
However, it is clear that the majority (62.5%) of samples will be allocated
to less promising regions, where the Hamming distance will be 2 or 3 from
both $(0, 0, 0, 0, 0)$ and $(1, 1, 1, 1, 1)$. This is a significant concern, which is
why recently EDAs have often been used in combination with local search
(e.g., see (Zhang, Sun, and Tsang, 2005)).

There have been several applications of probabilistic model-based evolution (EDA-style) in the areas of tree-based and linear GP. We review them
in the rest of this chapter.

8.2   Pure EDA GP

The first EDA-type GP system was effectively an extension of PBIL to trees
called *probabilistic incremental program evolution* (PIPE) (Salustowicz and
Schmidhuber, 1997; Sałustowicz, Wiering, and Schmidhuber, 1998; Salustowicz and Schmidhuber, 1999). In PIPE, the population is replaced by a
hierarchy of probability tables organised into a tree (such as the one in Figure 8.1). Each table represents the probability that a particular primitive
will be chosen at that specific location in a newly generated program tree.
At each generation a population of programs is created based on the current
tree of probability tables. The generation of a program begins by choosing a
root node based on the probabilities in the root table, and then continuing
down the hierarchy of probability tables until all branches of the tree are
complete (i.e., a terminal has been chosen on each branch). The fitness of
these new programs is computed, and the probability hierarchy is updated
on the basis of these fitnesses, so as to make the generation of above-average
fitness programs more likely in the next generation.

A positive feature of PIPE is that the probability of choosing a particular
primitive can vary with its depth (and, more generally, position) in the tree.
This makes it possible, for example, for terminals to become increasingly
probable as a node's depth increases. A limitation of PIPE, however, is that
the primitives forming a tree are chosen independently from each other,[2] so it
is impossible for PIPE to capture dependencies among primitives. Another
limitation is that the maximum size of the generated trees is constrained
by the size of the tree of probability tables. Ondas, Pelikan, and Sastry
(2005) compared the performance of PIPE and standard tree-based GP on

---

[1] The Hamming distance between two strings (whether binary or not) is the number
of positions where the two strings differ.

[2] There is a weak form of dependency, in that there can be a primitive in a particular
position only if the primitive just above it is a function. The choice of this parent primitive
does not, however, influence the choice of the child primitive.

a small set of artificial problems, including a GP version of one-max[3] and a GP version of the fully deceptive trap function[4]. Results suggest that PIPE and standard GP have similar scaling properties, but that standard subtree crossover inherently links neighbouring nodes whereas PIPE does not.

Sastry and Goldberg (2003) proposed an algorithm called *extended compact GP* (eCGP) which effectively extends the eCGA algorithm (Harik, 1999) to trees. Like PIPE, eCGA assumes that all trees will fit within a fixed maximal tree. It partitions the nodes in this maximal tree into groups. The nodes in a group are assumed to be linked and their co-occurrence is modelled by a full joint distribution table. As with eCGA, the probability of generating a particular tree is given by the product of the probabilities of generating each group of nodes using the groups' joint distributions. An advantage of this system is that, unlike PIPE, it captures dependencies among primitives. However, to the best of our knowledge this system has only been tested on the two artificial problems used by Ondas et al. (2005) to compare PIPE and GP. Consequently its behaviour on more typical GP problems is unknown.

Yanai and Iba (2003) proposed an EDA called *estimation of distribution programming* (EDP) which, in principle, can capture complex dependencies between a node in a program tree and the nodes directly above it or to its left.[5] As with eCGP and PIPE, programs are tree-like and are assumed to always fit within an ideal maximal full tree. A conditional probability table is necessary for each node in such a tree to capture the dependencies. To keep the size of data structures manageable, only pairwise dependencies between each node and its parent were stored and used. EDP was tested on both the Max problem (Gathercole and Ross, 1995) and the 6-multiplexer. A later hybrid algorithm combining EDP and GP was proposed (Yanai and Iba, 2004) which showed promise when tested on three symbolic regression problems.

An EDA based on a hierarchical BOA was used as the main mechanism to generate new individuals in *meta-optimising semantic evolutionary search* (MOSES) (Looks, 2007). This combined multiple strategies and used semantics to restrict and direct the search. BOA was also used to evolve programs in (Looks, Goertzel, and Pennachin, 2005) using a specialised representation for trees.

---

[3]One-max is a simple GA test problem where the goal is to maximise the number of 1's in a binary string.

[4]Trap functions are fitness functions that have a gradual slope leading to a sub-optimal local maxima, and a steep valley between that local maxima and the global optima. They therefore tend to "trap" populations on the local maxima

[5]In the general case a node can depend on the choices of any of the nodes that have already been chosen. Since the tree is constructed in a depth-first, left-to-right fashion, it can depend on any nodes that are its direct ancestors, or any nodes that are to its left in the tree. In practice, however, EDP only tracked the conditional probability of a node on its parent.

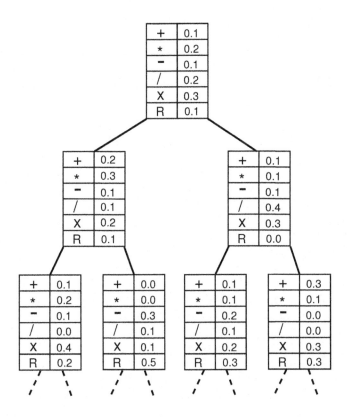

Figure 8.1: Example of probability tree used for the generation of programs in PIPE. New program trees are created starting from the root node at the top and moving through the hierarchy. Each node in an offspring tree is selected from the left hand side of the corresponding table with probability given by the right hand side. Each branch of the tree continues to expand until either the tree of probability tables is exhausted or a leaf (e.g., R) is selected.

Recently an EDA-based system called *N-gram GP* (Poli and McPhee, 2008a) has been proposed that allows the evolution of linear GP programs. To some extent, N-gram GP overcomes the common difficulties EDAs have in performing local search when using a centralised population model. The N-gram GP system is able to capture both the local and the global features of the optimal sampling distribution, albeit at the cost of imposing certain other constraints. This makes it possible, for example, for the search to focus on the neighbourhood of a small number of individuals without the need to choose among them. Tests on polynomial symbolic regression problems and the lawnmower problem were very encouraging.

8.3   Mixing Grammars and Probabilities

A variety of other systems have been proposed which combine the use of grammars and probabilities. We mention only a few here; a more extended review of these is available in (Shan, McKay, Essam, and Abbass, 2006).

Ratle and Sebag (2001) used a stochastic context-free grammar to generate program trees. The probability of applying each rewrite rule was adapted using a standard EDA approach so as to increase the likelihood of using successful rules. The system could also be run in a mode where rule probabilities depended upon the depth of the non-terminal symbol to which a rewrite rule was applied, thereby providing a higher degree of flexibility.

The approach taken in *program evolution with explicit learning* (PEEL) (Shan, McKay, Abbass, and Essam, 2003) was slightly more general. PEEL used a probabilistic L-system where rewrite rules were both depth- and location-dependent. The probabilities with which rules were applied were adapted by an *ant colony optimisation* (ACO) algorithm (Dorigo and Stützle, 2004). Another feature of PEEL was that the L-system's rules could be automatically refined via splitting and specialisation.

Other programming systems based on probabilistic grammars which are optimised via ant systems include *ant-TAG* (Abbass, Hoai, and McKay, 2002; Shan, Abbass, McKay, and Essam, 2002), which uses a tree-adjunct grammar as its main representation, and *generalised ant programming* (GAP) (Keber and Schuster, 2002), which is based on a context-free grammar. Other systems which learn and use probabilistic grammars include *grammar model based program evolution* (GMPE) (Shan, McKay, Baxter, Abbass, Essam, and Hoai, 2004), the system described in (Bosman and de Jong, 2004a,b) and *Baysian automatic programming* (BAP) (Regolin and Pozo, 2005).

Chapter 9

Multi-objective Genetic Programming

The area of *multi-objective GP* (MO GP) has been very active in the last decade. In a *multi-objective optimisation* (MOO) problem, one optimises with respect to multiple goals or fitness functions $f_1, f_2, \ldots$. The task of a MOO algorithm is to find solutions that are optimal, or at least acceptable, according to all the criteria *simultaneously*.

In most cases changing an algorithm from single-objective to multi-objective requires some alteration in the way selection is performed. This is how many MO GP systems deal with multiple objectives. However, there are other options. We review the main techniques in the following sections.

The complexity of evolved solutions is one of the most difficult things to control in evolutionary systems such as GP, where the size and shape of the evolved solutions is under the control of evolution. In some cases, for example, the size of the evolved solutions may grow rapidly, as if evolution was actively promoting it, without any clear benefit in terms of fitness. We will provide a detailed discussion of this phenomenon, which is know as *bloat*, and a variety of counter measures for it in Section 11.3. However, in this chapter we will review work where the size of evolved solutions has been used as an additional objective in multi-objective GP systems. Of course, we will also describe work where other objectives were used.

9.1 Combining Multiple Objectives into a Scalar Fitness Function

When given multiple fitness functions, it is natural to think of combining them in some way so as to produce an *aggregate scalar fitness function*. For example, one could use a linear combination of the form $f = \sum_i w_i f_i$, where the parameters w_1, w_2, ... are suitable constants. A MOO problem can then be solved by using any single-objective optimisation technique with f as a fitness function. This method has been used frequently in GP to control bloat. By combining program fitness and program size to form a parsimonious fitness function one can evolve solutions that satisfy both objectives (see Koza (1992); Zhang and Mühlenbein (1993, 1995); Zhang, Ohm, and Mühlenbein (1997) and Section 11.3.2).

A semi-linear aggregation of fitness and speed was used in (Langdon and Poli, 1998b) to improve the performance of GP on the Santa Fe Trail Ant problem. There, a threshold was used to limit the impact of speed to avoid providing an excessive bias towards ants that were fast but could not complete the trail.

A fitness measure which linearly combines two related objectives, the sum of squared errors and the number of hits (a hit is a fitness case in which the error falls below a pre-defined threshold), was used in (Langdon, Barrett, and Buxton, 2003) to predict biochemical interactions in drug discovery.

Zhang and Bhowan (2004) used a MO GP approach for object detection. Their fitness function was a linear combination of the detection rate (the percentage of small objects correctly reported), the false alarm rate (the percentage of non-objects incorrectly reported as objects), and the false alarm area (the number of false alarm pixels which were not object centres but were incorrectly reported as object centres).

O'Reilly and Hemberg (2007) used six objectives for the evolution of L-systems which developed into 3-D surfaces in response to a simulated environment. The objectives included the size of the surface, its smoothness, its symmetry, its undulation, the degree of subdivision of the surface, and the softness of its boundaries.

(Koza, Jones, Keane, and Streeter, 2004) used 16 different objectives in the process of designing analogue electrical circuits. In the case of an amplifier circuit these included: the 10dB initial gain, the supply current, the offset voltage, the gain ratio, the output swing, the variable load resistance signal output, etc. These objectives were combined in a complex heuristic way into a scalar fitness measure. In particular, objectives were divided into groups and many objectives were treated as penalties that were applied to the main fitness components only if they are outside certain acceptable tolerances.

9.2   Keeping the Objectives Separate

Since selection does not depend upon how the members of the population are represented, the MOO techniques developed for other evolutionary algorithms can be easily adapted to GP.

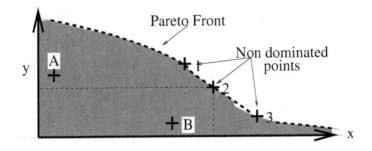

Figure 9.1: Two-dimensional example of Pareto optimality and the Pareto front, where the goal is to maximise along both the x and y axes. Solutions A and B do not dominate each other. However, solution B is dominated by solution 2. (Adapted from (Langdon, 1998).)

The main idea in MOO is the notion of *Pareto dominance*. Given a set of objectives, a solution is said to Pareto dominate another if the first is not inferior to the second in all objectives, and, additionally, there is at least one objective where it is better. This notion can lead to a *partial order*, where there is no longer a strict linear ordering of solutions. In Figure 9.1, for example, individual A dominates (is better than) individual B along the y axis, but B dominates A along the x axis. Thus there is no simple ordering between then. The individual marked '2', however dominates B on both axes and would thus be considered strictly better than B.

In this case the goal of the search algorithm becomes the identification of a *set* of solutions which are non-dominated by any others. Ideally, one would want to find the *Pareto front*, i.e., the set of *all* non-dominated solutions in the search space. However, this is often unrealistic, as the size of the Pareto front is often limited only by the precision of the problem representation. If x and y in Figure 9.1 are real-valued, for example, and the Pareto front is a continuous curve, then it contains an infinite number of points, making a complete enumeration impossible.

9.2.1 Multi-objective Bloat and Complexity Control

Rodriguez-Vazquez, Fonseca, and Fleming (1997) performed non-linear system identification using a MO GP system, where individuals were selected based on the Pareto dominance idea. The two objectives used were fitness and model complexity. In each generation individuals were ranked based on how many other individuals dominated them, and fitness was based on their rank. To better cover the Pareto front, niching via fitness sharing (Goldberg, 1989) was also performed. Preference information was also included to focus the selection procedure towards specific regions of the Pareto front. Hinchliffe, Willis, and Tham (1998) applied similar ideas to evolve parsimonious and accurate models of chemical processes using MO GP. Langdon and Nordin (2000) applied Pareto tournaments to obtain compact solutions in programmatic image compression, two machine learning benchmark problems and a consumer profiling task. Nicolotti, Gillet, Fleming, and Green (2002) used multi-objective GP to evolve quantitative structure–activity relationship models in chemistry; objectives included model fitting, the total number of terms and the occurrence of non-linear terms.

Ekart and Nemeth (2001) tried to control bloat using a variant of Pareto tournament selection where an individual is selected if it is not dominated by a set of randomly chosen individuals. If the test fails, another individual is picked from the population, until one that is non-dominated is found. In order to prevent very small individuals from taking over the population in the early generations of runs, the Pareto criterion was modified so as to consider as non-dominated solutions also those that were only slightly bigger, provided their fitness was not worse.

Bleuler, Brack, Thiele, and Zitzler (2001) suggested using the well-known multi-objective optimiser SPEA2 (Zitzler, Laumanns, and Thiele, 2001) to reduce bloat. de Jong, Watson, and Pollack (2001) and de Jong and Pollack (2003) proposed using a multi-objective approach to promote diversity and reduce bloat, stressing that without diversity enhancement (given by modern MOO methods) searches can easily converge to solutions that are too small to solve a problem. Tests with even parity and other problems were very encouraging. Badran and Rockett (2007) argued in favour of using mutation to prevent the population from collapsing onto single-node individuals when using a multi-objective GP.

As well as directly fighting bloat, MO GP can also be used to simplify solution trees. After GP has found a suitable (but large) model, for example, one can continue the evolutionary process, changing the fitness function to include a second objective that the model be as small as possible (Langdon, 1998). GP can then trim the trees while ensuring that the simplified program still fits the training data.

9.2.2   Other Objectives

Although much of the use of MOO techniques in GP has been aimed at controlling bloat, there are also genuinely MOO applications.

For example, Langdon (1998) made extensive use of Pareto dominance ranking to evolve different types of data structures. Up to six different criteria were used to indicate to what degree an evolved data structure met the requirements of the target data structure. The criteria were used in Pareto-type tournament selection, where, unlike in other systems, a second round of comparisons with the rest of the population was used as a tie breaker. The method successfully evolved queues, lists, and circular lists.

Langdon and Poli (1998b) used Pareto selection with two objectives, fitness and speed, to improve the performance of GP on the Santa Fe Trail Ant problem. Ross and Zhu (2004) used MO GP with different variants of Pareto selection to evolve 2-D textures. The objectives were feature tests that were used during fitness evaluation to rate how closely a candidate texture matched visual characteristics of a target texture image. Dimopoulos (2005) used MO GP to identify the Pareto set for a cell-formation problem related to the design of a cellular manufacturing production system. The objectives included the minimisation of total intercell part movement, and the minimisation of within-cell load variation.

Rossi, Liberali, and Tettamanzi (2001) used MO GP in electronic design automation to evolve VHDL code. The objectives used were the suitability of the filter transfer function and the transition activity of digital blocks. Cordon, Herrera-Viedma, and Luque (2002) used Pareto-dominance-based GP to learn Boolean queries in information retrieval systems. They used two objectives: precision (the ratio between the relevant documents retrieved in response to a query and the total number of documents retrieved) and recall (the ratio between the relevant documents retrieved and the total number of documents relevant to the query in the database).

Barlow (2004) used a GP extension of the well-known NSGA-II MOO algorithm (Deb, Agrawal, Pratap, and Meyarivan, 2000) for the evolution of autonomous navigation controllers for unmanned aerial vehicles. Their task was locating radar stations, and all work was done using simulators. Four objectives were used: the normalised distance from the emitter, the circling distance from the emitter, the stability of the flight, and the efficiency of the flight.

Araujo (2006) used MO GP for the joint solution of the tasks of statistical parsing and tagging of natural language. Their results suggest that solving these tasks jointly led to better results than approaching them individually.

Han, Zhou, and Wang (2006) used a MO GP approach for the identification of chaotic systems where the objectives included chaotic invariants obtained by chaotic time series analysis as well, as the complexity and performance of the models.

Khan (2006) used MO GP to evolve digital watermarking programs. The objectives were robustness in the decoding stage, and imperceptibility by the human visual system. Khan and Mirza (2007) added a third objective aimed at increasing the strength of the watermark in relation to attacks.

Kotanchek, Smits, and Vladislavleva (2006) compared different flavours of Pareto-based GP systems in the symbolic regression of industrial data. Weise and Geihs (2006) used MO GP to evolve protocols in sensor networks. The goal was to identify one node on a network to act as a communication relay. The following objectives were used: the number of nodes that know the designated node after a given amount of time, the size of the protocol code, its memory requirements, and a transmission count.

Agapitos, Togelius, and Lucas (2007) used MO GP to encourage the effective use of state variables in the evolution of controllers for toy car racing. Three different objectives were used: the ratio of the number of variables used within a program to the number of variables offered for use by the primitive language, the ratio of the number of variables being set within the program to the number of variables being accessed, and the average positional distance between memory setting instructions and corresponding memory reading instructions.

When two or three objectives need to be simultaneously optimised, the Pareto front produced by an algorithm is often easy to visualise. When more than three objectives are optimised, however, it becomes difficult to directly visualise the set of non-dominated solutions. Valdes and Barton (2006) proposed using GP to identify similarity mappings between high-dimensional Pareto fronts and 3-D space, and then use virtual reality to visualise the result.

9.2.3   Non-Pareto Criteria

Pareto dominance is not the only way to deal with multiple objectives without aggregating them into a scalar fitness function.

Schmiedle, Drechsler, Grosse, and Drechsler (2001) compared GP with four different MOO selection methods on the identification of binary decision diagrams. Linear weighting of the objectives was compared against: a) Pareto dominance; b) a weaker form of Pareto dominance where a solution is preferred to another if the *number* of objectives where the first is superior to the second is bigger than the number of objectives where the opposite is true; c) *lexicographic ordering* (where objectives are ordered based on the user's preference); and d) a new method based on *priorities*. The *lexicographic parsimony pressure* method proposed in (Luke and Panait, 2002; Ryan, 1994) is in fact a form of MOO with lexicographic ordering (in which shorter programs are preferred to longer ones whenever their fitness is the same or sufficiently similar). An approach which combines Pareto dominance and lexicographic ordering was proposed in (Panait and Luke, 2004).

9.3   Multiple Objectives via Dynamic and Staged Fitness Functions

Often it is possible to rank multiple objectives based on some notion of importance. In these cases, it is possible to use *dynamic* fitness functions which initially guide GP towards solutions that maximise the main objective. When enough of the population has reached reasonable levels in that objective, the fitness function is modified so as to guide the population towards the optimisation of a second objective. In principle this process can be iterated for multiple objectives. Of course, care needs to be taken to ensure that the functionality reached with a set of previous fitness measures is not wiped by the search for the optima of a later fitness function. This can be avoided by making sure each new fitness function somehow includes all the previous ones. For example, the fitness based on the new objectives can be added to the pre-existing objectives with some appropriate scaling factors.

A similar effect can be achieved via *static*, but *staged*, fitness functions. These are staged in the sense that certain levels of fitness are only be made available to an individual once it has reached a minimum acceptable performance on all objectives at the previous level. If each level represents one of the objectives, individuals are then encouraged to evolve in directions that ensure that good performance is achieved and retained on all objectives.

Koza et al. (1999) used this strategy when using GP for the evolution of electronic circuits where many criteria, such as input-output performance, power consumption, size, etc., must all be taken into account to produce good circuits. Kalganova and Miller (1999) used Cartesian GP (see Section 7.2.3) to design combinational logic circuits. A circuit's fitness was given by a value between 0 and 100 representing the percentage of output bits that were correct. If the circuit was 100% functional, then a further component was added which represented the number of gates in the graph that were not involved in the circuit. Since all individuals had the same number of gates available in the Cartesian GP grid, this could be used to minimise the number of gates actually used to solve the problem at hand.

9.4   MO GP via Operator Bias

While it is very common to use only modifications of the selection phase to perform multi-objective search, it is also possible to combine MOO selection with genetic operators exhibiting an inbuilt search bias which can steer the algorithm towards optimising certain objectives.

In some sense the classical *repair operators*, which are used in constrained optimisation to deal with hard constraints, are an extreme form of the idea of using operators to help MOO search.[1] More generally, it is possible to imagine search operators with softer biases which favour the achievement of one or more objectives. These can be the same or different from the objectives that bias the selection of parents.

---

[1]In combinatorial optimisation, repair operators are applied to invalid offspring to modify them in such a way as to ensure a problem's hard constraints are respected.

The *pygmies and civil servants* approach proposed in (Ryan, 1994, 1996) combines the separation typical of Pareto-based approaches with biased search operators. In this system two lists are built, one where individuals are ranked based on fitness and the other where individuals are ranked based on a linear combination of fitness and size (i.e., a parsimonious fitness function). During crossover, the algorithm draws one parent from the first list and the other from the second list. This can be seen as a form of *disassortative mating* aimed at maintain diversity in the population. Another example of this kind is (Zhang and Rockett, 2005) where crossover was modified so that an offspring is retained only if it dominates either of its parents.

Furthermore, as discussed in Sections 5.2 and 11.3.2, there are several mutation operators with a direct or indirect bias towards smaller programs. This provides a pressure towards the evolution of more parsimonious solutions throughout a run.

As with the staged fitness functions discussed in the previous section, it is also possible to activate operators with a known bias towards smaller programs only when the main objective — say a 100% correct solution — has been achieved. This was tested in (Pujol, 1999; Pujol and Poli, 1997), where GP was used to evolve neural networks. After a 100% correct solution was found, one hidden node of each network in the population was replaced by a terminal, and the evolution process was resumed. This pruning procedure was repeated until the specified number of generations had been reached.

Chapter 10

Fast and Distributed Genetic Programming

Users of all artificial intelligence tools are always eager to extend the boundaries of their techniques, for example by attacking more and more difficult problems. In fact, to solve hard problems it may be necessary to push GP to the limit — populations of millions of programs and/or long runs may be necessary.

There are a number of techniques to speed up, parallelise and distribute GP search. We start by looking at ways to reduce the number of fitness evaluations or increase their effectiveness (Section 10.1) and ways to speed up their execution (Section 10.2). We then look at the idea of running GP in parallel (Section 10.3) and point out that faster evaluation is not the only reason for doing so, as geographic distribution has advantages in its own right. In Section 10.4 we describe master–slave parallel architectures (Section 10.4.1), running GP on graphics hardware (Section 10.4.2) and FPGAs (Section 10.4.3). Section 10.4.4 describes a fast method to exploit the parallelism available on every computer. Finally, Section 10.5 concludes this chapter with a brief discussion of distributed, even global, evolution of programs.

10.1 Reducing Fitness Evaluations and/or Increasing their Effectiveness

While admirers of linear GP will suggest that machine code GP is the ultimate in speed, all forms of GP can be made faster in a number of ways. The first is to reduce the number of times a program is evaluated.

Many applications find the fitness of programs by running them on multiple training examples. The use of many examples provides an accurate evaluation of a program's quality. However, ultimately the point of fitness evaluation is to make a binary decision — does this individual get a child or not? The overwhelming proportion of GP's computational effort (or indeed the effort in any evolutionary computation technique) goes into adjusting the probability of this binary decision. However, it is not clear that a high-precision fitness evaluation is always necessary to decide well. Indeed, even when the fitness evaluation is very accurate, most selection algorithms,[1] being stochastic, inject noise into the decision of which points in the search space to proceed from and which to abandon. In these cases, reducing the number of times a program is evaluated is effectively an additional source of noise. If a program has already demonstrated it works poorly compared to the rest of the population on a fraction of the available training data, it not likely to be chosen as a parent. Conversely, if it has already exceeded many programs in the population after being tested on only a fraction of the training set, then it is likely to be chosen as a parent (Langdon, 1998). In either case, it is apparent that we do not gain much by running it on the remaining training examples. Teller and Andre (1997) developed these ideas into a useful algorithm called the *rational allocation of trials*.

As well as the computational cost, there are other negatives consequences that come from using all the training data all the time, as doing so gives rise to a static fitness function. In certain circumstances this may encourage the population to evolve into a cul-de-sac where it is dominated by offspring of a single initial program which did well on some fraction of the training cases, but was unable to fit others. A static fitness function can create conditions where good programs that perform moderately well on most portions of the training data have lower fitness than those that do very well in only a few small regions. With high selection pressure, it takes surprisingly little time for the best individual to dominate the whole population.[2]

Gathercole and Ross (1994, 1997) investigated a number of ways of dynamically changing training samples,[3] yielding a number of interacting effects. Firstly, by using only a subset of the available data, the GP fitness evaluation took less time. Secondly, by changing which examples were being

---

[1]Common selection algorithms include roulette wheel selection (Goldberg, 1989), SUS (Baker, 1987) and tournament selection.

[2]This is called the *take over time* (Goldberg, 1989). This can be formally analysed (Blickle, 1996; Droste, Jansen, Rudolph, Schwefel, Tinnefeld, and Wegener, 2003), but for tournament selection, a simple rule of thumb is often sufficient. If T is the tournament size, roughly $\log_T(\text{Pop size})$ generations are needed for the whole population to become descendants of a single individual. If, for example, we use binary tournaments ($T = 2$), then "take over" will require about ten generations for a population of 1,024. Alternatively, if we have a population of one million (10^6) and use ten individuals in each tournament ($T = 10$), then after about six generations more or less everyone will have the same great_6 great_5 great_4 great_3 grand_2 mother_1.

[3]Siegel (1994) proposed a rather different implementation.

used over time, the evolving population saw more of the training data and so was less liable to over fit a fraction of them. Thirdly, by randomly changing the fitness function, it became more difficult for evolution to produce an overspecialised individual which took over the population at the expense of solutions which were viable on other parts of the training data. *Dynamic subset selection* (DSS) appears to have been the most successful of Gathercole's suggested algorithms. It has been incorporated into Discipulus (see page 63), and was recently used in a large data mining application (Curry, Lichodzijewski, and Heywood, 2007).

Where each fitness evaluation may take a long time, it may be attractive to interrupt a long-running program in order to let others run. In GP systems which allow recursion or contain iterative elements (Brave, 1996; Langdon, 1998; Wilson and Heywood, 2007; Wong and Leung, 1996) it is common to enforce a time limit, a limit on the number of instructions executed, or a bound on the number of times a loop is executed. Maxwell (1994) proposed a solution to the question of what fitness to give to a program that has been interrupted. He allowed each program in the population a quantum of CPU time. When the program used up its quantum it was check-pointed.[4] In Maxwell's system, programs gained fitness as they ran, i.e., each time a program correctly processed a fitness case, its fitness was incremented. Tournament selection was then performed. If all members of the tournament had used the same number of CPU quanta, then the fitter program was the winner. If, however, one program had used less CPU than the others (and had a lower fitness) then it was restarted and run until it had used as much CPU as the others. Then fitnesses were compared in the normal way.

Teller (1994) had a similar but slightly simpler approach: every individual in the population was run for the same amount of time. When the allotted time elapsed a program was aborted and an answer extracted from it, regardless of whether it had terminated or not. Teller called this an "any time" approach. This suits graph systems like Teller's PADO (Section 7.2.2) or linear GP (Chapter 7.1) where it is easy to designate a register as the output register. The answer can then be extracted from this register or from an indexed memory cell at any point (including whilst the programming is running). Other any time approaches include (Spector and Alpern, 1995) and (Langdon and Poli, 2008).

A simple technique to speed up the evaluation of complex fitness functions is to organise the fitness function into stages of progressively increasing computational cost. Individuals are evaluated stage by stage. Each stage contributes to the overall fitness of a program. However, individuals need

---

[4]When a program is check-pointed, sufficient information (principally the program counter and stack) is saved so that it can later be restarted from where it was stopped. Many multi-tasking operating systems do something similar.

to reach a minimum fitness value in each stage in order for them to be allowed to progress to the next stage and acquire further fitness. Often different stages represent different requirements and constraints imposed on solutions.

Recently, a sophisticated technique called *backward chaining GP* has been proposed (Poli, 2005; Poli and Langdon, 2005a,b, 2006a). In GP and other evolutionary algorithms which use tournament selection with small tournament sizes, backward chaining can radically reduce the number of fitness evaluations. Tournament selection randomly draws programs from the population to construct tournaments, the winners of which are then selected. Although this process is repeated many times in each generation, when the tournaments are small there is a significant probability that an individual in the current generation is never chosen to become a member of any tournament. By reordering the way operations are performed, backward chaining GP exploits this. It not only avoids fitness calculations for individuals that are never included in a tournament, but can also achieve higher fitness sooner.

10.2   Reducing Cost of Fitness with Caches

In computer hardware it is common to use data caches which automatically hold copies of data locally in order to avoid the delays associated with fetching them from disk or over a network every time they are needed. This can work well when a small amount of data is needed many times over a short interval.

Caches can also be used to store results of calculations, thereby avoiding the re-calculation of data (Handley, 1994). GP populations have enormous amounts of common code (Langdon, 1998; Langdon and Banzhaf, 2005; Langdon and Poli, 2008). This is, after all, how genetic search works: it promotes the genetic material of fit individuals. So, typically in each generation we see many copies of successful code.

In many (but by no means all) GP systems, subtrees have no side-effects. This means results pass through a program's root node in a well organised and easy to understand fashion. Thus, if we remember a subtree's inputs and output when it was run before, we can avoid re-executing code whenever we are required to run the subtree again. Note that this is true irrespective of whether we need to run the same subtree inside a different individual or at a different time (i.e., a later generation). Thus, if we stored the output with the root node, we would only need to run the subtree once for any given set of inputs. Whenever the interpreter comes to evaluate the subtree, it needs only to check if the subtree's root contains a cache of the values the interpreter calculated last time, thus saving considerable computation time.

In order to achieve this, however, we need to overcome a problem: not only must the answer be stored, but the interpreter needs to know that the subtree's inputs are the same too. The common practices of GP come to our aid here. Usually every tree in the population is run on exactly the same inputs for each of the fitness cases. Thus, for a cache to work, the interpreter does not need to know a tree's inputs in detail, it need only know which of the fixed set of test cases was used.

A simple means of implementing this type of cache is to store a vector of values returned by each subtree for each of the test cases. Whenever a subtree is created (i.e., in the initial generation, by crossover or by mutations) the interpreter is run and the cache of values for its root node is set. Note this is recursive, so caches can also be calculated for subtrees within it at the same time. Now, when the interpreter is run and comes to a subtree's root node, it will simply retrieve the value it calculated earlier, using the test case's number as an index into the cache vector.

If a subtree is created by mutation, then its cache of values will be initially empty and will have to be calculated. However, this costs no more than it would without caches.

When code is inserted into an existing tree, be it by mutation or crossover, the chance that the new code behaves identically to the old code is normally very small. This means that the caches of every node between the new code and the root node may be invalid. The simplest solution is to re-evaluate them all. This may sound expensive, but the caches in all the other parts of the individual remain valid and can be used when the cache above them is re-evaluated. Thus, in effect, if the crossed over code is inserted at depth d, only d nodes need to be evaluated.

The whole question of monitoring how effective individual caches are, what their hit-rates are, etc. has been little explored. In practice, impressive savings have been achieved by simple implementations, with little monitoring and rudimentary garbage collection. Recent analysis (Ciesielski and Li, 2004; Dignum and Poli, 2007; Langdon and Poli, 2002; Poli et al., 2007) has shown that GP trees tend not to have symmetric shapes, and many leaves are very close to the root. This provides a theoretical explanation for why considerable computational saving can be made by using fitness caches. While it is possible to use hashing schemes to efficiently find common code, in practice assuming that common code only arises because it was inherited from the same location (e.g., by crossing over) is sufficient.

As well as the original Directed acyclic graph (DAG) implementation (Handley, 1994) other work includes (Ciesielski and Li, 2004; Keijzer, 1996; McPhee, Hopper, and Reierson, 1998; Yangiya, 1995). While so far we have only considered programs where no side effects take place, there are cases where caching can be extended outside this domain. For example, Langdon (1998) used fitness caches in evolved trees with side effects by exploiting syntax rules about where in the code the side-effects could lie.

10.3 Parallel and Distributed GP are Not Equivalent

There are two important aspects of parallel evolutionary algorithms which are equally important but are often confused. The first is the traditional aspect of parallel computing. That is, we port an existing algorithm onto a supercomputer so that it runs faster. The second aspect comes from the biological inspiration for evolutionary computation.

In nature everything happens in parallel. Individuals succeed or fail in producing and raising children at the same time as other members of their species. These individuals are spread across oceans, lakes, rivers, plains, forests, mountain chains, etc. It was this geographic spread that led Wright (1932) to propose that geography and changes to it are of great importance to the formation of new species and, so, to natural evolution as a whole.

Suppose a species occupies a range of hills. Individuals need not be able to move from one end of the range to another in their lifetime, but their descendents might. Wright (1932) proposed a mathematical model that can predict the amount of mixing between descendents across the entire range is needed to keep the whole population together as a single species. Based on his model, he predicted that only a few migrants per generation between hill tops are sufficient.

Now suppose the sea level rises. What was once a continuous range of hills becomes a chain of islands. Suppose members of this species have limited ability to swim. If the islands are close and the ocean currents are sometimes favourable, it may be that every year a few individuals cross between neighbouring islands. This may be enough to constrain diversification and allow the population to remain a single species. However, if the gaps between island become larger, the chance of an individual occasionally crossing the sea and breeding becomes remote. On each island, then, the sub-populations begin to diverge and over time new species, specific to each island, are formed (Darwin, 1859).

In nature, changes in conditions across regions can lead to corresponding differences in spatially distributed populations. Sometimes this can lead to new species, as in the example above. In other cases the variation can be gradual enough that there is no clear delineation that could be called a species boundary, but geographically distant individuals are unable or unwilling to mate, fulfilling a key property of different species. A particularly dramatic example of this is a *ring species*. The *Larus* gulls, for example, live along a ring that roughly follows the Arctic Circle. With one exception the variants can interbreed all along its range, despite often having differences significant enough that they have received different names. The key exception is in Europe, where the "ends" of the range meet. There the Herring Gull (*Larus argentatus*) and the Lesser Black-backed Gull (*Larus fuscus*) intermingle, but rarely interbreed.

The topology of the landscape is often a strong determiner of the spatial structure of a population. A large, fairly homogenous region, for example, might give rise to a species being spatially differentiated in two dimensions due to distance and climate. A river, on the other hand, may give rise to a linear distribution, especially if there are structures like water falls that restrict migration, and a river basin with several tributaries could lead to a tree structure.

In evolutionary computation we can choose whether we want to model some form of geography. We can run GP on parallel hardware so as to speed up runs, but without introducing a notion of proximity that limits which individuals are allowed to mate. Alternatively, we can model some form of geography, introducing spatial structure as a result.

In the following two sections we will discuss both ideas. It is important to note, however, that one does not need to use parallel hardware to use geographically distributed GP populations. Although parallel hardware naturally lends itself to the implementation of *physically-distributed* populations, one can obtain similar benefits by using *logically-distributed* populations in a single machine.

10.4 Running GP on Parallel Hardware

In contrast to much of computer science, evolutionary computation can be readily run on parallel computer hardware; indeed it is "embarrassingly parallel" (Andre and Koza, 1998). For example, when Openshaw and Turton (1994) ran GP on a Cray supercomputer they obtained about 30% of its theoretical peak performance, embarrassing their supercomputer savvy colleagues who rarely got better than a few percent out of it.

In Sections 10.4.1–10.4.3 we look at three ways of running GP on parallel hardware. Section 10.4.4 shows how to get 32 parallel operations from standard hardware.

10.4.1 Master–slave GP

If the objective is purely to speed up runs, we may want our parallel GP to work exactly the same as it did on a single computer. This is possible, but to achieve it we have to be very careful to ensure that, even if some parts of the population are evaluated more quickly, parallelisation does not change how we apply selection and which GP individual crosses over with which. Probably the easiest way to implement this is the master–slave model.

In the *master–slave model* (Oussaidène, Chopard, Pictet, and Tomassini, 1997) breeding, selection crossover, mutation etc. occur just as they would on a single computer and only fitness evaluation is spread across a network of computers. Each GP individual and its fitness cases are sent across the network to a different compute node. The central node waits for the compute nodes to return their individuals' fitnesses. Since individuals and fitness values are typically stored in small data structures, this can be quite efficient since transmission overheads are limited.

The central node is an obvious bottleneck. Also, a slow compute node or a lengthy fitness case will slow down the whole GP population, since eventually its result will be needed before moving onto the next generation.

10.4.2   GP Running on GPUs

Modern PC graphics cards contain powerful *graphics processing units* (GPUs) including a large number of computing components. For example, it is not atypical to have 128 streaming processors on a single PC's graphics card. In the last few years there has been an explosion of interest in porting scientific or general purpose computation to mass market graphics cards (Owens, Luebke, Govindaraju, Harris, Kruger, Lefohn, and Purcell, 2007).

Indeed, the principal manufactures (nVidia and ATI) claim faster than Moore's Law (Moore, 1965) increase in performance, suggesting that GPU floating point performance will continue to double every twelve months, rather than the 18–24 months observed for electronic circuits in general and personal computer CPUs in particular. In fact, the apparent failure of PC CPUs to keep up with Moore's law in the last few years makes GPU computing even more attractive. Even today's bottom-of-the-range GPUs greatly exceed the floating point performance of their hosts' CPU. However, this speed comes at a price, since GPUs provide a restricted type of parallel processing, often referred to a *single instruction multiple data* (SIMD) or *single program multiple data* (SPMD). Each of the many processors simultaneously runs the same program on different data items.

There have been a few genetic programming experiments with GPUs (Chitty, 2007; Ebner, Reinhardt, and Albert, 2005; Harding and Banzhaf, 2007; Langdon and Banzhaf, 2008; Langdon and Harrison, 2008; Loviscach and Meyer-Spradow, 2003; Meyer-Spradow and Loviscach, 2003; Reggia, Tagamets, Contreras-Vidal, Jacobs, Weems, Naqvi, Winder, Chabuk, Jung, and Yang, 2006). So far, in GP, GPUs have just been used for fitness evaluation.

Harding and Banzhaf (2007) used the Microsoft research GPU development DirectX^{TM} tools to compile (using a technique originally developed by Harris and Buxton (1996)) a whole population of Cartesian GP network programs into a single GPU program which was loaded onto a laptop's GPU to run the fitness cases. Chitty (2007) used a conversion technique, somewhat like an interpreter, to automatically convert each GP tree into a program

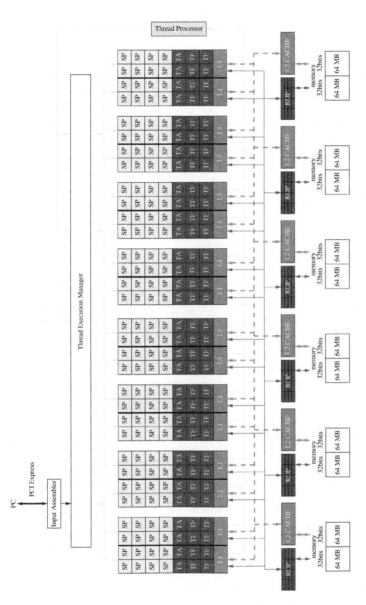

Figure 10.1: nVidia 8800 Block diagram. The 128 1360 MHz Stream Processors are arranged in 16 blocks of 8. Blocks share 16 KB memory (not shown), an 8/1 KB L1 cache, 4 Texture Address units and 8 Texture Filters. The 6×64 bit bus (dashed) links off chip RAM at 900 MHz. (Since there are two chips for each of the six off-chip memory banks, the bus is effectively running at up to 1800 Mhz per bank.) There are 6 Raster Operation Partitions. (nVidia, 2007).

that could be compiled for the GPU on the host PC. The compiled programs were transferred one at a time to a GPU for fitness evaluation. Both groups obtained impressive speedups by running many test cases in parallel.

Langdon and Banzhaf (2008) and Langdon and Harrison (2008) created a SIMD interpreter (Juille and Pollack, 1996) using RapidMind's GNU C++ OpenGL framework to simultaneously run up to a quarter of a million GP trees on an NVIDIA GPU (see Figure 10.1).[5] As discussed in Section 7.1.2, GP trees can be linearised. This avoids pointers and yields a very compact data structure; reducing the amount of memory needed in turn facilitates the use of large populations. To avoid recursive calls in the interpreter, Langdon used reverse polish notation (RPN), i.e., a post-fix rather than a pre-fix notation. Only small modifications are needed to crossover and mutation so that they act directly on the RPN expressions. This means the same representation is used on both the host and the GPU. Almost a billion GP primitives can be interpreted by a single graphics card per second. In both Cartesian and tree-based GP the genetic operations are done by the host CPU. Wong, Wong, and Fok (2005) showed, for a genetic algorithm, these too can be done by the GPU.

Although each of the GPU's processors may be individually quite fast and the manufacturers claim huge aggregate FLOPS ratings, the GPUs are optimised for graphics work. In practice, it is hard to keep all the processors fully loaded. Nevertheless 30 GFLOPS has been achieved (Langdon and Harrison, 2008). Given the differences in CPU and GPU architectures and clock speeds, often the speedup from using a GPU rather than the host CPU is the most useful statistic. This is obviously determined by many factors, including the relative importance of amount of computation and size of data. The measured RPN tree speedups were 7.6-fold (Langdon and Harrison, 2008) and 12.6-fold (Langdon and Banzhaf, 2008).

10.4.3   GP on FPGAs

Field programmable gate arrays (FPGAs) are chips which contain large arrays of simple logic processing units whose functionality and connectivity can be changed via software in microseconds by simply writing a configuration into a static memory. Once an FPGA is configured it can update all of its thousands of logic elements in parallel at the clock speed of the circuit. Although an FPGA's clock speed is often an order of magnitude slower than that of a modern CPU, its massive parallelism makes it a very powerful computational device. Because of this and of their flexibility there has been significant interest in using FPGAs in GP.

Work has ranged from the use of FPGAs to speed up fitness evaluation

---

[5]Bigger populations, e.g. five million programs (Langdon and Harrison, 2008), are possible by loading them onto the GPU in 256k units.

(Koza, Bennett, Hutchings, Bade, Keane, and Andre, 1997; Seok, Lee, and Zhang, 2000) to the definition of specialised operators (Martin and Poli, 2002). It is even possible to implement a complete GP on FPGAs, as suggested in (Heywood and Zincir-Heywood, 2000; Martin, 2001, 2002; Sidhu, Mei, and Prasanna, 1998). A massively parallel GP implementation has also been proposed by Eklund (2001, 2004) although to date all tests with that architecture have only been performed in simulation.

10.4.4 Sub-machine-code GP

We are nowadays so used to writing programs using high level sequential languages that it is very easy to forget that, underneath, computers have a high degree of parallelism. Internally, CPUs are made up of bit-slices which make it possible for the CPU to process all of the bits of the operands of an instruction in one go, in a single clock tick.

Sub-machine-code GP (SMCGP) (Poli and Langdon, 1999) is a technique to speed up GP and to extend its scope by exploiting the internal parallelism of sequential CPUs. In Boolean classification problems, SMCGP allows the parallel evaluation of 32 or 64 (depending on the CPU's word size) fitness cases per program execution, thereby providing a significant speed-up. This has made it possible to solve parity problems with up to 4 million fitness cases (Poli and Page, 2000). SMCGP has also been applied with success in binary image classification problems (Adorni, Cagnoni, and Mordonini, 2002; Quintana, Poli, and Claridge, 2003). The technique has also been extended to process multiple fitness cases per program execution in continuous symbolic regression problems where inputs and outputs are real-valued numbers (Poli, 1999b).

10.5 Geographically Distributed GP

Unless some type of synchronisation is imposed, the parallel forms of GP in which different parts of a population are evolved by different processing elements will not be running the same algorithm as the standard single-CPU version of GP. Therefore, almost certainly, different parallelisations will produce different answers. However, as we discussed in Section 10.3, this is not necessarily a bad thing.

Parallelisation itself can bring benefits similar to those hypothesised in natural populations by Wright (1932). In particular, the population is often divided into semi-independent sub-populations called *demes* (Collins, 1992; D'haeseleer and Bluming, 1994; Langdon, 1998; Popovici and De Jong, 2006). The flow of genetic material between demes is restricted by limiting the exchange of individuals between them. The limit can be on the number of individuals that are allowed to migrate per generation. Alternatively the

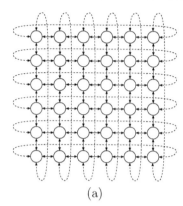
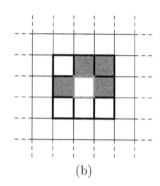

(a)   (b)

Figure 10.2: Spatially structured GP populations. (a) Toroidal grid of demes, where each deme (a node) contains a sub-population, and demes periodically exchange a small group of high-fitness individuals using a grid of communication channels. (b) Fine-grained distributed GP, where each grid cell contains one individual and where the selection of a mating partner for the individual in the centre cell is performed by executing a tournament among randomly selected individuals (e.g., the individuals shaded) in its 3×3 neighbourhood.

demes may be considered to be arranged in a "geographical" topology that constrains which demes can trade individuals. For example, it may be that with limited migration between compute nodes, the evolved populations on adjacent nodes will diverge, and that this increased diversity may lead to better solutions. Fernandez, Tomassini, and Vanneschi (2003), for example, report that distributing individuals between subpopulations offers an advantage in terms of quality of solutions and computational effort.

When Koza first started using GP on a network of Transputers (Andre and Koza, 1996), Andre experimentally determined the best *migration rate* for their problem. He suggested Transputers arranged in an asynchronous *2-D toroidal square grid* (such as the one in Figure 10.2a) should exchange 2% of their population with their four neighbours.

Densely connected grids have been widely adopted in parallel GP. Usually they allow innovative partial solutions to spread quickly. However, the GA community reported better results from less connected topologies, such as arranging the compute nodes' populations in a *ring*, so that they could transfer genes only between themselves and their two neighbours (Stender, 1993). Potter (1997) argues in favour of spatial separation in populations and fine-grained distributed forms of GP (see Figure 10.2b). Whitley (2001) gives some guidance on parallel genetic algorithms.

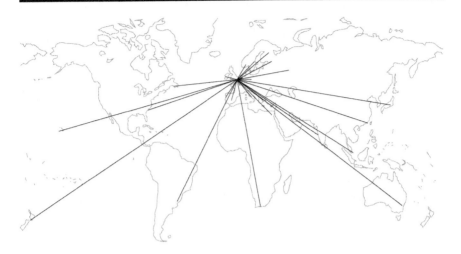

Figure 10.3: A globally distributed GP system (Langdon, 2005a). The server is the centre of the star architecture, with the lines connecting it to users around the world. The users evolved snowflake patterns using a continuously evolving L-System, and their (subjective) preferences provided the fitness measure used to drive the system.

While many have looked enviously at Koza's 1000 node Beowulf cluster (Sterling, 1998) and other supercomputer realisations of GP (Bennett, Koza, Shipman, and Stiffelman, 1999; Juille and Pollack, 1996), a supercomputer is often not necessary. Many businesses and research centres leave computers permanently switched on. During the night their computational resources tend to be wasted. This computing power can easily and efficiently be used to execute distributed GP runs overnight. Typically, GP does not demand a high performance bus to interconnect the compute nodes, and so existing office Ethernet networks are often sufficient. While parallel GP systems can be implemented using MPI (Walker, 2001) or PVM (Fernandez, Sanchez, Tomassini, and Gomez, 1999), the use of such tools is not necessary: simple Unix commands and port-to-port HTTP is sufficient (Poli, Page, and Langdon, 1999). The population can be split and stored on modest computers. With only infrequent interchange of parts of the population or fitness values little bandwidth is needed. Indeed a global population spread via the Internet (Chong and Langdon, 1999; Draves, 2006; Klein and Spector, 2007; Langdon, 2005a), à la seti@home, is perfectly feasible (see Figure 10.3).

Other parallel GPs include (Cheang, Leung, and Lee, 2006; Folino, Pizzuti, and Spezzano, 2003; Gustafson and Burke, 2006; Klein and Spector, 2007; Tanev, Uozumi, and Akhmetov, 2004).

Chapter 11

GP Theory and its Applications

Most of this book is about the mechanics of GP and its practical use for solving problems. In fact, as will become clear in Chapter 12, GP has been remarkably successful as a problem-solving and engineering tool. One might wonder how this is possible, given that GP is a non-deterministic algorithm, and as a result its behaviour varies from run to run. It is also a complex adaptive system which sometimes shows intricate and unexpected behaviours (such as bloat). Thus it is only natural to be interested in GP from the scientific point of view. That is, we want to understand why can GP solve problems, how it does it, what goes wrong when it cannot, what are the reasons for certain undesirable behaviours, what can we do to get rid of them without introducing new (and perhaps even less desirable) problems, and so on.

GP is a search technique that explores the space of computer programs. The search for solutions to a problem starts from a group of points (random programs) in this search space. Those points that are above average quality are then used to generate a new generation of points through crossover, mutation, reproduction and possibly other genetic operations. This process is repeated over and over again until a stopping criterion is satisfied. If we could *visualise* this search, we would often find that initially the population looks like a cloud of randomly scattered points, but that, generation after generation, this cloud changes shape and moves in the search space. Because GP is a stochastic search technique, in different runs we would observe different trajectories. If we could see regularities, these might provide us with a deep understanding of how the algorithm is searching the program space for the solutions, and perhaps help us see why GP is successful in finding solutions in certain runs and unsuccessful in others. Unfortunately, it is normally impossible to exactly visualise the program search space due to its high dimensionality and complexity, making it that much harder to understand.

An alternative approach to better understanding the dynamics of GP is to study *mathematical models of evolutionary search*. There are a number of cases where this approach has been very successful in illuminating some of the fundamental processes and biases in GP systems. In this chapter we will review several theoretical approaches to understanding GP, including mathematical models of GP (Section 11.1), analyses of the structure of GP search spaces (Section 11.2), and the use of theory to understand and combat the chronic problem of bloat in a principled fashion (Section 11.3).

11.1   Mathematical Models

Schema theories are among the oldest and the best known models of evolutionary algorithms (Holland, 1992; Whitley, 1994). Schema theories are based on the idea of partitioning the search space into subsets, called *schemata*. They are concerned with modelling and explaining the dynamics of the distribution of the population over the schemata. Modern genetic algorithm schema theory (Stephens and Waelbroeck, 1997, 1999) provides exact information about the distribution of the population at the next generation in terms of quantities measured at the current generation, without having to actually run the algorithm.

The theory of schemata in GP has had a difficult childhood. Some excellent early efforts led to different worst-case-scenario schema theorems (Altenberg, 1994; Koza, 1992; O'Reilly and Oppacher, 1994b; Poli and Langdon, 1997; Rosca, 1997; Whigham, 1995). Only very recently have the first exact schema theories become available (Poli, 2000a,b, 2001a) which give exact formulations (rather than lower bounds) for the expected number of individuals sampling a schema at the next generation. Initially (Poli, 2000b, 2001a), these exact theories were only applicable to GP with one-point crossover (see Section 5.3). However, more recently they have been extended to the class of homologous crossovers (Poli, McPhee, and Rowe, 2004) and to virtually all types of crossovers that swap subtrees (Poli and McPhee, 2003a,b), including standard GP crossover with and without uniform selection of the crossover points (Section 2.4), one-point crossover, context-preserving crossover and size-fair crossover (which have been described in Section 5.3), as well as more constrained forms of crossover such as strongly-typed GP crossover (see Section 6.2.2), and many others.

Other models of evolutionary algorithms include models based on Markov chain theory (e.g. (Davis and Principe, 1993; Nix and Vose, 1992)) and on statistical mechanics (e.g. (Prügel-Bennett and Shapiro, 1994)). Markov models have been applied to GP (Mitavskiy and Rowe, 2006; Poli et al., 2004; Poli, Rowe, and McPhee, 2001), but so far they have not been developed as fully as the schema theory model.

Exact mathematical models of GP are probabilistic descriptions of the operations of selection, reproduction, crossover and mutation. They explicitly represent how these operations determine which areas of the program space will be sampled by GP, and with what probability. These models treat the fitness function as a black box, however. That is, there is no representation of the fact that in GP, unlike in other evolutionary techniques, the fitness function involves the execution of computer programs on a variety of inputs. In other words, schema theories and Markov chains do not tell us how fitness is distributed in the search space. Yet, without this information, we have no way of closing the loop and fully characterising the behaviour of a GP systems which is always the result of the interaction between the fitness function and the search biases of the representation and genetic operations used in the system.

11.2   Search Spaces

The characterisation of the space of computer programs explored by GP has been another main topic of theoretical research (Langdon and Poli, 2002). Of course results describing the space of all possible programs are widely applicable, not only to GP and other search-based automatic programming techniques, but also to many other areas ranging from software engineering to theoretical computer science.

In this category are theoretical results showing that the distribution of functionality of non Turing-complete programs approaches a limit as program length increases. That is, although the number of programs of a particular length grows exponentially with length, beyond a certain threshold the fraction of programs implementing any particular functionality is effectively constant. For example, in Figure 11.1 we plot the proportion of binary program trees composed of NAND gates which implement each of the $2^{2^3} = 256$ Boolean functions of three inputs. Notice how, as the length of programs increases, the proportion of programs implementing each function approaches a limit.

This does not happen by accident. There is a very substantial body of empirical evidence indicating that this happens in a variety of other systems. In fact, there are also mathematical proofs of these convergence results for two important forms of programs: Lisp (tree-like) S-expressions (without side effects) and machine code programs without loops (Langdon, 2002a,b, 2003a,b, 2005b; Langdon and Poli, 2002). That the limiting distribution of functionality reaches a limit as program length increases was also proven for a variety of other non-Turing complete computers and languages, including: a) cyclic (increment, decrement and NOP), b) bit flip computer (flip bit and NOP), c) any non-reversible computer, d) any reversible computer,

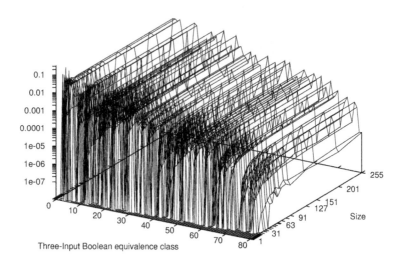

Three-Input Boolean equivalence class

Figure 11.1: Proportion of NAND trees that yield each three-input functions. As circuit size increases the distribution approaches a limit.

e) CCNOT (Toffoli gate) computer, f) quantum computers, g) the "average" computer and h) AND, NAND, OR, NOR expressions.

Recently, (Langdon and Poli, 2006; Poli and Langdon, 2006b) started extending these results to Turing complete machine code programs. For this purpose, a simple, but realistic, Turing complete machine code language, T7, was considered. It includes: directly accessed bit addressable memory, an addition operator, an unconditional jump, a conditional branch and four copy instructions. A mathematical analysis of the halting process based on a Markov chain model of program execution and halting was performed. The model can be used to estimate, for any given program length, important quantities, such as the halting probability and the run time of halting programs. This showed a scaling law indicating that the *halting probability* for programs of length L is of order $1/\sqrt{L}$, while the expected number of instructions executed by halting programs is of order $\sqrt{L}$. In contrast to many proposed Markov models, this can be done very efficiently, making it possible to compute these quantities for programs of tens of million instructions in a few minutes. Experimental results confirmed the theory.

11.3   Bloat

Starting in the early 1990s, researchers began to notice that in addition to progressively increasing their mean and best fitness, GP populations also showed certain other dynamics. In particular, it was noted that very often the average size (number of nodes) of the programs in a population, after a certain number of generations in which it was largely static, at some point would start growing at a rapid pace. Typically the increase in program size was not accompanied by any corresponding increase in fitness. The origin of this phenomenon, which is known as *bloat*, has effectively been a mystery for over a decade.

Note that there are situations where one would expect to see program growth as part of the process of solving a problem. For example, GP runs typically start from populations of small random programs, and it may be necessary for the programs to grow in complexity for them to be able to comply with all the fitness cases (a situation which often arises in continuous symbolic regression problems). So, we should not equate growth with bloat and we should define *bloat as program growth without (significant) return in terms of fitness*.

Bloat is not only surprising, it also has significant practical effects: large programs are computationally expensive to evolve and later use, can be hard to interpret, and may exhibit poor generalisation. For these reasons bloat has been a subject of intense study in GP. Over the years, many theories have been proposed to explain various aspects of bloat, and while great strides have been made, we still lack a single, universally-accepted unifying theory to explain the broad range of empirical observations. We review the key theoretical results on bloat in Section 11.3.1.

While discussions on the causes of bloat were going on, practitioners have still had to face the reality of combating bloat in their runs. Consequently, a variety of effective practical techniques have been proposed to counteract bloat. We review these in Section 11.3.2, where we will particularly focus on the *parsimony pressure method* (Koza, 1992; Zhang and Mühlenbein, 1993, 1995; Zhang et al., 1997), which is perhaps the simplest and most frequently used method to control bloat in genetic programming.

11.3.1   Bloat in Theory

As mentioned above, there are several theories of bloat. Let us start by looking at three of the oldest ones: the replication accuracy theory, the removal bias theory and the nature of program search spaces theory.

Three Classic Explanations for Bloat

The *replication accuracy theory* (McPhee and Miller, 1995) states that the success of a GP individual depends on its ability to have offspring that are functionally similar to the parent. As a consequence, GP evolves towards (bloated) representations that increase replication accuracy.

The nodes in a GP tree can often be crudely categorised into two classes: active code and inactive code. Roughly speaking, *inactive code* is code that is not executed, or is executed but its output is then discarded. All remaining code is *active code*. The *removal bias theory* (Soule and Foster, 1998a) observes that inactive code in a GP tree tends to be low in the tree, residing, therefore, in smaller-than-average-size subtrees. Crossover events excising inactive subtrees produce offspring with the same fitness as their parents. On average the inserted subtree is bigger than the excised one, so such offspring are bigger than average while retaining the fitness of their parent, leading ultimately to growth in the average program size.

Finally, the *nature of program search spaces theory* (Langdon and Poli, 1997; Langdon, Soule, Poli, and Foster, 1999) predicts that above a certain size, the distribution of fitnesses does not vary with size. Since there are more long programs, the number of long programs of a given fitness is greater than the number of short programs of the same fitness. Over time GP samples longer and longer programs simply because there are more of them.

Executable Models of Bloat

The explanations for bloat provided by these three theories are largely qualitative. There have, however, been some efforts to mathematically formalise and verify these theories. For example, Banzhaf and Langdon (2002) defined an *executable model of bloat* where only the fitness, the size of active code and the size of inactive code were represented (i.e., there was no representation of program structures). Fitnesses of individuals were drawn from a bell-shaped distribution, while active and inactive code lengths were modified by a size-unbiased mutation operator. Various interesting effects were reported which are very similar to corresponding effects found in GP runs. Rosca (2003) proposed a similar, but slightly more sophisticated model which also included an analogue of crossover. This provided further interesting evidence.

A strength of these executable models is their simplicity. A weakness is that they suppress or remove many details of the representation and operators typically used in GP. This makes it difficult to verify if all the phenomena observed in the model have analogues in GP runs, and if all important behaviours of GP in relation to bloat are captured by the model.

Size Evolution Equation

In (Poli, 2001b; Poli and McPhee, 2003b), a *size evolution equation* for genetic programming was developed, which provided an exact formalisation of the dynamics of average program size. The original equation was derived from the exact schema theory for GP, and expressed mean program size as a function of the size and selection probabilities of particular schemata representing program shapes. The equation has recently been simplified (Poli and McPhee, 2008b) giving:

$$E[\mu(t+1)] = \sum_{\ell} \ell \times p(\ell, t), \tag{11.1}$$

where $\mu(t+1)$ is the mean size of the programs in the population at generation $t+1$, E is the expectation operator, ℓ is a program size, and $p(\ell, t)$ is the probability of selecting programs of size ℓ from the population in generation t.

This equation can be rewritten in terms of the expected change in average program size as:

$$E[\mu(t+1) - \mu(t)] = \sum_{\ell} \ell \times (p(\ell, t) - \Phi(\ell, t)), \tag{11.2}$$

where $\Phi(\ell, t)$ is the proportion of programs of size ℓ in the current generation. Both equations apply to a GP system with selection and any form of symmetric subtree crossover.[1]

Note that Equations (11.1) and (11.2) do not directly explain bloat. They are, however, important because *they constrain what can and cannot happen size-wise* in GP populations. Any explanation for bloat (including the theories summarised above) has to agree with Equations (11.1) and (11.2).

In particular, Equation (11.1) predicts that, for symmetric subtree-swapping crossover operators, the mean program size evolves *as if selection only was acting* on the population. This means that if there is a change in mean size (bloat, for example) it must be the result of some form of positive or negative selective pressure on some or all of the length classes ℓ. Equation (11.2) shows that there can be bloat only if the selection probability $p(\ell, t)$ is different from the proportion $\Phi(\ell, t)$ for at least some ℓ. In particular, for bloat to happen there will have to be some small ℓ's for which $p(\ell, t) < \Phi(\ell, t)$ and also some bigger ℓ's for which $p(\ell, t) > \Phi(\ell, t)$ (at least on average).

---

[1] In a symmetric operator the probability of selecting particular crossover points in the parents does not depend on the order in which the parents are drawn from the population.

Crossover Bias Theory of Bloat

We conclude this review on theories of bloat with a recent explanation for bloat called the *crossover bias theory* (Dignum and Poli, 2007; Poli et al., 2007). This is based on and is consistent with the size evolution equation (Equation 11.1).

On average, each application of subtree crossover removes as much genetic material as it inserts; consequently crossover on its own does not produce growth or shrinkage. While the *mean* program size is unaffected, however, *higher moments* of the distribution are. In particular, crossover pushes the population towards a particular distribution of program sizes, known as a *Lagrange distribution of the second kind*, where small programs have a much higher frequency than longer ones. For example, crossover generates a very high proportion of single-node individuals. In virtually all problems of practical interest, however, very small programs have no chance of solving the problem. As a result, programs of above average size have a selective advantage over programs of below average size, and the mean program size increases.

Because crossover will continue to create small programs, which will then be ignored by selection (in favour of the larger programs), the increase in average size will continue generation by generation.

11.3.2 Bloat Control in Practice

Numerous empirical techniques have been proposed to control bloat (Langdon et al., 1999; Soule and Foster, 1998b). We cannot look at them all. However, we briefly review some of the most important.

Size and Depth Limits

Rather naturally, the first and simplest method to control code growth is the use of hard limits on the size or depth of the offspring programs generated by the genetic operators.

Many implementations of this idea (e.g., (Koza, 1992)) apply a genetic operator and then check whether the offspring is beyond the size or depth limit. If it isn't, the offspring enters the population. If, instead, the offspring exceeds the limit, one of the parents is returned. Obviously, this implementation does not allow programs to grow too large. However, there is a serious problem with this way of applying size limits, or more generally, constraints to programs: parent programs that are more likely to violate a constraint will tend to be copied (unaltered) more often than programs that don't. That is, the population will tend to be filled up with programs that nearly infringe the constraint, which is typically not what is desired.

It is well known, for example, that depth thresholds lead to the population filling up with very bushy programs where most branches reach the depth limit (being effectively full trees). On the contrary, size limits produce populations of stringy programs which tend to all approach the size limit. See (Crane and McPhee, 2005; McPhee, Jarvis, and Crane, 2004) for more on the impact of size and depth limits, and the differences between them.

The problem can be fixed by *not returning parents* if the offspring violates a constraint. This can be realised with two different strategies. Firstly, one can just return the oversize offspring, but give it a fitness of 0, so that selection will get rid of it at the next generation. Secondly, one can simply declare the genetic operation failed, and try again. This can be done in two alternative ways: a) the same parent or parents are used again, but new mutation or crossover points are randomly chosen (which can be done up to a certain number of times before giving up on those parents), or b) new parents are selected and the genetic operation is attempted again.

If a limit is used, programs must not be so tightly constrained that they cannot express any solution to the problem. As a rule of thumb, one should try to estimate the size of the minimum possible solution (using the terminals and functions given to GP) and add some percentage (e.g., 50-200%) as a safety margin. In general, however, it may be hard to heuristically come up with good limits, so some trial and error may be required. Alternatively, one can use one of the many techniques that have been proposed to adjust size limits during runs. These can be both at the level of individuals and the population. See for example the work by Silva and Almeida (2003); Silva and Costa (2004, 2005a,b); Silva, Silva, and Costa (2005).

Anti-bloat Genetic Operators

One can control bloat by using genetic operators which directly or indirectly have an anti-bloat effect.

Among the most recent bloat-control methods are *size fair crossover* and *size fair mutation* (Crawford-Marks and Spector, 2002; Langdon, 2000). These work by constraining the choices made during the execution of a genetic operation so as to actively prevent growth. In size-fair crossover, for example, the crossover point in the first parent is selected randomly, as in standard crossover. Then the size of the subtree to be excised is calculated. This is used to constrain the choice of the second crossover point so as to guarantee that the subtree chosen from the second parent will not be "unfairly" big.

Older methods include several *mutation operators* that may help control the average tree size in the population while still introducing new genetic material. Kinnear (1993) proposes a mutation operator which prevents the offspring's depth being more than 15% larger than its parent. Langdon (1998) proposes two mutation operators in which the new random subtree is on average the same size as the code it replaces. In *Hoist mutation* (Kinnear, 1994a) the new subtree is selected from the subtree being removed from the parent, guaranteeing that the new program will be smaller than its parent. *Shrink mutation* (Angeline, 1996) is a special case of subtree mutation where the randomly chosen subtree is replaced by a randomly chosen terminal. McPhee and Poli (2002) provides theoretical analysis and empirical evidence that combinations of subtree crossover and subtree mutation operators can control bloat in linear GP systems.

Other methods which control bloat by exploiting the bias of the operators were discussed in Section 9.4.

Anti-Bloat Selection

As clarified by the size evolution equation discussed in the previous section, in systems with symmetric operators, bloat can only happen if there are some longer-than-average programs that are fitter than average or some shorter-than-average programs that are less fit than average, or both. So, it stands to reason that in order to control bloat one needs to somehow modulate the selection probabilities of programs based on their size.

As we have discussed in Section 9.2.1, recent methods also include the use of *multi-objective optimisation* to control bloat. This typically involves the use of a modified selection based on the Pareto criterion.

A recent technique, the *Tarpeian method* (Poli, 2003), controls bloat by acting directly on the selection probabilities in Equation (11.2). This is done by setting the fitness of randomly chosen longer-than-average programs to 0. This prevents them being parents. By changing how frequently this is done the anti-bloat intensity of Tarpeian control can be modulated. An advantage of the method is that the programs whose fitness is zeroed are never executed, thereby speeding up runs.

The well-known *parsimony pressure* method (Koza, 1992; Zhang and Mühlenbein, 1993, 1995; Zhang et al., 1997) changes the selection probabilities by subtracting a value based on the size of each program from its fitness. Bigger programs have more subtracted and, so, have lower fitness and tend to have fewer children. That is, the new fitness function is $f(x) - c \times \ell(x)$, where $\ell(x)$ is the size of program x, $f(x)$ is its original fitness and c is a constant known as the *parsimony coefficient*.[2] Zhang and Mühlenbein (1995) showed some benefits of adaptively adjusting the coefficient c at each generation but most implementations actually keep the parsimony coefficient constant.

---

[2]While the new fitness is used to guide evolution, one still needs to use the original fitness function to recognise solutions and stop runs.

The parsimony pressure method can be seen as a way to address the generalisation–accuracy tradeoff common in machine learning (Rosca and Ballard, 1996b; Zhang and Mühlenbein, 1995). There are also connections between this method and the Minimum Description Length (MDL) principle used to control bloat in (Iba, 1997; Iba et al., 1994; Iba, de Garis, and Sato, 1995a). The MDL approach uses a fitness function which combines program complexity (expressed as the number of bits necessary to encode the program's tree) and classification error (expressed as the number of bits necessary to encode the errors on all fitness cases). Rosca also linked the parsimony pressure method to his approximate evolution equations for rooted-tree schemata (Rosca, 1996, 1997; Rosca and Ballard, 1996b, 1999).

Controlling bloat while at the same time maximising fitness turns the evolution of programs into either a multi-objective optimisation problem or, at least, into a constrained optimisation problem. The parsimony pressure method effectively treats the minimisation of size as a soft constraint and attempts to enforce this constraint using the *penalty method*, i.e., by decreasing the fitness of programs by an amount that depends on their size. The penalty is typically simply proportional to program size. The intensity with which bloat is controlled is, therefore, determined by the parsimony coefficient. The value of this coefficient is very important: too small a value and runs will still bloat wildly; too large a value and GP will take the minimisation of size as its main target and will almost ignore fitness, thus converging towards extremely small but useless programs (Soule, 1998). However, good values of the parsimony coefficient are highly dependent on particulars such as the problem being solved, the choice of functions and terminals, and various parameter settings. Furthermore, with a constant parsimony coefficient the method can only achieve *partial control* over the dynamics of the average program size over time.

Recently, a theoretically sound method for setting the parsimony coefficient in a principled manner has been proposed (Poli and McPhee, 2008b). The *covariant parsimony pressure* method is based on an analysis of the size evolution Equation (11.1), and is easy to implement. It recalculates the parsimony coefficient c at each generation using $c = \mathrm{Cov}(\ell, f)/\mathrm{Var}(\ell)$, where $\mathrm{Cov}(\ell, f)$ is the covariance between program size ℓ and program fitness f in the population, and $\mathrm{Var}(\ell)$ is the variance of program sizes. Note that c needs to be recalculated each generation because both $\mathrm{Cov}(\ell, f)$ and $\mathrm{Var}(\ell)$ change from generation to generation. As shown in Figure 11.2 (in the portion labelled "Local"), using this equation ensures that the mean program size remains at the value set by the initialisation procedure (although there can be a small amount of drift). There is a variant of the method that allows the user to even decide what function the mean program size should follow over time. As shown in the figure this provides complete control over the population size dynamics.

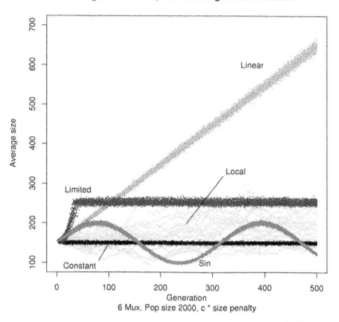

Figure 11.2: Plots of the evolution average size over 500 generations for multiple runs of the 6-MUX problem with various forms of covariant parsimony pressure. The "Constant" runs had a constant target size of 150. In the "Sin" runs the target size was $\sin((\text{generation} + 1)/50.0) \times 50.0 + 150$. For the "Linear" runs the target size was $150 + \text{generation}$. The "Limited" runs used no size control until the size reached 250, then the target was held at 250. Finally, the "Local" runs used $c = \text{Cov}(\ell, f)/\text{Var}(\ell)$, which allowed a certain amount of drift but still avoided runaway bloat (see text).

Part III

Practical Genetic Programming

Three little pigs provide a demonstration of construction techniques...

and Goldilocks finally gets it just *right.*

Chapter 12

Applications

Since its early beginnings, GP has produced a cornucopia of results. The literature, which covers more than 5000 recorded uses of GP, reports an enormous number of applications where GP has been successfully used as an automatic programming tool, a machine learning tool or an automatic problem-solving engine. It is impossible to list all such applications here. In the following sections we start with a discussion of the general kinds of problems where GP has proved successful (Section 12.1) and then review a representative subset for each of the main application areas of GP (Sections 12.2–12.11), devoting particular attention to the important areas of symbolic regression (Section 12.2) and human-competitive results (Section 12.3).

12.1 Where GP has Done Well

Based on the experience of numerous researchers over many years, it appears that GP and other evolutionary computation methods have been especially productive in areas having some or all of the following properties:

The interrelationships among the relevant variables is unknown or poorly understood (or where it is suspected that the current understanding may possibly be wrong). One of the particular values of GP (and other evolutionary algorithms) is in exploring poorly understood domains. If the problem domain is well understood, there may well be analytical tools that will provide quality solutions without the uncertainty inherent in a stochastic search process such as GP. GP, on the other hand, has proved successful where the application is new or otherwise not well understood. It can help discover which variables and operations are important; provide novel solutions to individual problems; unveil unexpected relationships among variables; and, sometimes GP can discover new concepts that can then be applied in a wide variety of circumstances.

Finding the size and shape of the ultimate solution is a major part of the problem. If the form of the solution is known, then alternative search mechanisms that work on fixed size representations (e.g., genetic algorithms) may be more efficient because they won't have to discover the size and shape of the solution.

Significant amounts of test data are available in computer-readable form. GP (and most other machine learning and search techniques) benefit from having significant pools of test data. At a minimum there needs to be enough data to allow the system to learn the salient features, while leaving enough at the end to use for validation and over-fitting tests. It is also useful if the test data are as clean and accurate as possible. GP is capable of dealing gracefully with certain amounts of noise in the data (especially if steps are taken to reduce over-fitting), but cleaner data make the learning process easier for any system, GP included.

There are good simulators to test the performance of tentative solutions to a problem, but poor methods to directly obtain good solutions. In many domains of science and engineering, simulators and analysis tools have been constructed that allow one to evaluate the behaviour and performance of complex artifacts such as aircraft, antennas, electronic circuits, control systems, optical systems, games, etc. These simulators contain enormous amounts of knowledge of the domain and have often required several years to create. These tools solve the so-called *direct problem* of working out the behaviour of a solution or tentative solution to a problem, given the solution itself. However, the knowledge stored in such systems cannot be easily used to solve the *inverse problem* of designing an artifact from a set of functional or performance requirements. A great advantage of GP is that it is able to connect to simulators and analysis tools and to "data-mine" the simulator to solve the inverse problem automatically. That is, the user need not specify (or know) much about the form of the eventual solution before starting.

Conventional mathematical analysis does not, or cannot, provide analytic solutions. If there is a good exact analytic solution, one probably wants to use it rather than spend the energy to evolve what is likely to be an approximate solution. That said, GP might still be a valuable option if the analytic solutions have undesirable properties (e.g., unacceptable run times for large instances), or are based on assumptions that don't apply in one's circumstances (e.g., noise-free data).

An approximate solution is acceptable (or is the only result that is ever likely to be obtained). Evolution in general, and GP in particular, is typically about being "good enough" rather than "the best". (A rabbit doesn't have to be the fastest animal in the world: it just has to be fast enough to escape that particular fox.) As a result, evolutionary algorithms tend to work best in domains where close approximations are both possible and acceptable.

Small improvements in performance are routinely measured (or easily measurable) and highly prized. Technological efforts tend to concentrate in areas of high economic importance. In these domains, the state of the art tends to be fairly advanced, and, so, it is difficult to improve over existing solutions. However, in these same domains small improvements can be extremely valuable. GP can sometimes discover small, but valuable, relationships.

Two (of many) examples of successful applications of GP that satisfy many of these properties are the work of Lohn, Hornby, and Linden (2004) on satellite antenna design and Spector's evolution of new quantum computing algorithms that out-performed all previous approaches (Spector, Barnum, and Bernstein, 1998; Spector, Barnum, Bernstein, and Swamy, 1999). Both of these domains are complex, without analytic solutions, yet in both cases good simulators existed which could be used to evaluate the fitness of solutions. In other words, people didn't know how to solve the problems but they could (automatically) recognise a good solution when they saw one. Both of these applications resulted in the discovery of highly successful and unexpected designs. The key component of the evolved quantum algorithm could in fact be extracted and applied in a wide variety of other settings, leading to major improvements in a number of related quantum algorithms as well as the ones under specific study.

12.2 Curve Fitting, Data Modelling and Symbolic Regression

In principle, there are as many possible applications of GP as there are applications for programs—in other words, virtually infinite. However, before one can try to solve a new problem with GP, one needs to define an appropriate fitness function. In problems where only the side effects of a program are of interest, the fitness function usually compares the effects of the execution of a program in some suitable environments with a desired behaviour, often in a very application-dependent manner. However, in many problems the goal is to *find a function* whose output has some desired property, e.g., the function matches some target values (as in the example given in Section 4.1). This is generally known as a *symbolic regression* problem.

Many people are familiar with the notion of *regression*. Regression means finding the coefficients of a predefined function such that the function best fits some data. A problem with regression analysis is that, if the fit is not good, the experimenter has to keep trying different functions by hand until a good model for the data is found. Not only is this laborious, but also the results of the analysis depend very much on the skills and inventiveness of the experimenter. Furthermore, even expert users tend to have strong mental biases when choosing functions to fit. For example, in many application areas there is a considerable tradition of using only linear or quadratic models, even when the data might be better fit by a more complex model.

Symbolic regression attempts to go beyond this. It consists of finding a function that fits the given data points without making any assumptions about the structure of that function. Since GP makes no such assumption, it is well suited to this sort of discovery task. Symbolic regression was one of the earliest applications of GP (Koza, 1992), and continues to be widely studied (Cai, Pacheco-Vega, Sen, and Yang, 2006; Gustafson, Burke, and Krasnogor, 2005; Keijzer, 2004; Lew, Spencer, Scarpa, Worden, Rutherford, and Hemez, 2006).

The steps necessary to solve symbolic regression problems include the five preparatory steps mentioned in Chapter 2. We practiced them in the example in Chapter 4, which was an instance of a symbolic regression problem. There is an important difference here, however: the data points provided in Chapter 4 were computed using a simple formula, while in most realistic situations each point represents the measured values taken by some variables at a certain time in some dynamic process, in a repetition of an experiment, and so on. So, the collection of an appropriate set of data points for symbolic regression is an important and sometimes complex task.

For instance, consider the case of using GP to evolve a *soft sensor* (Jordaan, Kordon, Chiang, and Smits, 2004). The intent is to evolve a function that will provide a reasonable estimate of what a sensor (in an industrial production facility) would report, based on data from other actual sensors in the system. This is typically done in cases where placing an actual sensor in that location would be difficult or expensive. However, it is necessary to place at least one instance of such a sensor in a working system in order to collect the data needed to train and test the GP system. Once the sensor is placed, one would collect the values reported by that sensor and by all the other real sensors that are available to the evolved function, at various times, covering the various conditions under which the evolved system will be expected to act.

Such experimental data typically come in large tables where numerous quantities are reported. Usually we know which variable we want to predict (e.g., the soft sensor value), and which other quantities we can use to make the prediction (e.g., the hard sensor values). If this is not known, then experimenters must decide which are going to be their *dependent variables* before applying GP. Sometimes, in practical situations, the data tables include hundreds or even thousands of variables. It is well known that in these cases the efficiency and effectiveness of any machine learning or program induction method, including GP, can dramatically drop as most of the variables are typically redundant or irrelevant. This forces the system to waste considerable energy on isolating the key features. To avoid this, it is necessary to perform some form of *feature selection*, i.e., we need to decide which *independent variables* to keep and which to leave out. There are many techniques to do this, but these are beyond the scope of this book. However, it is worth noting that GP itself can be used to do feature selection as shown in (Langdon and Buxton, 2004).

There are problems where more than one output (prediction) is required. For example, Table 12.1 shows a data set with four variables controlled during data collection (left) and six dependent variables (right). The data were collected for the purpose of solving an inverse kinematics problem in the Elvis robot (Langdon and Nordin, 2001). The robot is shown in Figure 12.1 during the acquisition of a data sample. The roles of the independent and dependent variables are swapped when GP is given the task of controlling the arm given data from the robot's eyes.

There are several GP techniques which might be used to deal with applications where multiple outputs are required: GP individuals including multiple trees (as in Figure 2.2, page 11), linear GP with multiple output registers (see Section 7.1), graph-based GP with multiple output nodes (see Section 7.2), a single GP tree with primitives operating on vectors, and so forth.

Once a suitable data set is available, its independent variables must all be represented in the primitive set. What other terminals and functions are included depends very much on the type of the data being processed (are they numeric? are they strings? etc.) and is often guided by the information available to the experimenter and the process that generated the data. If something is known (or strongly suspected) about the desired structure of the function to be evolved, it may be very beneficial to use this information (or to apply some constraints, like those discussed in Section 6.2). For example, if the data are known to be periodic, then the function set should probably include something like the sine function.

What is common to virtually all symbolic regression problems is that the fitness function must measure how close the outputs produced by each program are to the values of the dependent variables, when the corresponding values of the independent ones are used as inputs for the program. So,

Table 12.1: Samples showing the size and location of `Elvis`'s finger tip as apparent to this two eyes, given various right arm actuator set points (4 degrees of freedom). Cf. Figure 12.1. When the data are used for training, GP is asked to invert the mapping and evolve functions from data collected by both cameras showing a target location to instructions to give to `Elvis`'s four arm motors so that its arm moves to the target.

Arm actuator				Left eye			Right eye		
				x	y	size	x	y	size
-376	-626	1000	-360	44	10	29	-9	12	25
-372	-622	1000	-380	43	7	29	-9	12	29
-377	-627	899	-359	43	9	33	-20	14	26
-385	-635	799	-319	38	16	27	-17	22	30
-393	-643	699	-279	36	24	26	-21	25	20
-401	-651	599	-239	32	32	25	-26	28	18
-409	-659	500	-200	32	35	24	-27	31	19
-417	-667	399	-159	31	41	17	-28	36	13
-425	-675	299	-119	30	45	25	-27	39	8
-433	-683	199	-79	31	47	20	-27	43	9
-441	-691	99	-39	31	49	16	-26	45	13
⋮	⋮	⋮	⋮	⋮	⋮	⋮	⋮	⋮	⋮

continues for a total of 691 lines

most symbolic regression fitness functions tend to include summing the errors measured for each record in the data set, as we did in Section 4.2.2. Usually either the absolute difference or the square of the error is used.

The fourth preparatory step typically involves choosing a size for the population (which is often done initially based on the perceived difficulty of the problem, and is then refined based on the actual results of preliminary runs). The user also needs to set the balance between the selection strength (normally tuned via the tournament size) and the intensity of variation (which can be varied by modifying the mutation and crossover rates, but many researchers tend to fix to some standard values).

FINGER TIP

Figure 12.1: Elvis sitting with its right hand outstretched. The apparent position and size of a bright red laser attached to its finger tip is recorded (see Table 12.1). The data are then used to train a GP to move the robot's arm to a spot in three dimensions using only its eyes.

12.3 Human Competitive Results: The *Humies*

Getting machines to produce human-like results is the very reason for the existence of the fields of artificial intelligence and machine learning. However, it has always been very difficult to assess how much progress these fields have made towards their ultimate goal. Alan Turing understood that in order to avoid human biases when assessing machine intelligence, machine behaviour must be evaluated *objectively*. This led him to propose an imitation game, now known as the *Turing test* (Turing, 1950). Unfortunately, the Turing test is not usable in practice, and so, there is a need for more workable objective tests of machine intelligence.

Koza, Bennett, and Stiffelman (1999) suggested shifting attention from the notion of intelligence to the notion of *human competitiveness*. A result cannot acquire the rating of "human competitive" merely because it is endorsed by researchers *inside* the specialised fields that are attempting to create machine intelligence. A result produced by an automated method must earn the rating of "human competitive" independently of the fact that it was generated by an automated method.

Koza proposed that an automatically-created result should be considered "human-competitive" if it satisfies at least one of these eight criteria:

1. The result was patented as an invention in the past, is an improvement over a patented invention or would qualify today as a patentable new invention.

2. The result is equal to or better than a result that was accepted as a new scientific result at the time when it was published in a peer-reviewed scientific journal.

3. The result is equal to or better than a result that was placed into a database or archive of results maintained by an internationally recognised panel of scientific experts.

4. The result is publishable in its own right as a new scientific result, independent of the fact that the result was mechanically created.

5. The result is equal to or better than the most recent human-created solution to a long-standing problem for which there has been a succession of increasingly better human-created solutions.

6. The result is equal to or better than a result that was considered an achievement in its field at the time it was first discovered.

7. The result solves a problem of indisputable difficulty in its field.

8. The result holds its own or wins a regulated competition involving human contestants (in the form of either live human players or human-written computer programs).

These criteria are independent of, and at arm's length from, the fields of artificial intelligence, machine learning, and GP.

Over the years, dozens of results have passed the human-competitiveness test. Some pre-2004 human-competitive results include:

- Creation of quantum algorithms, including a better-than-classical algorithm for a database search problem and a solution to an AND/OR query problem (Spector et al., 1998, 1999).

- Creation of a competitive soccer-playing program for the RoboCup 1997 competition (Luke, 1998).

- Creation of algorithms for the transmembrane segment identification problem for proteins (Koza, 1994, Sections 18.8 and 18.10) and (Koza et al., 1999, Sections 16.5 and 17.2).

- Creation of a sorting network for seven items using only 16 steps (Koza et al., 1999, Sections 21.4.4, 23.6, and 57.8.1).

- Synthesis of analogue circuits (with placement and routing, in some cases), including: 60- and 96-decibel amplifiers (Koza et al., 1999, Section 45.3); circuits for squaring, cubing, square root, cube root, logarithm, and Gaussian functions (Koza et al., 1999, Section 47.5.3); a circuit for time-optimal control of a robot (Koza et al., 1999, Section 48.3); an electronic thermometer (Koza et al., 1999, Section 49.3); a voltage-current conversion circuit (Koza, Keane, Streeter, Mydlowec, Yu, and Lanza, 2003, Section 15.4.4).

- Creation of a cellular automaton rule for the majority classification problem that is better than all known rules written by humans (Andre et al., 1996).

- Synthesis of topology for controllers, including: a PID (proportional, integrative, and derivative) controller (Koza et al., 2003, Section 9.2) and a PID-D2 (proportional, integrative, derivative, and second derivative) controller (Koza et al., 2003, Section 3.7); PID tuning rules that outperform the Ziegler-Nichols and Astrom-Hagglund tuning rules (Koza et al., 2003, Chapter 12); three non-PID controllers that outperform a PID controller that uses the Ziegler-Nichols or Astrom-Hagglund tuning rules (Koza et al., 2003, Chapter 13).

In total (Koza and Poli, 2005) lists 36 human-competitive results. These include 23 cases where GP has duplicated the functionality of a previously patented invention, infringed a previously patented invention, or created a patentable new invention. Specifically, there are fifteen examples where GP has created an entity that either infringes or duplicates the functionality of a previously patented 20th-century invention, six instances where GP has done the same with respect to an invention patented after 1 January 2000, and two cases where GP has created a patentable new invention. The two new inventions are general-purpose controllers that outperform controllers employing tuning rules that have been in widespread use in industry for most of the 20th century.

Many of the pre-2004 results were obtained by Koza. However, since 2004, a competition has been held annually at ACM's *Genetic and Evolutionary Computation Conference* (termed the Human-Competitive awards – the *Humies*). The $10,000 prize is awarded to projects that have produced automatically-created results which equal or better those produced by humans.

The Humies Prizes have typically been awarded to applications of evolutionary computation to high-tech fields. Many used GP. For example, the 2004 gold medals were given for the design, via GP, of an antenna for

Figure 12.2: Award winning human-competitive antenna design produced by GP.

deployment on NASA's Space Technology 5 Mission (see Figure 12.2) (Lohn et al., 2004) and for evolutionary quantum computer programming (Spector, 2004). There were three silver medals in 2004: one for the evolution of local search heuristics for SAT using GP (Fukunaga, 2004), one for the application of GP to the synthesis of complex kinematic mechanisms (Lipson, 2004) and one for organisation design optimisation using GP (KHosraviani, 2003; KHosraviani, Levitt, and Koza, 2004). Also, four of the 2005 medals were awarded for GP applications: the invention of optical lens systems (Al-Sakran, Koza, and Jones, 2005; Koza, Al-Sakran, and Jones, 2005), the evolution of a quantum Fourier transform algorithm (Massey, Clark, and Stepney, 2005), evolving assembly programs for `Core War` (Corno, Sanchez, and Squillero, 2005) and various high-performance game players for Backgammon, Robocode and Chess endgame (Azaria and Sipper, 2005a,b; Hauptman and Sipper, 2005; Shichel, Ziserman, and Sipper, 2005). In 2006, GP again scored a gold medal with the synthesis of interest point detectors for image analysis (Trujillo and Olague, 2006a,b), while it scored a silver medal in 2007 with the evolution of an efficient search algorithm for the Mate-in-N problem in Chess (Hauptman and Sipper, 2007) (see Figure 12.3).

Note that many human competitive results were presented at the Humies 2004–2007 competitions (e.g., 11 of the 2004 entries were judged to be human competitive). However, only the very best were awarded medals. So, at the

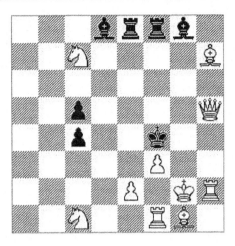

Figure 12.3: Example mate-in-2 problem.

time of writing we estimate that there are at least 60 human competitive results obtained by GP. This shows GP's potential as a powerful invention machine.

12.4   Image and Signal Processing

Hampo and Marko (1992) were among the first people from industry to consider using GP for signal processing. They evolved algorithms for pre-processing electronic motor vehicle signals for possible use in engine monitoring and control.

Several applications of GP for image processing have been for military uses. For example, Tackett (1993) evolved algorithms to find tanks in infrared images. Howard, Roberts, and Brankin (1999); Howard, Roberts, and Ryan (2006) evolved programs to pick out ships from SAR radar mounted on satellites in space and to locate ground vehicles from airborne photo reconnaissance. They also used GP to process surveillance data for civilian purposes, such as predicting motorway traffic jams from subsurface traffic speed measurements (Howard and Roberts, 2004).

Using satellite SAR radar, Daida, Hommes, Bersano-Begey, Ross, and Vesecky (1996) evolved algorithms to find features in polar sea ice. Optical satellite images can also be used for environmental studies (Chami and Robilliard, 2002) and for prospecting for valuable minerals (Ross, Gualtieri, Fueten, and Budkewitsch, 2005).

Alcazar used GP to find recurrent filters (including artificial neural networks (Esparcia-Alcazar and Sharman, 1996)) for one-dimensional electronic signals (Sharman and Esparcia-Alcazar, 1993). Local search (simulated annealing or gradient descent) can be used to adjust or fine-tune "constant" values within the structure created by genetic search (Smart and Zhang, 2004).

Yu and Bhanu (2006) have used GP to preprocess images, particularly of human faces, to find regions of interest for subsequent analysis. See also (Trujillo and Olague, 2006a).

Zhang has been particularly active at evolving programs with GP to visually classify objects (typically coins) (Zhang and Smart, 2006). He has also applied GP to human speech (Xie, Zhang, and Andreae, 2006).

"Parisian GP" is a system in which the image processing task is split across a swarm of evolving agents ("flies"). In (Louchet, 2001; Louchet, Guyon, Lesot, and Boumaza, 2002) the flies reconstruct three dimensions from pairs of stereo images. For example, in (Louchet, 2001), as the flies buzz around in three dimensions their position is projected onto the left and right of a pair of stereo images. The fitness function tries to minimise the discrepancy between the two images, thus encouraging the flies to settle on visible surfaces in the 3-D space. So, the true 3-D space is inferred from pairs of 2-D images taken from slightly different positions.

While the likes of Google have effectively indexed the written word, for speech and pictures indexing has been much less effective. One area where GP might be applied is in the automatic indexing of images. Some initial steps in this direction are given in (Theiler, Harvey, Brumby, Szymanski, Alferink, Perkins, Porter, and Bloch, 1999).

To some extent, extracting text from images (OCR) can be done fairly reliably, and the accuracy rate on well formed letters and digits is close to 100%. However, many interesting cases remain (Cilibrasi and Vitanyi, 2005) such as Arabic (Klassen and Heywood, 2002) and oriental languages, handwriting (De Stefano, Cioppa, and Marcelli, 2002; Gagne and Parizeau, 2006; Krawiec, 2004; Teredesai and Govindaraju, 2005) (such as the MNIST examples), other texts (Rivero, nal, Dorado, and Pazos, 2004) and musical scores (Quintana, Poli, and Claridge, 2006).

The scope for applications of GP to image and signal processing is almost unbounded. A promising area is medical imaging (Poli, 1996b). GP image techniques can also be used with sonar signals (Martin, 2006). Off-line work on images includes security and verification. For example, Usman, Khan, Chamlawi, and Majid (2007) have used GP to detect image watermarks which have been tampered with. Recent work by Zhang has incorporated multi-objective fitness into GP image processing (Zhang and Rockett, 2006).

In 1999 Poli, Cagnoni and others founded the annual *European Workshop on Evolutionary Computation in Image Analysis and Signal Processing* (EvoIASP). *EvoIASP* is held every year with the *EuroGP*. Whilst not solely dedicated to GP, many GP applications have been presented at *EvoIASP*.

12.5   Financial Trading, Time Series Prediction and Economic Modelling

GP is very widely used in the areas of financial trading, time series prediction and economic modelling and it is impossible to describe all its applications. It this section we will hint at just a few areas.

Chen has written more than 60 papers on using GP in finance and economics. Recent papers have looked at the modelling of agents in stock markets (Chen and Liao, 2005), game theory (Chen, Duffy, and Yeh, 2002), evolving trading rules for the S&P 500 (Yu and Chen, 2004) and forecasting the Heng-Sheng index (Chen, Wang, and Zhang, 1999).

The *efficient markets hypothesis* is a tenet of economics. It is founded on the idea that everyone in a market has "perfect information" and acts "rationally". If the efficient markets hypothesis held, then everyone would see the same value for items in the market and so agree the same price. Without price differentials, there would be no money to be made from the market itself. Whether it is trading potatoes in northern France or dollars for yen, it is clear that traders are not all equal and considerable doubt has been cast on the efficient markets hypothesis. So, people continue to play the stock market. Game theory has been a standard tool used by economists to try to understand markets but is increasingly supplemented by simulations with both human and computerised agents. GP is increasingly being used as part of these simulations of social systems.

Neely, Weller, and Dittmar (1997), Neely and Weller (1999, 2001) and Neely (2003) of the US Federal Reserve Bank used GP to study intra-day technical trading on the foreign exchange markets to suggest the market is "efficient" and found no evidence of excess returns. This negative result was criticised by Marney, Miller, Fyfe, and Tarbert (2001). Later work by Neely, Weller, and Ulrich (2006) suggested that data after 1995 are consistent with Lo's *adaptive markets hypothesis* rather than the *efficient markets hypothesis*. Note that here GP and computer tools are being used in a novel data-driven approach to try and resolve issues which were previously a matter of dogma.

From a more pragmatic viewpoint, Kaboudan shows GP can forecast international currency exchange rates (Kaboudan, 2005), stocks (Kaboudan, 2000) and stock returns (Kaboudan, 1999). Tsang and his co-workers continue to apply GP to a variety of financial arenas, including: betting (Tsang, Li, and Butler, 1998), forecasting stock prices (Li and Tsang, 1999; Tsang and Li, 2002; Tsang, Yung, and Li, 2004), studying markets (Martinez-Jaramillo and Tsang, 2007), approximating Nash equilibrium in game theory (Jin, 2005; Jin and Tsang, 2006; Tsang and Jin, 2006) and arbitrage (Tsang, Markose, and Er, 2005). Dempster and HSBC also use GP in foreign exchange trading (Austin, Bates, Dempster, Leemans, and Williams,

2004; Dempster and Jones, 2000; Dempster, Payne, Romahi, and Thompson, 2001). Pillay has used GP in social studies and teaching aids in education, e.g. (Pillay, 2003). As well as trees (Koza, 1990), other types of GP have been used in finance, e.g. (Nikolaev and Iba, 2002).

Since 1995 the *International Conference on Computing in Economics and Finance* (CEF) has been held every year. It regularly attracts GP papers, many of which are on-line. In 2007 Brabazon and O'Neill established the *European Workshop on Evolutionary Computation in Finance and Economics* (EvoFIN). EvoFIN is held with EuroGP.

12.6   Industrial Process Control

There is evidence that GP is frequently used in industrial process control, although, of course, most industrialists have little time to spend on academic reporting. A notable exception is Dow Chemical, where a group has been very active in publishing results (Castillo, Kordon, and Smits, 2006a; Castillo, Kordon, Smits, Christenson, and Dickerson, 2006b; Jordaan, den Doelder, and Smits, 2006; Kordon, Castillo, Smits, and Kotanchek, 2005; Kotanchek et al., 2006; Mercure, Smits, and Kordon, 2001). Kordon (2006) describes where industrial GP stands now and how it will progress.

Another active collaboration is that of Kovacic and Balic, who used GP in the computer numerical control of industrial milling and cutting machinery (Kovacic and Balic, 2003). The partnership of Deschaine and Francone (Francone and Deschaine, 2004) is most famous for their use of Discipulus (Foster, 2001) for detecting bomb fragments and unexploded ordnance (Deschaine, 2006). Discipulus has also been used as an aid in the development of control systems for rubbish incinerators (Deschaine, Patel, Guthrie, Grimski, and Ades, 2001).

One of the earliest users of GP in control was Willis' Chemical Engineering group at Newcastle, which used GP to model flow in a plasticating extruder (Willis, Hiden, and Montague, 1997a). Other GP applications in the plastics industry include (Brezocnik, Balic, and Gusel, 2000). McKay, Willis, Searson, and Montague (2000) also modelled extruding food. Searson, Montague, and Willis (1998) modelled control of chemical reactions in continuous stirred tank reactors. Marenbach (1998) investigated GP in the control of biotech reactors. Willis, Hiden, Marenbach, McKay, and Montague (1997b) surveyed GP applications, including in the area of control.

Lewin, Lachman-Shalem, and Grosman (2006) and Dassau, Grosman, and Lewin (2006) applied GP to the control of an integrated circuit fabrication plant. Domingos worked on simulations of nuclear reactors (PWRs to be exact) to devise better ways of preventing xenon oscillations (Domingos, Schirru, and Martinez, 2005). GP has also been used to identify the state of a plant to be controlled (in order to decide which of various alternative control laws to apply). For example, Fleming's group in Sheffield used multi-objective GP (Hinchliffe and Willis, 2003; Rodriguez-Vazquez, Fonseca, and Fleming, 2004) to reduce the cost of running aircraft jet engines (Arkov, Evans, Fleming, Hill, Norton, Pratt, Rees, and Rodriguez-Vazquez, 2000; Evans, Fleming, Hill, Norton, Pratt, Rees, and Rodriguez-Vazquez, 2001).

Alves da Silva and Abrao (2002) surveyed GP and other AI techniques applied in the electrical power industry.

12.7 Medicine, Biology and Bioinformatics

GP has long been applied to medicine, biology and bioinformatics. Early work by Handley (1993) and Koza and Andre (1996) used GP to make predictions about the behaviour and properties of biological systems, principally proteins. Oakley, a practising medical doctor, used GP to model blood flow in toes (Oakley, 1994) as part of his long term interests in frostbite.

In 2002 Banzhaf and Foster organised BioGEC: the first GECCO workshop on biological applications of genetic and evolutionary computation. BioGEC has become a bi-annual feature of the annual GECCO conference. Half a year later Marchiori and Corne organised EvoBio: the European conference on evolutionary computation, machine learning and data mining in bioinformatics. EvoBio is held every year alongside EuroGP. GP figures heavily in both BioGEC and EvoBIO.

GP is often used in biomedical data mining. Of particular medical interest are very wide data sets, with many inputs per sample (Lavington, Dewhurst, Wilkins, and Freitas, 1999). Examples include infrared spectra (Ellis, Broadhurst, and Goodacre, 2004; Ellis, Broadhurst, Kell, Rowland, and Goodacre, 2002; Goodacre, 2003; Goodacre, Shann, Gilbert, Timmins, McGovern, Alsberg, Kell, and Logan, 2000; Harrigan, LaPlante, Cosma, Cockerell, Goodacre, Maddox, Luyendyk, Ganey, and Roth, 2004; Johnson, Gilbert, Winson, Goodacre, Smith, Rowland, Hall, and Kell, 2000; McGovern, Broadhurst, Taylor, Kaderbhai, Winson, Small, Rowland, Kell, and Goodacre, 2002; Taylor, Goodacre, Wade, Rowland, and Kell, 1998; Vaidyanathan, Broadhurst, Kell, and Goodacre, 2003), single nuclear polymorphisms (Barrett, 2003; Reif, White, and Moore, 2004; Shah and Kusiak, 2004), chest pain (Bojarczuk, Lopes, and Freitas, 2000), and Affymetrix GeneChip microarray data (de Sousa, de C. T. Gomes, Bezerra, de Castro, and Von Zuben, 2004; Eriksson and Olsson, 2004; Heidema, Boer, Nagelkerke, Mariman, van der A, and Feskens, 2006; Ho, Hsieh, Chen, and Huang, 2006; Hong and Cho, 2006; Langdon and Buxton, 2004; Li, Jiang, Li, Moser, Guo, Du, Wang, Topol, Wang, and Rao, 2005; Linden and Bhaya, 2007; Yu, Yu, Almal, Dhanasekaran, Ghosh, Worzel, and Chinnaiyan, 2007).

Kell and his colleagues in Aberystwyth have had great success in applying GP widely in bioinformatics (see infrared spectra above and (Allen, Davey, Broadhurst, Heald, Rowland, Oliver, and Kell, 2003; Day, Kell, and Griffith, 2002; Gilbert, Goodacre, Woodward, and Kell, 1997; Goodacre and Gilbert, 1999; Jones, Young, Taylor, Kell, and Rowland, 1998; Kell, 2002a,b,c; Kell, Darby, and Draper, 2001; Shaw, Winson, Woodward, McGovern, Davey, Kaderbhai, Broadhurst, Gilbert, Taylor, Timmins, Goodacre, Kell, Alsberg, and Rowland, 2000; Woodward, Gilbert, and Kell, 1999)). Another very active group is that of Moore and his colleagues (Moore, Parker, Olsen, and Aune, 2002; Motsinger, Lee, Mellick, and Ritchie, 2006; Ritchie, Motsinger, Bush, Coffey, and Moore, 2007; Ritchie, White, Parker, Hahn, and Moore, 2003).

Computational chemistry is widely used in the drug industry. The properties of simple molecules can be calculated. However, the interactions between chemicals which might be used as drugs and medicinal targets within the body are beyond exact calculation. Therefore, there is great interest in the pharmaceutical industry in approximate *in silico* models which attempt to predict either favourable or adverse interactions between proto-drugs and biochemical molecules. Since these are computational models, they can be applied very cheaply in advance of the manufacturing of chemicals, to decide which of the myriad of chemicals might be worth further study. Potentially, such models can make a huge impact both in terms of money and time without being anywhere near 100% correct. Machine learning and GP have both been tried. GP approaches include (Bains, Gilbert, Sviridenko, Gascon, Scoffin, Birchall, Harvey, and Caldwell, 2002; Barrett and Langdon, 2006; Buxton, Langdon, and Barrett, 2001; Felton, 2000; Globus, Lawton, and Wipke, 1998; Goodacre, Vaidyanathan, Dunn, Harrigan, and Kell, 2004; Harrigan et al., 2004; Hasan, Daugelat, Rao, and Schreiber, 2006; Krasnogor, 2004; Si, Wang, Zhang, Hu, and Fan, 2006; Venkatraman, Dalby, and Yang, 2004; Weaver, 2004).

12.8   GP to Create Searchers and Solvers – Hyper-heuristics

Hyper-heuristics could simply be defined as "heuristics to choose other heuristics" (Burke, Kendall, Newall, Hart, Ross, and Schulenburg, 2003). A *heuristic* is considered as a rule-of-thumb or "educated guess" that reduces the search required to find a solution. The difference between meta-heuristics and hyper-heuristics is that the former operate directly on the problem search space with the goal of finding optimal or near-optimal solutions. The latter, instead, operate on the heuristics search space (which consists of the heuristics used to solve the target problem). The goal then is finding or generating high-quality heuristics for a problem, for a certain class of instances of a problem, or even for a particular instance.

GP has been very successfully used as a hyperheuristic. For example, GP has evolved competitive SAT solvers (Bader-El-Den and Poli, 2007a,b; Fukunaga, 2002; Kibria and Li, 2006), state-of-the-art or better than state-of-the-art bin packing algorithms (Burke, Hyde, and Kendall, 2006; Burke, Hyde, Kendall, and Woodward, 2007; Poli, Woodward, and Burke, 2007), particle swarm optimisers (Poli, Di Chio, and Langdon, 2005; Poli, Langdon, and Holland, 2005), evolutionary algorithms (Oltean, 2005), and travelling salesman problem solvers (Keller and Poli, 2007a,b,c; Oltean and Dumitrescu, 2004).

12.9 ³/₄ Entertainment and Computer Games

Today, a major usage of computers is interactive games (Priesterjahn, Kramer, Weimer, and Goebels, 2006). There has been some work on incorporating artificial intelligence into mainstream commercial games. The software owners are not keen on explaining exactly how much AI they use or giving away sensitive information on how they use AI. Work on GP and games includes (Azaria and Sipper, 2005a; Langdon and Poli, 2005; Vowk, Wait, and Schmidt, 2004) as well as the human-competitive game players mentioned in Section 12.3, page 120. Funes reports experiments which attracted thousands of people via the Internet who were entertained by evolved Tron players (Funes, Sklar, Juille, and Pollack, 1998b).

Since 2004, the annual IEEE CEC conference has included sessions on evolutionary computation in games. After chairing the IEEE Symposium on Computational Intelligence and Games 2005, at Essex University, Simon Lucas founded the IEEE Computational Intelligence Society's Technical Committee on Games. GP features heavily in the Games TC's activities having being applied to Othello, poker, backgammon, draughts, chess, Ms Pac-Man, robotic football and radio controlled model car racing.

12.10 The Arts

Computers have long been used to create purely aesthetic artifacts. Much of today's computer art tends to ape traditional drawing and painting, producing static pictures on a computer monitor. However, the immediate advantage of the computer screen — movement — can also be exploited. In both cases evolutionary computation can and has been exploited. Indeed, with evolution's capacity for unlimited variation, evolutionary computation offers the artist the scope to produce ever changing works. Some artists have also worked with sound.

The use of GP in computer art can be traced back at least to the work of Sims (Sims, 1991) and Latham.[1] Jacob's work (Jacob, 2000, 2001) provides many examples. McCormack (2006) considers the recent state of play in evolutionary art and music. Many recent techniques are described in (Machado and Romero, 2008).

Evolutionary music (Todd and Werner, 1999) has been dominated by Jazz (Spector and Alpern, 1994). An exception is Bach (Federman, Sparkman, and Watt, 1999). Most approaches to evolving music have made at least some use of interactive evolution (Takagi, 2001) in which the fitness of programs is provided by users, often via the Internet (Ando, Dahlsted, Nordahl, and Iba, 2007; Chao and Forrest, 2003). The limitation is almost always finding enough people willing to participate (Langdon, 2004). Costelloe and Ryan (2007) tried to reduce the human burden. Algorithmic approaches are also possible (Cilibrasi, Vitanyi, and de Wolf, 2004; Inagaki, 2002).

One of the sorrows of AI is that as soon as it works it stops being AI (and celebrated as such) and becomes computer engineering. For example, the use of computer generated images has recently become cost effective and is widely used in Hollywood. One of the standard state-of-the-art techniques is the use of Reynold's swarming "boids" (Reynolds, 1987) to create animations of large numbers of rapidly moving animals. This was first used in *Cliffhanger* (1993) to animate a cloud of bats. Its use is now commonplace (herds of wildebeest, schooling fish, and even large crowds of people). In 1997 Reynold was awarded an Oscar.

Since 2003, EvoMUSART (the European Workshop on Evolutionary Music and Art) has been held every year along with the EuroGP conference as part of the EvoStar event.

12.11   Compression

Koza (1992) was the first to use genetic programming to perform compression. He considered, in particular, the lossy compression of images. The idea was to treat an image as a function of two variables (the row and column of each pixel) and to use GP to evolve a function that matches as closely as possible the original. One can then use the evolved GP tree as a lossy compressed version of the image, since it is possible to obtain the original image by evaluating the program at each row-column pair of interest. The technique, which was termed *programmatic compression*, was tested on one small synthetic image with good success. Programmatic compression was further developed and applied to realistic data (images and sounds) by Nordin and Banzhaf (1996).

---

[1]http://www.williamlatham1.com/

Iterated Functions System (IFS) are important in the domain of fractals and the fractal compression algorithm. Lutton, Levy-Vehel, Cretin, Glevarec, and Roll (1995a,b) used genetic programming to solve the inverse problem of identifying a mixed IFS whose attractor is a specific binary (black and white) image of interest. The evolved program can then be taken to represent the original image. In principle, this can then be further compressed. The technique is lossy, since rarely the inverse problem can be solved exactly. No practical application or compression ratio results were reported in (Lutton et al., 1995a,b). Using similar principles, Sarafopoulos (1999) used GP to evolve affine IFSs whose attractors represent a binary image containing a square (which was compressed exactly) and one containing a fern (which was achieved with some error in the finer details).

Wavelets are frequently used in lossy image and signal compression. Klappenecker and May (1995) used GP to evolve wavelet compression algorithms (internal nodes represented conjugate quadrature filters, leaves represented quantisers). Results on a small set of real-world images were impressive, with the GP compression outperforming JPEG at all compression ratios.

The first lossless compression technique (Fukunaga and Stechert, 1998) used GP to evolve non-linear predictors for images. These were used to predict the gray level a pixel will take based on the gray values of a subset of its neighbours (those that have already been computed in a row-by-row and column-by-column scan of the image array). The prediction errors together with the model's description represent a compressed version of the image. These were compressed using the Huffman encoding. Results on five images from the NASA Galileo Mission database were very promising with GP compression outperforming some of the best human-designed lossless compression algorithms.

In many compression algorithms some form of pre-processing or transformation of the original data is performed before compression. This often improves compression ratios. Parent and Nowe (2002) evolved pre-processors for image compression using GP. The objective of the pre-processor was to reduce losslessly the entropy in the original image. In tests with five images from the Canterbury corpus, GP was successful in significantly reducing the image entropy. As verified via the application of bzip2, the resulting images were markedly easier to compress.

In (Krantz, Lindberg, Thorburn, and Nordin, 2002) the use of programmatic compression was extended from images to natural videos. A program was evolved that generates intermediate frames of video sequence, where each frame is composed by a series of transformed regions from the adjacent frames. The results were encouraging in the sense that a good approximation to frames was achieved. While a significant improvement in compression was achieved, programmatic compression was very slow in comparison with standard compression methods, the time needed for compression being measured in hours or even days. Acceleration in GP image compression was achieved in (He, Wang, Zhang, Wang, and Fang, 2005), where an optimal linear predictive technique was proposed which used a less complex fitness function.

Recently Kattan and Poli (2008) proposed a GP system called *GP-ZIP* for lossless data compression based on the idea of optimally combining well-known lossless compression algorithms. The file to be compressed was divided into chunks of a predefined length, and GP was asked to find the best possible compression algorithm for each chunk in such a way as to minimise the total length of the compressed file. The compression algorithms available to GP-ZIP included arithmetic coding, Lempel-Ziv-Welch, unbounded prediction by partial matching, and run length encoding among others. Experimentation showed that when the file to be compressed is composed of heterogeneous data fragments (as it is the case, for example, in archive files), GP-zip is capable of achieving compression ratios that are significantly superior to those obtained with other compression algorithms.

Chapter 13

Troubleshooting GP

The dynamics of evolutionary algorithms (including GP) are often very complex, and the behaviour of an EA is typically challenging to predict or understand. As a result it is often difficult to troubleshoot such systems when they are not performing as expected. While we obviously cannot provide troubleshooting suggestions that are specific to every GP implementation and application, we can suggest some general issues to keep in mind. To a large extent the advice in (Kinnear, 1994b; Koza, 1992; Langdon, 1998) also remains sound.

13.1   Is there a Bug in the Code?

Machine learning systems are notoriously difficult to protect from coding and logical mistakes. Unless a mistake produces a runtime error, it may remain hidden in a system for a long time and may contribute to the system achieving unsatisfactory results. Such mistakes are difficult to find because the system, being adaptive, will still work to some degree. This is also true of GP.

The most common reaction to a system not producing satisfactory results is to start playing with the parameters, the fitness function, the primitive set, etc. However, one should also consider the possibility of a coding mistake. The normal program validation techniques, such as inspection of critical regions of code, should be used to ensure everything is alright.

If the code is part of an established GP implementation, coding errors are less likely.[1] A more probable source of coding errors is stretching the GP library beyond its original intended use. Reading the manual carefully is sometimes a good preventive cure for problems.

---

[1] Coding errors cannot be entirely excluded, though, especially if a GP library is large and provides a rich set of features and functionalities.

13.2   Can you Trust your Results?

Since GP is a stochastic search algorithm, different runs may have different outcomes and yield different results. Because of this, one needs to be very careful in making inferences regarding the degree of success of the system from a small set of runs.

It is possible, for example, to run a GP system 10 times on a particular problem, observe that all 10 runs failed to find a solution, and conclude that GP cannot solve the problem. However, if the success probability is say 5% with a particular choice of parameters and representation, the probability of doing 10 runs and all of them failing is almost 60%! So, the failure to solve the problem in these 10 runs should not come as a surprise, even though there's a reasonable chance that you would find a solution if you did more runs.

For precisely this reason, it is very important to do enough runs and use appropriate statistical tests to ensure that conclusions are statistically significant.

GP runs can often be very time consuming, especially if the fitness function is computationally expensive. While parallel and distributed computing (see Section 10.4) can significantly speed up the process, tools from the *design of experiments* literature (Bartz-Beielstein, 2006) can also be used to reduce the number of different runs that are necessary to explore the space in a statistically sound manner.

A common GP application is classification, e.g., evolving a program or function that can classify patient biopsy data into two categories: cancerous or benign. There are numerous pitfalls in this type of work, such as using all the available data as training data, thereby leaving nothing to use for validating your evolved solution on unseen data. There is a broad literature on this and related subjects, and numerous tools such as cross-validation that one can use when not enough data are available. (See, for example, (Hastie, Tibshirani, and Friedman, 2001).) The aim must be to ensure that your results can be trusted to work in the real world, rather than in just the synthetic environment created by the fitness cases we chose.

13.3   There are No Silver Bullets

When working on real problems there are not likely to be any silver bullets. No technique (including GP) is likely to solve all instances of an NP-hard problem in an amount of time that grows linearly with the size of the problem. GP has proven extremely successful in a wide variety of domains (e.g., Chapter 12) but that doesn't mean that it will work immediately or easily in every domain, or even that it is the best tool for a specific domain.

While some of the successes in the field have been "easy", most were the result of significant effort by experienced practitioners. It is likely that for every GP approach that has successfully solved a problem, several others have failed. It is in the nature of academic publishing that one does not get to hear about failures.

So, don't expect immediate success, and don't become too discouraged by poor early results.

13.4 Small Changes can have Big Effects

Don't assume "a little fiddling" with parameters, operators, fitness functions, etc., is harmless. One of the awkward realities of many widely applicable tools is that they typically have numerous tunable parameters. Evolutionary algorithms such as GP are no exception. Often changing a parameter or two can have a fairly minimal impact, and averaging over many runs is required to reliably detect those effects. Some parameter changes, however, can produce more dramatic effects. Changing the function set, for example, can significantly change the distribution of the sizes and shapes of trees, especially in the early generations, and potentially bias the system in unexpected ways.

Another source of change can be the problem domain. A common mistake is to hope that parameter settings that worked well for one problem will also work well for what appears to be a very similar problem. Problems that appear similar to humans, however, may have quite different search characteristics.

In addition, there are many small differences in GP implementations that are rarely considered important or even reported. However, our experience is that they may produce significant changes in the behaviour of a GP system. Differences as small as an '$>$' in place of a '$\geq$' in an `if` statement can have an important effect. For example, the substitution '$>$' $\leftrightarrow$ '$\geq$' may influence the winners of tournaments, the designation of the best-of-run individual, the choice of which elements are cloned when elitism is used, or the offspring produced by operators which accept the offspring only if it is better or not worse than a parent.

13.5 Big Changes can have No Effect

When big changes appear to make little difference, this can sometimes be used to identify problems with the domain representation and fitness measure. Alternatively it may be that the problem is simply too difficult, and no change is likely to make a significant difference.

Suppose that you're not making much progress during a set of runs. One might react by sweeping the parameter space, doing runs with a variety of different parameter settings in the hope of finding a better collection of parameter values. What if changing the parameter values really does not have much impact? That may mean that GP just is not able to gain any traction given your current representation of the problem domain and fitness function. You might, therefore, reconsider how the problem is posed to GP. If the representation and fitness make the problem essentially a search for a needle in a haystack, then GP will mostly be lost searching through highly sub-optimal solutions. If so, altering parameter values is unlikely to help.

Note that essentially the same symptoms are also observed if the problem is really beyond the capabilities of your computing resources. For example, if the solutions are exceptionally rare, unless there are nice fitness gradients guiding GP towards them, finding any solution will likely be beyond the capacity of current computer technology.

How can one distinguish which is the cause of the lack of success? Is it a bad choice of representation and fitness or is it just an extremely hard problem? To answer these questions, it is important to look at what happened when the population size was varied. Even in the absence of fitness guidance, GP will search. In fact, it will perform a sort of random exploration of the search space. It may not be a particularly rational exploration — we know, for example, that GP with subtree crossover tends to oversample and re-sample short programs — yet, it is still a form of stochastic search. Thus, one may expect that, if the problem is solvable, as the population size is progressively increased, sooner or later we should start seeing some variation in the fitness of programs. This may be sufficient for evolution to work with, particularly if we help it by improving the representation and fitness function. If, instead, nothing interesting happened as the population size was increased, then perhaps you don't have enough computing power to solve the problem as posed, or the problem has no solution.

13.6   Study your Populations

If you're not getting your desired results, it is important to take the time to dig around in the populations and see what is actually being evolved.[2] For example, if you're using ADFs because you think that your problem would benefit from a modular solution, examine the individuals that you're evolving. Are they using ADFs? (Sometimes the result producing branch simply will not refer to the ADFs at all.) Are they using them in a modular way? Are ADFs being used multiple times? Do the ADFs encapsulate some interesting logic, or are they just re-naming an input variable? If you're using grammatical evolution, on the other hand, are your evolved individuals using your grammar as you expected? Or is the grammar in fact biasing

---

[2]If the system you're using doesn't allow you to dump individuals from a run, add that functionality or use a different system.

the system in an undesirable and unexpected way? Similar questions can be asked for almost any flavour of GP; think about your goals and expectations, and explore your populations to see to what degree those are being met.

Similarly, it can be valuable to look at the way your population changes over time in more detail than that provided by the standard plot of fitness vs. time. You might look at the distribution of tree sizes during your run, or the distribution of fitness values. The distribution of fitness values might suggest things about the structure of the search space as seen by your GP system. If it seems to be dominated by disjoint values with large gaps between them, then jumping those gaps may be a major challenge for your system and it may be the cause for poor performance.

While it is important to look inside your populations, the time and effort required to do so is effectively a function of how much information is recorded. Computer algorithms can easily generate enormous amounts of data, especially if you produce a detailed log of events and individuals generated during your runs. Consequently, processing those results may become a challenging data-mining exercise. Finding good ways to visualise those large data sets can be extremely valuable. While there are a handful of papers that specifically address visualisation, e.g., (Daida, Hilss, Ward, and Long, 2005; Pohlheim, 1999; Yamashiro, Yoshikawa, and Furuhashi, 2006), and even the occasional workshop (Smith, Bullock, and Bird, 2002), most visualisation techniques are scattered through the literature and we are unaware of any comprehensive review. Where we can provide a bit more guidance is program visualisation.

An obvious (but easy to forget) advantage of GP is that we create *visible* programs. This need not be the case with other approaches. So, when presenting GP results, as a matter of routine one should consider making a figure which contains the whole evolved program. The dot component of the Graphviz package[3] can be particularly helpful in this regard; Figure 6.2 is an example of a tree diagram generated with a simple dot input file. The program lisp2dot[4] can help with the conversion from Lisp-style expressions to dot input files.

As the evolved trees can often be very large, it is usually helpful to perform at least some basic simplifications such as removing excess significant digits in constants and combining constant terms. Naturally, after cleaning up the evolved program, one should make sure it still works; you should also clearly indicate in any presentation or write-up that the program you're presenting has been cleaned and is not the actual tree generated by GP.

There are methods to automatically simplify expressions (e.g., in Mathematica and Emacs). However, since in general there is an exponentially large number of equivalent expressions, automatic simplification is hard. Another

---

[3]http://www.graphviz.org/
[4]http://www.cs.ucl.ac.uk/staff/W.Langdon/lisp2dot.html

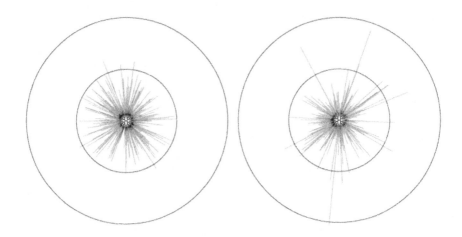

Figure 13.1: Visualisation of the size and shape of the entire population of 1,000 individuals in the final generation of runs using a depth limit of 50 (on the left) and a size limit of 600 (on the right). The inner circle is at depth 50, and the outer circle is at depth 100. These plots are from (Crane and McPhee, 2005) and were drawn using the techniques described in (Daida et al., 2005).

way is to use GP as a multi-objective evolutionary algorithm (cf. Chapter 9.)

In some cases the details of the trees are less important than their general size and shape. Daida et al. (2005) presented a particularly useful set of visualisation techniques for this situation.[5] These techniques allow one to see the size and shape of both individual trees as well as an aggregate view of entire populations. Figure 13.1, for example, shows the impact of size and depth limits on the size and shape of trees in two different runs with very similar *average* sizes and depths. The plots make it clear, however, that the shapes of the resulting trees were quite different.

13.7   Encourage Diversity

One important property to keep an eye on is population diversity. Two particular measures that can be useful sources of information are:

Frequency of primitives Recognising when a primitive has been completely lost from the population (or its frequency has fallen to a low level, consistent with the mutation rate) may help to diagnose problems.

---

[5]A Mathematica implementation of this technique can be downloaded from http://library.wolfram.com/infocenter/MathSource/5163/.

Population variety If the variety —the number of distinct individuals in the population— falls below 90% of the population size, this may indicate that there is a problem. However, a high variety does not mean the reverse. GP populations often contain introns (Section 11.3), and so programs which are not identical may behave identically (Gustafson, 2004; McPhee and Hopper, 1999). Being different, these individuals contribute to a high variety. So, a high variety need not indicate all is well. Measuring phenotypic variation (i.e., diversity of behaviour) may also be useful (McPhee, Ohs, and Hutchison, 2008).

Insufficient diversity may cause significant problems. Panmictic[6] steady-state populations with tournament selection, reproduction and crossover, for example, are prone to premature convergence. If you find this to be an issue, measures should be taken to encourage population diversity such as:

- Not using the reproduction operator.

- Adding one or more mutation operators.

- Using a weaker selection mechanism, e.g., using smaller tournament sizes.

- Using uniform random selection (instead of the standard negative tournaments) to decide which individuals to remove from the population.[7]

- Using a generational population model instead of a steady-state model.

- Splitting large populations into semi-isolated demes (Section 10.5).[8]

- Using fitness sharing to encourage the formation of many fitness niches.

13.8 Embrace Approximation

There is a widespread belief that computer programs are fragile and that any change to any bit in them will cause them to stop working. This is fostered by the common knowledge that a small typing mistake by a human programmer can sometimes introduce a troublesome bug into a program.

---

[6]In a panmictic population no mating restrictions are imposed as to which individual mates with which.

[7]Doing this means that the selection scheme is no longer elitist, and it may be worthwhile to protect the best individual(s) to preserve the elitism.

[8]What is meant by a "large population" has changed over time. In the early days of GP, populations of 1,000 or more could be considered large. However, CPU speeds and computer memory have increased exponentially over time. So, at the time of writing it is not unusual to see populations of hundred of thousands or millions of individuals being used in the solution of hard problems. Research indicates that there are benefits in splitting populations into demes even for much smaller populations. See Section 10.5.

Programmers know from painful experience, however, that far from proving immediately fatal, errors can lay hidden for years. Further, not all errors are created equal. Some are indeed critical and must be dealt with immediately, while others are rare or largely inconsequential and so never become a major priority. The worst are arguably the severe bugs that rarely express themselves, as they can be extremely difficult to pin down yet still have dire consequences when they appear.

In summary, *there is no such thing as a perfect (non-trivial) human-written program and all such programs include a variety of errors of different severity and with a different frequency of manifestation.*[9]

This sort of variability is also very common in GP work. It provides the sort of toehold that evolution can exploit in the early generations of GP runs. The population of programs just needs to contain a few which move vaguely in the right direction. Many of their offspring may be totally blind or have no legs, just so long as a few continue to slime towards the light. Over generations evolution may hopefully cobble together some useful features from this initially unpromising ooze. *The results, however, are unlikely to be perfect or pretty.* If you as a GP engineer insist on only accepting solutions that are beautifully symmetric and walk on two legs on day one, you are likely to be disappointed. As we have argued above, even human-written programs often only approximate their intended functionality. So, why should we not accept the same from GP?

If you accept this notion, then it is important to provide your system with some sort of gradient upon which to act, allowing it to evolve ever better approximations. It is also important to ensure that your test environment (usually encapsulated in the fitness function) places appropriate emphasis on the most important features of the space from a user perspective. Consider a problem with five test cases, four of which are fairly easy and consequently less important, with the fifth being crucial and quite difficult. A likely outcome in such a setting is that individuals that can do the four easier tasks, but are unable to make the jump to the fifth. There are several things you could try: 1) weighting the hard task more heavily, 2) dividing it up in some way into additional sub-tasks, or 3) changing it from being a binary condition (meaning that an individual does or does not succeed on the fifth task) to a continuous condition, so that an individual GP program can partially succeed on the fifth task. The first of these options is the simplest to implement. The second two, however, create a smoother gradient for the evolutionary process to follow, and so may yield better results.

---

[9]This is, of course, no excuse for writing shoddy, bug-ridden code.

13.9 Control Bloat

If you are running out of memory or your execution times seem inordinately high, look at how your average program size is changing over time. If programs are growing extremely fast, you may want to implement some form of bloat control (see Section 11.3). Naturally, long runs may simply be the result of the population being very large or the fitness evaluation being slow. In these cases, you may find the techniques described in Chapter 10 helpful.

Controlling bloat is also important if your goal is to find a comprehensible model, since in practice smaller models are easier to understand. A large model will not only be difficult to understand but also may over-fit the training data (Gelly, Teytaud, Bredeche, and Schoenauer, 2006).

13.10 Checkpoint Results

Where GP run time is long, it is important to periodically save the current state of the run. Should the system crash, the run can be restarted from part way through rather than at the start. Care should be taken to save the entire state, so restarting a run does not introduce any unknown variation. The bulk of the state to be saved is the current population. This can be compressed, e.g., using `gzip`. While compression can add a few percent to run time, reductions in disk space to less than one bit per primitive in the population have been achieved. Checkpointing also allows you to later continue runs that seemed particularly promising when they reached whatever maximum generation you set initially.

13.11 Report Well

There are many potential reasons why work may be poorly received. Here are a few: insufficient explanation of methods and algorithms, insufficient experimental evidence, insufficient analysis, lack of statistical significance, lack of replicability, reading too much into one's results, insufficient novelty, poor presentation and poor English. In scientific, rather than commercial, work it is vital to report enough details so that someone else can reproduce your results. One very useful idea is to publish a table summarising your GP run. Table 4.1 (page 31) contains an example tableau.

As explained in Section 13.2, it is essential to ensure that results are statistically significant so that nobody can dismiss them as the consequence of a lucky fluke. Complex ideas are often best explained by diagrams. When possible, descriptions of non-trivial algorithms should be accompanied by pseudocode, along with text describing the most important components of the algorithm.

In addition to reporting your results, make sure you also discuss their implications. If, for example, what GP has evolved means the customer can save money or could improve their process in some way, then this should be highlighted. Also be careful to not construct excessively complex explanations for the observations. It is very tempting to say "X is probably due to Y", but for this to be believable one should at least have made some attempt to check if Y is indeed taking place, and whether modulations or suppression of Y in fact produce modulations and/or suppression of X.

Finally, the most likely outcomes of a text that is badly written or badly presented are: 1) your readers will misunderstand you, and 2) you will have fewer readers. Spell checkers can help with typos, but whenever possible one should ensure a native English speaker has proofread the text.

13.12   Convince your Customers

For any work in science, engineering, industry or commerce to make an impact it must be presented in a form that can convince others of the validity of its results and conclusions. This might include: a pitch within a corporation seeking continued financial support for a project, the submission of a research paper to a journal or the presentation of a GP-based product to potential customers.

The burden of proof is on the users of GP, and it is important to use the customer's language. If the fact that GP discovers a particular chemical is important in a reaction or drug design, for example, one should make this stand out during the presentation. A great advantage of GP over many AI techniques in that its results are often simple equations. Ensure these are intelligible to your customer, e.g., by simplification. Also make an effort to present your results using your customer's terminology. Your GP system may produce answers as trees, but if the customers use spreadsheets, consider translating the tree into a spreadsheet formula. Alternatively, your customer may not be particularly interested in the details of the solution, but instead care a great deal about which inputs the evolutionary process tended to use.

Also, one should try to discover how the customers intend to validate GP's answer. Do not let them invent some totally new data which has nothing to do with the data they supplied for training ("just to see how well it does..."). Avoid customers with contrived data: GP is not omnipotent and knows nothing about things it has not seen. At the same time you should be scrupulous about your own use of holdout data. GP is a very powerful machine learning technique, and with this comes the ever present danger of over-fitting. One should never allow performance on data reserved for validation to be used to choose which answer to present to the customer.

Chapter 14

Conclusions

In his seminal paper entitled "Intelligent Machinery", Turing (1948) identified three ways by which human-competitive machine intelligence might be achieved. In connection with one of those ways, Turing said:

> There is the genetical or evolutionary search by which a combination of genes is looked for, the criterion being the survival value. (Turing, 1948)

Turing did not specify how to conduct the "genetical or evolutionary search" for machine intelligence. In particular, he did not mention the idea of a population-based parallel search in conjunction with sexual recombination (crossover) as described in Holland's 1975 book *Adaptation in Natural and Artificial Systems* (Holland, 1992, second edition). However, in Turing's paper "Computing Machinery and Intelligence" (Turing, 1950), he did point out:

> We cannot expect to find a good child-machine at the first attempt. One must experiment with teaching one such machine and see how well it learns. One can then try another and see if it is better or worse. There is an obvious connection between this process and evolution:

> 'Structure of the child machine' = Hereditary material
> 'Changes of the child machine' = Mutations
> 'Natural selection' = Judgement of the experimenter

In other words, Turing perceived that one possibly productive approach to machine intelligence would involve an evolutionary process in which a description of a computer program (the hereditary material) undergoes progressive modification (mutation) under the guidance of natural selection (that is, selective pressure in the form of what we now call "fitness").

141

Today, decades later, we can see that indeed Turing was right. GP has started fulfilling his dream by providing us with a systematic method, based on Darwinian evolution, for getting computers to automatically solve hard real-life problems. To do so, it simply requires a high-level statement of what needs to be done and enough computing power.

Turing also understood the need to evaluate objectively the behaviour exhibited by machines, to avoid human biases when assessing their intelligence. This led him to propose an imitation game, now known as the *Turing test for machine intelligence*, whose goals are wonderfully summarised by Samuel's position statement quoted in the introduction of this book (page 1). The eight criteria for human competitiveness we discussed in Section 12.3 are essentially motivated by the same goals.

At present GP is unable to produce computer programs that would pass the full Turing test for machine intelligence, and it might not be ready for this immense task for centuries. Nonetheless, thanks to the constant improvements in GP technology, in its theoretical foundations and in computing power, GP has been able to solve dozens of difficult problems with human-competitive results and to provide valuable solutions to many other problems (see Chapter 12). These are a small step towards fulfilling Turing and Samuel's dreams, but they are also early signs of things to come. It is reasonable to predict that in a few years time GP will be able to *routinely* and *competently* solve important problems for us, in a variety of application domains with human-competitive performance. Genetic programming will then become an essential collaborator for many human activities. This will be a remarkable step forward towards achieving true human-competitive machine intelligence.

This field guide is an attempt to chart the terrain of techniques and applications we have encountered in our journey in the world of genetic programming. Much is still unmapped and undiscovered. We hope this book will make it easier for other travellers to start many long and profitable journeys in this exciting world.

If you have found this book to be useful, please feel free to redistribute it (see page ii). Should you want to cite this book, please refer to the entry for (Poli et al., 2008) in the bibliography.

Part IV

Tricks of the Trade

In the end we find that Mary does indeed have a little GP...

and the wolf is shown to have a very large bibliography.

Appendix A

Resources

The field of GP took off in the early 1990's, driven in significant part by the publication of (Koza, 1992). Those early days were characterised by the exponential growth common in the initial stages of successful technologies. Many influential papers from that period can be found in the proceedings of the International Conference on Genetic Algorithms (ICGA-93, ICGA-95), the IEEE conferences on Evolutionary Computation (EC-1994), and the Evolutionary Programming conferences. A surprisingly large number of these are now available on-line, and we've included as many URLs as we could in the bibliography.[1] After almost twenty years, GP has matured and is used in a wondrous array of applications from banking to betting, from bomb detection to architectural design, from the steel industry to the environment, from space to biology, and many others (as we have seen in Section 12).

In 1996 it was possible to list almost all the studies and applications of GP (Langdon, 1996), but today the range is far too great. In this appendix we will review some of the wide variety of available sources on GP which should assist readers who wish to explore further. Consulting information available on the Web is certainly a good way to get quick answers for someone who wants to know what GP is. These answers, however, will often be too shallow for someone who really wants to then apply GP to solve practical problems. People in this position should probably invest some time going through more detailed accounts; some of the key books in the field include (Banzhaf, Nordin, Keller, and Francone, 1998a; Koza, 1992; Langdon and Poli, 2002), and others are listed in Section A.1. Technical papers in the extensive GP literature may be the next stage. Although this literature is easily accessible thanks to the complete on-line bibliography (Langdon et al., 1995-2008), newcomers will often need to be selective in what they read. The

---

[1]Each included URL was tested and was operational at the time of writing.

objective here may be different for different types of readers. Practitioners may wish to focus initially on papers which deal with the same problem they are interested in. Researchers and PhD students interested in developing a deeper understanding of GP should also make sure they identify and read as many seminal papers as possible, including papers or books on empirical and theoretical studies on the inner mechanisms and behaviour of GP. These are frequently cited in other papers and, so, can be easily identified.

A.1 Key Books

There are today more than 31 books written in English principally on GP or its applications with more being written. These start with John Koza's *Genetic Programming* 1992 (often referred to as Jaws). Koza has subsequently published three additional books on GP: *Genetic Programming II: Automatic Discovery of Reusable Programs* (1994) deals with ADFs; *Genetic Programming 3* (1999) covers, in particular, the evolution of analogue circuits; *Genetic Programming 4* (2003) uses GP for automatic invention. MIT Press published three volumes in the series *Advances in Genetic Programming* (Angeline and Kinnear, 1996; Kinnear, 1994c; Spector, Langdon, O'Reilly, and Angeline, 1999). The joint GP / genetic algorithms Kluwer book series edited by Koza and Goldberg now contains 14 books starting with *Genetic Programming and Data Structures* (Langdon, 1998). Apart from Jaws, these tend to be for the GP specialist. The late 1990s saw the introduction of the first textbook dedicated to GP (Banzhaf et al., 1998a). Eiben and Smith (2003) and Goldberg (1989) provide general treatments of evolutionary algorithms.

Other titles include: *Genetic Programming* (in Japanese) (Iba, 1996b), *Principia Evolvica – Simulierte Evolution mit Mathematica* (in German) (Jacob, 1997) (English version (Jacob, 2001)), *Data Mining Using Grammar Based Genetic Programming and Applications* (Wong and Leung, 2000), *Grammatical Evolution: Evolutionary Automatic Programming in a Arbitrary Language* (O'Neill and Ryan, 2003), *Humanoider: Sjavlarande robotar och artificiell intelligens* (in Swedish) (Nordin and Johanna, 2003), and *Linear Genetic Programming* (Brameier and Banzhaf, 2007).

Readers interested in mathematical and empirical analyses of GP behaviour may find *Foundations of Genetic Programming* (Langdon and Poli, 2002) useful.

Each of Koza's four books has an accompanying video. These videos are now available in DVD format. Also, a small set of videos on specific GP techniques and applications is available via on-line resources such as Google Video and YouTube.

A.2 Key Journals

In addition to GP's own *Genetic Programming and Evolvable Machines* journal, *Evolutionary Computation*, the *IEEE transaction on Evolutionary Computation*, *Complex Systems* (Complex Systems Publication, Inc.), the new
Journal on Artificial Evolution and Applications and many others publish
GP articles. The GP bibliography (Langdon et al., 1995-2008) lists a further
375 different journals worldwide that have published articles related to GP.

A.3 Key International Meetings

EuroGP – the European Conference on Genetic Programming – has been
held every year since 1998. All EuroGP papers are available on line as part of
Springer's LNCS series. The original annual *Genetic Programming* conference ran for three years (1996-1998) before combining in 1999 with the International Conference on Genetic Algorithms (ICGA) to form GECCO. 98%
of GECCO papers are available on-line. The Michigan-based *Genetic Programming Theory and Practice* workshop (O'Reilly, Yu, Riolo, and Worzel,
2004; Riolo and Worzel, 2003; Riolo, Soule, and Worzel, 2007a; Yu, Riolo,
and Worzel, 2005) has recently published its fifth proceedings (Riolo, Soule,
and Worzel, 2007b). Other EC conferences, such as CEC, PPSN, Evolution
Artificielle and WSC, also regularly contain GP papers.

A.4 GP Implementations

One of the reasons behind the success of GP is that it is easy to implement
own versions, and implementing a simple GP system from scratch remains
an excellent way to make sure one really understands the mechanics of GP.
In addition to being an exceptionally useful exercise, it is often easier to
customise (e.g., adding new, application specific genetic operators or implementing unusual, knowledge-based initialisation strategies) a system one has
built for new purposes than a large GP distribution. All of this, however,
requires reasonable programming skills and the will to thoroughly test the
resulting system until it behaves as expected.

   This is actually an extremely tricky issue in highly stochastic systems
such as GP, as we discussed in Section 13.1. The problem is that almost
any system will produce "interesting" behaviour, but it is typically very
hard to test whether it is exhibiting the *correct* interesting behaviour. It
is remarkably easy for small mistakes to go unnoticed for extended periods
of time (even years).[2] It is also easy to incorrectly assume that "minor"

---

[2]Several years ago Nic and some of his students discovered that one of their systems
had been performing addition instead of subtraction for several months due to a copy-

implementation decisions will not significantly affect the behaviour of the system (see Section 13.4).

An alternative is to use one of the many public domain GP implementations and adapt this for one's purposes. This process is faster, and good implementations are often robust, efficient, well documented and comprehensive. The small price to pay is the need to study the available documentation and examples. These often explain how to modify the GP system to some extent. However, deeper modifications (such as the introduction of new or unusual operators) will often require studying the actual source code and a substantial amount of trial and error. Good publicly available GP implementations include: Lil-GP (Punch and Zongker, 1998), ECJ (Luke, Panait, Balan, Paus, Skolicki, Popovici, Harrison, Bassett, Hubley, and Chircop, 2000-2007), Open Beagle (Gagné and Parizeau, 2002) and GPC++ (Fraser and Weinbrenner, 1993-1997). The most prominent commercial implementation remains Discipulus (RML Technologies, 1998-2007); see (Foster, 2001) for a review. A number of older unsupported tools can be found at `ftp://cs.ucl.ac.uk/genetic/ftp.io.com/`.

While the earliest GP systems were implemented in Lisp, people have since coded GP in a huge range of different languages, including C/C++, Java (see an example in Appendix B), JavaScript, Perl, Prolog, Mathematica, Pop-11, MATLAB, Fortran, Occam and Haskell. Typically, these evolve expressions and programs which look like simplified Lisp. More complex target languages can be supported, however, especially with the use of more advanced tools such as grammars and type systems (see Chapter 6). Conversely, many successful programs in machine code or low-level languages have also climbed from the primordial ooze of initial randomness.

A.5   On-Line Resources

On-line resources appear, disappear, and move with great speed, so all the addresses here (and elsewhere in the book), which were correct at the time of writing, are obviously subject to change without notice after publication. Hopefully, the most valuable resources should be readily findable using standard search tools.

One of the key on-line resources is the GP bibliography (Langdon et al., 1995-2008).[3] At the time of writing, this bibliography contains about 5,000 GP entries, roughly half of which can be downloaded immediately.[4]

---

paste error. Fortunately no published results were affected, but it was a very unsettling experience.

[3]`http://www.cs.bham.ac.uk/~wbl/biblio/`

[4]The GP bibliography is a volunteer effort and depends crucially on submissions from users. Authors are encouraged to check that their *GP* publications are listed, and send missing entries to the bibliography's maintainers.

The GP bibliography has a variety of interfaces, including a graphical representation of GP's collaborative network (see Figure A.1). The bibliography allows for quick jumps between papers linked by authors and allows one to sort the author list by the number of GP publications. Full references are provided in both BibTeX and Refer formats for direct inclusion in papers written in LaTeX and Microsoft Word, respectively. The GP bibliography is also part of the Collection of Computer Sciences Bibliographies (Achilles and Ortyl, 1995-2008), which provides a comprehensive Lucerne syntax search engine.

From early on there has been an active, open email discussion list: the Genetic Programming mailing list (2001-2008). The EC-Digest (1985-2008) is a moderated list covering evolutionary computation more broadly, and often contains GP related announcements.

Koza's `http://www.genetic-programming.org/` contains a ton of useful information for the novice, including a short tutorial on "What is Genetic Programming" and the Lisp implementation of GP from *Genetic Programming* (Koza, 1992).

Figure A.1: Co-authorship connections within GP. Each of the 1,141 dots indicates an author, and edges link people who have co-authored one or more GP papers. (To reduce clutter only links to first authors are shown.) The size of each dot indicates the number of entries. The on-line version is annotated using JavaScript and contains hyperlinks to authors and their GP papers. The graph was created by GraphViz twopi, which tries to place strongly connected people close together. This diagram displays just the "centrally connected component" (Tomassini et al., 2007) and contains approximately half of all GP papers. The remaining papers are not linked by co-authorship to this graph. Several other large components are also available on-line via the GP Bibliography (Langdon et al., 1995-2008).

Appendix B

TinyGP

TinyGP[1] i s a highly optimised GP system that was originally developed to meet the specifications set out in the TinyGP competition of the Genetic and Evolutionary Computation Conference (GECCO) 2004. We include it as a working example of a real GP system, to show that GP software tools are not necessarily big, complex and difficult to understand. The system can be used *as is* or can be modified or extended for a user's specific applications. Furthermore, TinyGP may serve as a guide to other implementations of genetic programming.

The following section provides a description of the main characteristics of TinyGP. Section B.2 describes the format for the input files for TinyGP. Section B.3 provides further details on the implementation and the source code for a Java version of TinyGP. Finally, Section B.4 describes a sample run of the system.

There are numerous other GP systems available on-line. See Section A.4 for a discussion of some of the options.

B.1 Overview of TinyGP

TinyGP is a symbolic regression system with the following characteristics:

1. The terminal set includes a user-definable number of floating point variables (named X1 to XN).

2. The function set includes multiplication, protected division, subtraction and addition.

3. The fitness cases are read from a file (the format is given below).

---

[1]http://cswww.essex.ac.uk/staff/rpoli/TinyGP/

4. The system is steady state. A "generation" is considered concluded when POPSIZE (see below) crossover/mutation events have been performed.

5. Selection is performed using tournament selection.

6. Negative tournaments are used for the selection of the individuals to be replaced at each steady-state-GP iteration.

7. Subtree crossover is used. The selection of crossover points is uniform, so every node is chosen equally likely.

8. Point mutation is used. That is, points (nodes) in the tree are randomly chosen. If a point is a terminal, then it is replaced by another randomly chosen terminal. If it is a function, then it is replaced by another randomly chosen function with the same number of inputs.

9. The following parameters are implemented as static class variables:

   • The maximum length any GP program can take: MAX_LEN.

   • The size of the population: POPSIZE.

   • The maximum depth initial programs can have: DEPTH. Note 0 represents the depth of programs containing just one terminal.

   • The maximum number of generations allowed for a run: GENERATIONS.

   • The probability of creating new individuals via crossover: CROSSOVER_PROB. The mutation probability is 1 - CROSSOVER_PROB.

   • The mutation probability (per node) when point mutation is chosen as the variation operator: PMUT_PER_NODE.

   • The tournament size: TSIZE.

10. The parameters and the random seed are printed when each run starts.

11. The fitness function is minus the sum of the absolute differences between the actual program output and the desired output for each fitness case. TinyGP maximises it.

12. The grow initialisation method is used to create the initial population.

13. At each generation the following statistics are calculated and printed:

   • The generation number.

   • The average fitness of the individuals in the population.

   • The fitness of the best individual in the population.

- The average size of the programs in the current generation.

- The best individual in the population.

14. The random number generator can be seeded via the command line. If this command line parameter is absent, the system uses the current time to seed the random number generator.

15. The name of the file containing the fitness cases can be passed to the system via the command line. If the command line parameter is absent, the system assumes the data are stored in the current directory in a file called "problem.dat".

16. If the total error made by the best program goes below 10^{-5} TinyGP prints a message indicating success and stops. If the problem has not been solved after the maximum number of generations, it prints a message indicating failure and stops.

B.2 Input Data Files for TinyGP

The input files for TinyGP have the following plain ASCII format:

```
HEADER          // See below
FITNESSCASE1 // The fitness cases (one per line)
FITNESSCASE2
FITNESSCASE3
. . . .
```

Each fitness case is of the form

X1 ... XN TARGET

where X1 to XN represent a set of input values for a program, while TARGET represents the desired output for the given inputs.

The header has the following entries

NVAR NRAND MINRAND MAXRAND NFITCASES

where NVAR is an integer representing the number of variables the system should use, NRAND is an integer representing the number of random constants to be provided in the primitive set, MINRAND is a float representing the lower limit of the range used to generate random constants, MAXRAND is the corresponding upper limit, and NFITCASES is an integer representing the number of fitness cases. NRAND can be set to 0, in which case MINRAND and MAXRAND are ignored. For example:

```
1 100 -5 5 63
0.0 0
```

```
0.1 0.0998334166468282
0.2 0.198669330795061
0.3 0.29552020666134
....
55 LINES OMITTED
....
5.9 -0.373876664830236
6.0 -0.279415498198926
6.1 -0.182162504272095
6.2 -0.0830894028174964
```

These fitness cases are $\sin(x)$ for $x \in \{0.0,\ 0.1,\ 0.2,\ \dots\ 6.2\}$

B.3   Source Code

The original TinyGP system was implemented, in the C programming language, to maximise efficiency and minimise the size of the executable.[2] The version presented here is a Java re-implementation of TinyGP. The original version did not allow the use of random numerical constants.

How does TinyGP work? The system is based on the standard flattened (linear) representation for trees, which effectively corresponds to listing the primitives in prefix notation but without any brackets. Each primitive occupies one byte. A program is simply a vector of characters. The parameters of the system are as specified in Section B.1. They are fixed at compile time through a series of static class variable assignments. The operators used are subtree crossover and point mutation. The selection of the crossover points is performed at random with uniform probability. The primitive set and fitness function are as indicated above. The code uses recursion for the creation of the initial population (`grow`), for the identification of the subtree rooted at a particular crossover point (`traverse`), for program execution (`run`), and for printing programs (`print_indiv`). A small number of global variables have been used. For example, the variable `program` is a program counter used during the recursive interpretation of programs, which is automatically incremented every time a primitive is evaluated. Although using global variables is normally considered bad programming practice, this was done purposely, after extensive experimentation, to reduce the executable's size.

---

[2]The C version of TinyGP is probably the world's smallest tree-based symbolic-regression GP system. The source code, in C, is 5,906 bytes. The original version included a compilation script which, with a variety of tricks, created a self-extracting executable occupying 2,871 bytes (while the actual size of the executable after self-extraction was 4,540 bytes). All optimisations in the code were aimed at bringing the executable size (as opposed to the source code size) down, the main purpose being to show that, against popular belief, it is possible to have really tiny and efficient GP systems.

The code reads command line arguments using the standard **args** array.

Generally the code is quite standard and should be self-explanatory for anyone who can program in Java, whether or not they have implemented a GP system before. Therefore very few comments have been provided in the source code.

The source is provided below.

```
1   /*
2    * Program:     tiny_gp.java
3    *
4    * Author:      Riccardo Poli (email: rpoli@essex.ac.uk)
5    *
6    */
7
8   import java.util.*;
9   import java.io.*;
10  import java.text.DecimalFormat;
11
12  public class tiny_gp {
13     double [] fitness;
14     char [][] pop;
15     static Random rd = new Random();
16     static final int
17       ADD = 110,
18       SUB = 111,
19       MUL = 112,
20       DIV = 113,
21       FSET_START = ADD,
22       FSET_END = DIV;
23     static double [] x = new double[FSET_START];
24     static double minrandom, maxrandom;
25     static char [] program;
26     static int PC;
27     static int varnumber, fitnesscases, randomnumber;
28     static double fbestpop = 0.0, favgpop = 0.0;
29     static long seed;
30     static double avg_len;
31     static final int
32       MAX_LEN = 10000,
33       POPSIZE = 100000,
34       DEPTH   = 5,
35       GENERATIONS = 100,
36       TSIZE = 2;
37     public static final double
38       PMUT_PER_NODE  = 0.05,
39       CROSSOVER_PROB = 0.9;
40     static double [][] targets;
41
42     double run() { /* Interpreter */
43       char primitive = program[PC++];
44       if ( primitive < FSET_START )
45         return(x[primitive]);
46       switch ( primitive ) {
```

```
47      case ADD : return( run() + run() );
48      case SUB : return( run() - run() );
49      case MUL : return( run() * run() );
50      case DIV : {
51        double num = run() , den = run();
52        if ( Math.abs( den ) <= 0.001 )
53          return( num );
54        else
55          return( num / den );
56        }
57      }
58    return( 0.0 ); // should never get here
59  }
60
61  int traverse( char [] buffer , int buffercount ) {
62    if ( buffer[buffercount] < FSET_START )
63      return( ++buffercount );
64
65    switch(buffer[buffercount]) {
66      case ADD:
67      case SUB:
68      case MUL:
69      case DIV:
70      return( traverse( buffer , traverse( buffer , ++buffercount
          ) ) );
71      }
72    return( 0 ); // should never get here
73  }
74
75  void setup_fitness(String fname) {
76    try {
77      int i,j;
78      String line;
79
80      BufferedReader in =
81      new BufferedReader(
82                      new
83                      FileReader(fname));
84      line = in.readLine();
85      StringTokenizer tokens = new StringTokenizer(line);
86      varnumber = Integer.parseInt(tokens.nextToken().trim());
87      randomnumber = Integer.parseInt(tokens.nextToken().trim())
          ;
88      minrandom =              Double.parseDouble(tokens.nextToken().
          trim());
89      maxrandom =   Double.parseDouble(tokens.nextToken().trim())
          ;
90      fitnesscases = Integer.parseInt(tokens.nextToken().trim())
          ;
91      targets = new double[fitnesscases][varnumber+1];
92      if (varnumber + randomnumber >= FSET_START )
93        System.out.println("too_many_variables_and_constants");
94
95      for (i = 0; i < fitnesscases; i ++ ) {
```

```
96        line = in.readLine();
97        tokens = new StringTokenizer(line);
98        for ( j = 0; j <= varnumber; j++) {
99          targets[i][j] = Double.parseDouble(tokens.nextToken().
              trim());
100       }
101     }
102     in.close();
103   }
104   catch(FileNotFoundException e) {
105     System.out.println("ERROR:_Please_provide_a_data_file");
106     System.exit(0);
107   }
108   catch(Exception e ) {
109     System.out.println("ERROR:_Incorrect_data_format");
110     System.exit(0);
111   }
112 }
113
114 double fitness_function( char [] Prog ) {
115   int i = 0, len;
116   double result, fit = 0.0;
117
118   len = traverse( Prog, 0 );
119   for ( i = 0; i < fitnesscases; i ++ ) {
120     for ( int j = 0; j < varnumber; j ++ )
121         x[j] = targets[i][j];
122     program = Prog;
123     PC = 0;
124     result = run();
125     fit += Math.abs( result - targets[i][varnumber]);
126     }
127   return(-fit );
128 }
129
130 int grow( char [] buffer, int pos, int max, int depth ) {
131   char prim = (char) rd.nextInt(2);
132
133   if ( pos >= max )
134     return( -1 );
135
136   if ( pos == 0 )
137     prim = 1;
138
139   if ( prim == 0 || depth == 0 ) {
140     prim = (char) rd.nextInt(varnumber + randomnumber);
141     buffer[pos] = prim;
142     return(pos+1);
143     }
144   else  {
145     prim = (char) (rd.nextInt(FSET_END - FSET_START + 1) +
            FSET_START);
146     switch(prim) {
147     case ADD:
148     case SUB:
```

```
149        case MUL:
150        case DIV:
151          buffer[pos] = prim;
152          return( grow( buffer, grow( buffer, pos+1, max, depth-1),
153                    max, depth-1 ) );
154        }
155      }
156      return( 0 ); // should never get here
157    }
158
159    int print_indiv( char [] buffer, int buffercounter ) {
160      int a1=0, a2;
161      if ( buffer[buffercounter] < FSET_START ) {
162        if ( buffer[buffercounter] < varnumber )
163          System.out.print( "X"+ (buffer[buffercounter] + 1 )+ "_"
                    );
164        else
165          System.out.print( x[buffer[buffercounter]]);
166        return( ++buffercounter );
167        }
168      switch(buffer[buffercounter]) {
169        case ADD: System.out.print( "(");
170          a1=print_indiv( buffer, ++buffercounter );
171          System.out.print( "_+_");
172          break;
173        case SUB: System.out.print( "(");
174          a1=print_indiv( buffer, ++buffercounter );
175          System.out.print( "_-_");
176          break;
177        case MUL: System.out.print( "(");
178          a1=print_indiv( buffer, ++buffercounter );
179          System.out.print( "_*_");
180          break;
181        case DIV: System.out.print( "(");
182          a1=print_indiv( buffer, ++buffercounter );
183          System.out.print( "_/_");
184          break;
185        }
186      a2=print_indiv( buffer, a1 );
187      System.out.print( ")");
188      return( a2);
189    }
190
191
192    static char [] buffer = new char[MAX_LEN];
193    char [] create_random_indiv( int depth ) {
194      char [] ind;
195      int len;
196
197      len = grow( buffer, 0, MAX_LEN, depth );
198
199      while (len < 0 )
200        len = grow( buffer, 0, MAX_LEN, depth );
201
```

```
202        ind = new char[len];
203
204        System.arraycopy(buffer, 0, ind, 0, len );
205        return( ind );
206    }
207
208    char [][] create_random_pop(int n, int depth, double []
            fitness ) {
209        char [][] pop = new char[n][];
210        int i;
211
212        for ( i = 0; i < n; i ++ ) {
213            pop[i] = create_random_indiv( depth );
214            fitness[i] = fitness_function( pop[i] );
215        }
216        return( pop );
217    }
218
219
220    void stats( double [] fitness, char [][] pop, int gen ) {
221        int i, best = rd.nextInt(POPSIZE);
222        int node_count = 0;
223        fbestpop = fitness[best];
224        favgpop = 0.0;
225
226        for ( i = 0; i < POPSIZE; i ++ ) {
227            node_count += traverse( pop[i], 0 );
228            favgpop += fitness[i];
229            if ( fitness[i] > fbestpop ) {
230            best = i;
231            fbestpop = fitness[i];
232            }
233        }
234        avg_len = (double) node_count / POPSIZE;
235        favgpop /= POPSIZE;
236        System.out.print("Generation="+gen+" _Avg_Fitness="+(-favgpop
            )+
237                "_Best_Fitness="+(-fbestpop)+"_Avg_Size="+
                    avg_len+
238                "\nBest_Individual:_");
239        print_indiv( pop[best], 0 );
240        System.out.print( "\n");
241        System.out.flush();
242    }
243
244    int tournament( double [] fitness, int tsize ) {
245        int best = rd.nextInt(POPSIZE), i, competitor;
246        double fbest = -1.0e34;
247
248        for ( i = 0; i < tsize; i ++ ) {
249            competitor = rd.nextInt(POPSIZE);
250            if ( fitness[competitor] > fbest ) {
251            fbest = fitness[competitor];
252            best = competitor;
253            }
```

```
254        }
255        return( best );
256      }
257
258      int negative_tournament( double [] fitness , int tsize ) {
259        int worst = rd.nextInt(POPSIZE) , i , competitor;
260        double fworst = 1e34;
261
262        for ( i = 0; i < tsize; i ++ ) {
263          competitor = rd.nextInt(POPSIZE);
264          if ( fitness[competitor] < fworst ) {
265            fworst = fitness[competitor];
266            worst = competitor;
267            }
268        }
269        return( worst );
270      }
271
272      char [] crossover( char [] parent1 , char [] parent2 ) {
273        int xo1start , xo1end , xo2start , xo2end;
274        char [] offspring;
275        int len1 = traverse( parent1 , 0 );
276        int len2 = traverse( parent2 , 0 );
277        int lenoff;
278
279        xo1start =  rd.nextInt(len1);
280        xo1end = traverse( parent1 , xo1start );
281
282        xo2start =  rd.nextInt(len2);
283        xo2end = traverse( parent2 , xo2start );
284
285        lenoff = xo1start + (xo2end - xo2start) + (len1-xo1end);
286
287        offspring = new char[lenoff];
288
289        System.arraycopy( parent1 , 0 , offspring , 0 , xo1start );
290        System.arraycopy( parent2 , xo2start , offspring , xo1start ,
291                    (xo2end - xo2start) );
292        System.arraycopy( parent1 , xo1end , offspring ,
293                    xo1start + (xo2end - xo2start) ,
294                    (len1-xo1end) );
295
296        return( offspring );
297      }
298
299      char [] mutation( char [] parent , double pmut ) {
300        int len = traverse( parent , 0 ) , i;
301        int mutsite;
302        char [] parentcopy = new char [len];
303
304        System.arraycopy( parent , 0 , parentcopy , 0 , len );
305        for (i = 0; i < len; i ++ ) {
306          if ( rd.nextDouble() < pmut ) {
307          mutsite =  i;
308          if ( parentcopy[mutsite] < FSET_START )
```

```
309          parentcopy [ mutsite ] = (char) rd . nextInt ( varnumber ) ;
310        else
311          switch ( parentcopy [ mutsite ] ) {
312          case ADD:
313          case SUB:
314          case MUL:
315          case DIV:
316             parentcopy [ mutsite ] =
317                (char) ( rd . nextInt (FSET_END - FSET_START + 1)
318                   + FSET_START ) ;
319          }
320        }
321      }
322    return ( parentcopy ) ;
323    }
324
325    void print_parms () {
326      System . out . print ("---_TINY_GP_ ( Java_version )_---\n" ) ;
327      System . out . print ("SEED="+seed+"\nMAX_LEN="+MAX_LEN+
328              "\nPOPSIZE="+POPSIZE+"\nDEPTH="+DEPTH+
329              "\nCROSSOVER_PROB="+CROSSOVER_PROB+
330              "\nPMUT_PER_NODE="+PMUT_PER_NODE+
331              "\nMIN_RANDOM="+minrandom+
332              "\nMAX_RANDOM="+maxrandom+
333              "\nGENERATIONS="+GENERATIONS+
334              "\nTSIZE="+TSIZE+
335              "\n————————————————————\n" ) ;
336    }
337
338    public tiny_gp ( String fname , long s ) {
339      fitness = new double [POPSIZE] ;
340      seed = s ;
341      if ( seed >= 0 )
342          rd . setSeed ( seed ) ;
343      setup_fitness ( fname ) ;
344      pop = create_random_pop (POPSIZE, DEPTH, fitness ) ;
345      for ( int i = 0; i < FSET_START; i ++ )
346        x [ i ]= ( maxrandom-minrandom )* rd . nextDouble ()+minrandom ;
347    }
348
349    void evolve () {
350      int gen = 0, indivs , offspring , parent1 , parent2 , parent ;
351      double newfit ;
352      char [] newind ;
353      print_parms () ;
354      stats ( fitness , pop , 0 ) ;
355      for ( gen = 1; gen < GENERATIONS; gen ++ ) {
356        if ( fbestpop > -1e-5 ) {
357        System . out . print ("PROBLEM_SOLVED\n" ) ;
358        System . exit ( 0 ) ;
359        }
360        for ( indivs = 0; indivs < POPSIZE; indivs ++ ) {
361        if ( rd . nextDouble () > CROSSOVER_PROB ) {
362          parent1 = tournament ( fitness , TSIZE ) ;
363          parent2 = tournament ( fitness , TSIZE ) ;
```

```
364              newind = crossover ( pop [ parent1 ] , pop [ parent2 ] );
365          }
366          else {
367              parent = tournament ( fitness , TSIZE );
368              newind = mutation ( pop [ parent ] , PMUT_PER_NODE );
369          }
370          newfit = fitness_function ( newind );
371          offspring = negative_tournament ( fitness , TSIZE );
372          pop [ offspring ] = newind;
373          fitness [ offspring ] = newfit;
374          }
375          stats ( fitness , pop , gen );
376      }
377      System . out . print ( "PROBLEM_*NOT*_SOLVED\n" );
378      System . exit ( 1 );
379  }

381  public static void main ( String [] args ) {
382      String fname = " problem . dat";
383      long s = −1;

385      if ( args . length == 2 ) {
386          s = Integer . valueOf ( args [ 0 ] ) . intValue ();
387          fname = args [ 1 ];
388      }
389      if ( args . length == 1 ) {
390          fname = args [ 0 ];
391      }

393      tiny_gp gp = new tiny_gp ( fname , s );
394      gp . evolve ();
395  }
396  };
```

B.4   Compiling and Running TinyGP

It is very common, nowadays, for people to write and execute code within some development environment. Each has its own way of doing these operations, but the process is typically very straightforward.

If one wants to compile TinyGP from the operating system's shell, this can be done by issuing the command javac -O tiny_gp.java. This applies to both Unix and Windows users. Windows users will have to click on Start→Run and then issue the command cmd to launch a shell. Of course, if the javac Java compiler and/or the tiny_gp.java source file are not in the current directory/folder, then full path names must be provided when issuing the compilation command.

If the dataset is stored in a file problem.dat, the program can then simply be launched with the command java tiny_gp. Otherwise, the user can specify a different datafile on the command line, by giving the command java tiny_gp FILE, where FILE is the dataset file name (which can include the full path to the file). Finally, the user can specify both the datafile and a *seed* for the random number generator on the command line, by giving the command java tiny_gp SEED FILE, where SEED is an integer.

As an example, we ran TinyGP on the $\sin(x)$ dataset described in Section B.2 (which is available at http://cswww.essex.ac.uk/staff/rpoli/ TinyGP/sin-data.txt). The output produced by the program was something like the following

```
--- TINY GP (Java version) ---
SEED=-1
MAX_LEN=10000
POPSIZE=100000
DEPTH=5
CROSSOVER_PROB=0.9
PMUT_PER_NODE=0.05
MIN_RANDOM=-5.0
MAX_RANDOM=5.0
GENERATIONS=100
TSIZE=2
```

```
Generation=0 Avg Fitness=42.53760218120066 Best Fitness
    =39.997953686554816 Avg Size=10.9804
Best Individual: (1.589816334458055 / -2.128280559500907)
Generation=1 Avg Fitness=1226.404415960088 Best Fitness
    =24.441994244449372 Avg Size=10.97024
Best Individual: (((-0.3839867944222206 / -2.2796127162428403) +
    (-1.8386812853617673 / -1.06553859601892)) -
    (((4.984026635222818 * (0.17196413319878445 -
    0.1294044215655923)) + (X1 - -1.8956001614031734)) *
    0.3627020733460027))
...
```

The flip-o-rama animation in the footer of the bibliography and index include plots of the best and mean fitness, the mean program size and the behaviour of the best-so-far individual at each generation. The animation should be viewed by rapidly flipping the pages of the book from the beginning of the bibliography onward. For convenience, the plots corresponding to the final generation are also reported in Figure B.1.

As one can see, GP progressively evolves better and better approximations to the sine function. The best individual at the end of the run had an error of 1.88. Its unsimplified version as produced by the system is

```
(X1 / ((-2.766097899954383 * (X1 / (((X1 / ((((X1 / (X1 *
    -3.2001163763204445)) * X1 ) - -3.2001163763204445) *
    -3.2001163763204445)) + X1 ) + (X1 * (X1 -
    3.9532436938954376))))) - (((X1 * X1 ) / (((X1 /
    (3.9532436938954376 * -3.2001163763204445)) * X1 ) -
    -3.2001163763204445)) / (((X1 + X1 ) / (X1 * X1 )) + X1 ))
    ))
```

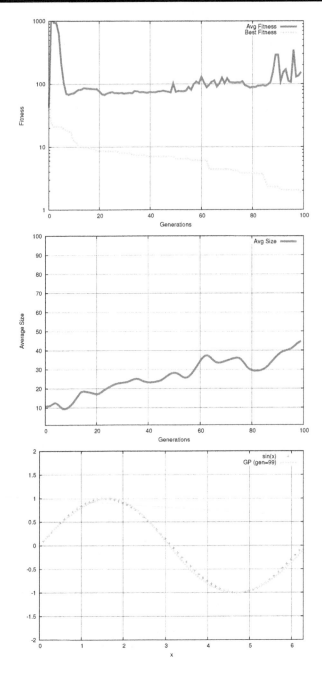

Figure B.1: Final generation of a TinyGP sample run: best and mean fitness (top), mean program size (middle) and behaviour of the best-so-far individual (bottom).

which can be simplified to

$$\cfrac{x}{\cfrac{-a \times x}{\frac{x}{x-b} + x + x \times (x-c)} - \cfrac{x^2}{\left(\frac{2}{x} + x\right) \times \left(d - \frac{x^2}{e}\right)}}$$

where

$$a = 2.76609789995$$
$$b = 10.240744822$$
$$c = 3.9532436939$$
$$d = 3.20011637632$$
$$e = 12.6508398844$$

Hardly an obvious approximation for the sine function, but still a very accurate one, at least over the test range.

Bibliography

H. Abbass, N. Hoai, and R. McKay. Anttag: A new method to compose computer programs using colonies of ants. In *IEEE Congress on Evolutionary Computation, 2002.*, 2002. URL http://citeseer.ist.psu.edu/abbass02anttag.html.

A.-C. Achilles and P. Ortyl. The Collection of Computer Science Bibliographies, 1995-2008. URL http://liinwww.ira.uka.de/bibliography/.

G. Adorni, S. Cagnoni, and M. Mordonini. Efficient low-level vision program design using sub-machine-code genetic programming. In M. Gori, editor, *AIIA 2002, Workshop sulla Percezione e Visione nelle Macchine*, Siena, Italy, 10-13 September 2002. URL http://www-dii.ing.unisi.it/aiia2002/paper/PERCEVISIO/adorni-aiia02.pdf. GPBiB

A. Agapitos, J. Togelius, and S. M. Lucas. Multiobjective techniques for the use of state in genetic programming applied to simulated car racing. In D. Srinivasan and L. Wang, editors, *2007 IEEE Congress on Evolutionary Computation*, pages 1562–1569, Singapore, 25-28 September 2007. IEEE Computational Intelligence Society, IEEE Press. ISBN 1-4244-1340-0. GPBiB

S. H. Al-Sakran, J. R. Koza, and L. W. Jones. Automated re-invention of a previously patented optical lens system using genetic programming. In M. Keijzer, et al., editors, *Proceedings of the 8th European Conference on Genetic Programming*, volume 3447 of *Lecture Notes in Computer Science*, pages 25–37, Lausanne, Switzerland, 30 March - 1 April 2005. Springer. ISBN 3-540-25436-6. URL http://springerlink.metapress.com/openurl.asp?genre=article&issn=0302-9743&volume=3447&spage=25. GPBiB

R. Aler, D. Borrajo, and P. Isasi. Using genetic programming to learn and improve control knowledge. *Artificial Intelligence*, 141(1-2):29–56, October 2002. URL http://scalab.uc3m.es/~dborrajo/papers/aij-evock.ps.gz. GPBiB

J. Allen, H. M. Davey, D. Broadhurst, J. K. Heald, J. J. Rowland, S. G. Oliver, and D. B. Kell. High-throughput classification of yeast mutants for functional genomics using metabolic footprinting. *Nature Biotechnology*, 21(6):692–696, June 2003. URL http://dbkgroup.org/Papers/NatureBiotechnology21(692-696).pdf. GPBiB

L. Alonso and R. Schott. *Random Generation of Trees*. Kluwer Academic Publishers, Boston, MA, USA, 1995. ISBN 0-7923-9528-X.

L. Altenberg. Emergent phenomena in genetic programming. In A. V. Sebald and L. J. Fogel, editors, *Evolutionary Programming — Proceedings of the Third Annual Conference*, pages 233–241, San Diego, CA, USA, 24-26 February 1994. World Scientific Publishing. ISBN 981-02-1810-9. URL http://dynamics.org/~altenber/PAPERS/EPIGP/. GPBiB

A. P. Alves da Silva and P. J. Abrao. Applications of evolutionary computation in electric power systems. In D. B. Fogel, et al., editors, *Proceedings of the 2002 Congress on Evolutionary Computation CEC2002*, pages 1057–1062. IEEE Press, 2002. ISBN 0-7803-7278-6.   GPBiB

D. Ando, P. Dahlsted, M. Nordahl, and H. Iba. Interactive GP with tree representation of classical music pieces. In M. Giacobini, et al., editors, *Applications of Evolutionary Computing, EvoWorkshops2007: EvoCOMNET, EvoFIN, EvoIASP, EvoInteraction, EvoMUSART, EvoSTOC, EvoTransLog*, volume 4448 of *LNCS*, pages 577–584, Valencia, Spain, 11-13 April 2007. Springer Verlag.   GPBiB

D. Andre, F. H. Bennett, III, and J. R. Koza. Discovery by genetic programming of a cellular automata rule that is better than any known rule for the majority classification problem. In J. R. Koza, et al., editors, *Genetic Programming 1996: Proceedings of the First Annual Conference*, pages 3–11, Stanford University, CA, USA, 28–31 July 1996. MIT Press. URL http://www.genetic-programming.com/jkpdf/gp1996gkl.pdf. GPBiB

D. Andre and J. R. Koza. Parallel genetic programming: A scalable implementation using the transputer network architecture. In P. J. Angeline and K. E. Kinnear, Jr., editors, *Advances in Genetic Programming 2*, chapter 16, pages 317–338. MIT Press, Cambridge, MA, USA, 1996. ISBN 0-262-01158-1.   GPBiB

D. Andre and J. R. Koza. A parallel implementation of genetic programming that achieves super-linear performance. *Information Sciences*, 106(3-4):201–218, 1998. ISSN 0020-0255. URL http://www.sciencedirect.com/science/article/B6V0C-3TKS65B-21/2/22b9842f820b08883990bbae1d889c03.   GPBiB

P. J. Angeline. An investigation into the sensitivity of genetic programming to the frequency of leaf selection during subtree crossover. In J. R. Koza, et al., editors, *Genetic Programming 1996: Proceedings of the First Annual Conference*, pages 21–29, Stanford University, CA, USA, 28–31 July 1996. MIT Press. URL http://www.natural-selection.com/Library/1996/gp96.zip.   GPBiB

P. J. Angeline. Subtree crossover: Building block engine or macromutation? In J. R. Koza, et al., editors, *Genetic Programming 1997: Proceedings of the Second Annual Conference*, pages 9–17, Stanford University, CA, USA, 13-16 July 1997. Morgan Kaufmann.   GPBiB

P. J. Angeline and K. E. Kinnear, Jr., editors. *Advances in Genetic Programming 2*. MIT Press, Cambridge, MA, USA, 1996. ISBN 0-262-01158-1. URL http://www.cs.bham.ac.uk/~wbl/aigp2.html.   GPBiB

P. J. Angeline and J. B. Pollack. The evolutionary induction of subroutines. In *Proceedings of the Fourteenth Annual Conference of the Cognitive Science Society*, pages 236–241, Bloomington, Indiana, USA, 1992. Lawrence Erlbaum. URL http://www.demo.cs.brandeis.edu/papers/glib92.pdf.   GPBiB

L. Araujo. Multiobjective genetic programming for natural language parsing and tagging. In T. P. Runarsson, et al., editors, *Parallel Problem Solving from Nature - PPSN IX*, volume 4193 of *LNCS*, pages 433–442, Reykjavik, Iceland, 9-13 September 2006. Springer-Verlag. ISBN 3-540-38990-3. URL http://ppsn2006.raunvis.hi.is/proceedings/055.pdf.   GPBiB

V. Arkov, C. Evans, P. J. Fleming, D. C. Hill, J. P. Norton, I. Pratt, D. Rees, and K. Rodriguez-Vazquez. System identification strategies applied to aircraft gas turbine engines. *Annual Reviews in Control*, 24(1):67–81,

2000. URL http://www.sciencedirect.com/science/article/B6V0H-482MDPD-8/2/
dd470648e2228c84efe7e14ca3841b7e.   GPBiB

M. P. Austin, G. Bates, M. A. H. Dempster, V. Leemans, and S. N. Williams.
Adaptive systems for foreign exchange trading. *Quantitative Finance*, 4(4):37–
45, August 2004. ISSN 1469-7688. URL http://www-cfr.jbs.cam.ac.uk/archive/
PRESENTATIONS/seminars/2006/dempster2.pdf.   GPBiB

Y. Azaria and M. Sipper. GP-gammon: Genetically programming backgammon players.
Genetic Programming and Evolvable Machines, 6(3):283–300, September 2005a. ISSN
1389-2576. URL http://www.cs.bgu.ac.il/~sipper/papabs/gpgammon.pdf. Published online: 12 August 2005.   GPBiB

Y. Azaria and M. Sipper. Using GP-gammon: Using genetic programming to evolve
backgammon players. In M. Keijzer, et al., editors, *Proceedings of the 8th European Conference on Genetic Programming*, volume 3447 of *Lecture Notes in Computer
Science*, pages 132–142, Lausanne, Switzerland, 30 March - 1 April 2005b. Springer.
ISBN 3-540-25436-6. URL http://springerlink.metapress.com/openurl.asp?genre=
article&issn=0302-9743&volume=3447&spage=132.   GPBiB

V. Babovic. *Emergence, evolution, intelligence; Hydroinformatics - A study of distributed
and decentralised computing using intelligent agents*. A. A. Balkema Publishers, Rot-
terdam, Holland, 1996. ISBN 90-5410-404-X.   GPBiB

M. Bader-El-Den and R. Poli. Generating sat local-search heuristics using a gp hyper-
heuristic framework. In *Proceedings of Evolution Artificielle*, October 2007a.

M. B. Bader-El-Den and R. Poli. A GP-based hyper-heuristic framework for evolving
3-SAT heuristics. In D. Thierens, et al., editors, *GECCO '07: Proceedings of the 9th
annual conference on Genetic and evolutionary computation*, volume 2, pages 1749–
1749, London, 7-11 July 2007b. ACM Press. URL http://www.cs.bham.ac.uk/~wbl/
biblio/gecco2007/docs/p1749.pdf.   GPBiB

K. M. S. Badran and P. I. Rockett. The roles of diversity preservation and mutation in
preventing population collapse in multiobjective genetic programming. In D. Thierens,
et al., editors, *GECCO '07: Proceedings of the 9th annual conference on Genetic
and evolutionary computation*, volume 2, pages 1551–1558, London, 7-11 July 2007.
ACM Press. URL http://www.cs.bham.ac.uk/~wbl/biblio/gecco2007/docs/p1551.
pdf.   GPBiB

W. Bains, R. Gilbert, L. Sviridenko, J.-M. Gascon, R. Scoffin, K. Birchall, I. Harvey,
and J. Caldwell. Evolutionary computational methods to predict oral bioavailability
QSPRs. *Current Opinion in Drug Discovery and Development*, 5(1):44–51, January
2002.   GPBiB

J. E. Baker. Reducing bias and inefficiency in the selection algorithm. In J. J. Grefenstette,
editor, *Proceedings of the Second International Conference on Genetic Algorithms
and their Application*, pages 14–21, Cambridge, MA, USA, 1987. Lawrence Erlbaum
Associates. ISBN 0-8058-0158-8.

J. Balic. *Flexible Manufacturing Systems; Development - Structure - Operation - Han-
dling - Tooling*. Manufacturing technology. DAAAM International, Vienna, 1999. ISBN
3-901509-03-8.   GPBiB

S. Baluja and R. Caruana. Removing the genetics from the standard genetic algorithm.
In A. Prieditis and S. Russell, editors, *Machine Learning: Proceedings of the Twelfth
International Conference*, pages 38–46. Morgan Kaufmann Publishers, San Francisco,
CA, 1995.

Generation 0
(see Sec. B.4)

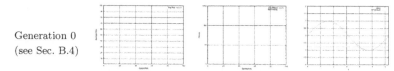

W. Banzhaf and W. B. Langdon. Some considerations on the reason for bloat. *Genetic Programming and Evolvable Machines*, 3(1):81–91, March 2002. ISSN 1389-2576. URL http://web.cs.mun.ca/~banzhaf/papers/genp_bloat.pdf. GPBiB

W. Banzhaf. Genetic programming for pedestrians. In S. Forrest, editor, *Proceedings of the 5th International Conference on Genetic Algorithms, ICGA-93*, page 628, University of Illinois at Urbana-Champaign, 17-21 July 1993. Morgan Kaufmann. URL http://www.cs.ucl.ac.uk/staff/W.Langdon/ftp/ftp.io.com/papers/GenProg_forPed.ps.Z. GPBiB

W. Banzhaf, F. D. Francone, and P. Nordin. The effect of extensive use of the mutation operator on generalization in genetic programming using sparse data sets. In H.-M. Voigt, et al., editors, *Parallel Problem Solving from Nature IV, Proceedings of the International Conference on Evolutionary Computation*, volume 1141 of *LNCS*, pages 300–309, Berlin, Germany, 22-26 September 1996. Springer Verlag. ISBN 3-540-61723-X. GPBiB

W. Banzhaf, P. Nordin, R. E. Keller, and F. D. Francone. *Genetic Programming – An Introduction; On the Automatic Evolution of Computer Programs and its Applications*. Morgan Kaufmann, San Francisco, CA, USA, January 1998a. ISBN 1-55860-510-X. URL http://www.elsevier.com/wps/find/bookdescription.cws_home/677869/description#description. GPBiB

W. Banzhaf, R. Poli, M. Schoenauer, and T. C. Fogarty, editors. *Genetic Programming*, volume 1391 of *LNCS*, Paris, 14-15 April 1998b. Springer-Verlag. ISBN 3-540-64360-5. URL http://www.springer.de/cgi-bin/search_book.pl?isbn=3-540-64360-5. GPBiB

W. Banzhaf, J. Daida, A. E. Eiben, M. H. Garzon, V. Honavar, M. Jakiela, and R. E. Smith, editors. *GECCO-99: Proceedings of the Genetic and Evolutionary Computation Conference*, Orlando, Florida, USA, 13-17 July 1999. Morgan Kaufmann. ISBN 1-55860-611-4. URL http://www.amazon.com/exec/obidos/ASIN/1558606114/qid%3D977054373/105-7666192-3217523. GPBiB

G. J. Barlow. Design of autonomous navigation controllers for unmanned aerial vehicles using multi-objective genetic programming. Master's thesis, North Carolina State University, Raleigh, NC, USA, March 2004. URL http://www.andrew.cmu.edu/user/gjb/includes/publications/thesis/barlow2004-thesis/barlow2004-thesis.pdf. GPBiB

S. J. Barrett. Recurring analytical problems within drug discovery and development. In T. Scheffer and U. Leser, editors, *Data Mining and Text Mining for Bioinformatics: Proceedings of the European Workshop*, pages 6–7, Dubrovnik, Croatia, 22 September 2003. URL http://www2.informatik.hu-berlin.de/~scheffer/publications/ProceedingsWS2003.pdf. Invited talk. GPBiB

S. J. Barrett and W. B. Langdon. Advances in the application of machine learning techniques in drug discovery, design and development. In A. Tiwari, et al., editors, *Applications of Soft Computing: Recent Trends*, Advances in Soft Computing, pages 99–110, On the World Wide Web, 19 September - 7 October 2005 2006. Springer. ISBN ISBN 3-540-29123-7. URL http://www.cs.ucl.ac.uk/staff/W.Langdon/ftp/papers/barrett_2005_WSC.pdf. GPBiB

T. Bartz-Beielstein. *Experimental research in evolutionary computation : the new experimentalism*. Springer, 2006.

F. H. Bennett, III. Automatic creation of an efficient multi-agent architecture using genetic programming with architecture-altering operations. In J. R. Koza, et al., editors, *Genetic Programming 1996: Proceedings of the First Annual Conference*, pages 30–38, Stanford University, CA, USA, 28–31 July 1996. MIT Press. URL http://cognet.mit.edu/library/books/view?isbn=0262611279. GPBiB

F. H. Bennett, III, J. R. Koza, J. Shipman, and O. Stiffelman. Building a parallel computer system for $18,000 that performs a half peta-flop per day. In W. Banzhaf, et al., editors, *Proceedings of the Genetic and Evolutionary Computation Conference*, volume 2, pages 1484–1490, Orlando, Florida, USA, 13-17 July 1999. Morgan Kaufmann. ISBN 1-55860-611-4. URL http://www.genetic-programming.com/jkpdf/gecco1999beowulf.pdf. GPBiB

H.-G. Beyer, U.-M. O'Reilly, D. V. Arnold, W. Banzhaf, C. Blum, E. W. Bonabeau, E. Cantu-Paz, D. Dasgupta, K. Deb, J. A. Foster, E. D. de Jong, H. Lipson, X. Llora, S. Mancoridis, M. Pelikan, G. R. Raidl, T. Soule, A. M. Tyrrell, J.-P. Watson, and E. Zitzler, editors. *GECCO 2005: Proceedings of the 2005 conference on Genetic and evolutionary computation*, Washington DC, USA, 25-29 June 2005. ACM Press. ISBN 1-59593-010-8. URL http://portal.acm.org/citation.cfm?id=1068009&jmp=cit&coll=GUIDE&dl=GUIDE&CFID=48779769&CFTOKEN=55479664#supp. GPBiB

B. Bhanu, Y. Lin, and K. Krawiec. *Evolutionary Synthesis of Pattern Recognition Systems*. Monographs in Computer Science. Springer-Verlag, New York, 2005. ISBN 0-387-21295-7. URL http://www.springer.com/west/home/computer/imaging?SGWID=4-149-22-39144807-detailsPage=ppmmedia|aboutThisBook. GPBiB

A. S. Bickel and R. W. Bickel. Tree structured rules in genetic algorithms. In J. J. Grefenstette, editor, *Genetic Algorithms and their Applications: Proceedings of the second International Conference on Genetic Algorithms*, pages 77–81, MIT, Cambridge, MA, USA, 28-31 July 1987. Lawrence Erlbaum Associates. GPBiB

S. Bleuler, M. Brack, L. Thiele, and E. Zitzler. Multiobjective genetic programming: Reducing bloat using SPEA2. In *Proceedings of the 2001 Congress on Evolutionary Computation CEC2001*, pages 536–543, COEX, World Trade Center, 159 Samseong-dong, Gangnam-gu, Seoul, Korea, 27-30 May 2001. IEEE Press. ISBN 0-7803-6658-1. URL ftp://ftp.tik.ee.ethz.ch/pub/people/zitzler/BBTZ2001b.ps.gz. GPBiB

T. Blickle. *Theory of Evolutionary Algorithms and Application to System Synthesis*. PhD thesis, Swiss Federal Institute of Technology, Zurich, November 1996. URL http://www.handshake.de/user/blickle/publications/diss.pdf. GPBiB

W. Bohm and A. Geyer-Schulz. Exact uniform initialization for genetic programming. In R. K. Belew and M. Vose, editors, *Foundations of Genetic Algorithms IV*, pages 379–407, University of San Diego, CA, USA, 3–5 August 1996. Morgan Kaufmann. ISBN 1-55860-460-X. GPBiB

C. C. Bojarczuk, H. S. Lopes, and A. A. Freitas. Genetic programming for knowledge discovery in chest-pain diagnosis. *IEEE Engineering in Medicine and Biology Magazine*, 19(4):38–44, July-August 2000. ISSN 0739-5175. URL http://ieeexplore.ieee.org/iel5/51/18543/00853480.pdf. GPBiB

P. A. N. Bosman and E. D. de Jong. Grammar transformations in an EDA for genetic programming. In R. Poli, et al., editors, *GECCO 2004 Workshop Proceedings*, Seattle, Washington, USA, 26-30 June 2004a. URL http://www.cs.bham.ac.uk/~wbl/biblio/gecco2004/WOBU001.pdf. GPBiB

Generation 1
(see Sec. B.4)

P. A. N. Bosman and E. D. de Jong. Learning probabilistic tree grammars for genetic programming. In X. Yao, et al., editors, *Parallel Problem Solving from Nature - PPSN VIII*, volume 3242 of *LNCS*, pages 192–201, Birmingham, UK, 18-22 September 2004b. Springer-Verlag. ISBN 3-540-23092-0. URL http://www.cs.uu.nl/~dejong/publications/edagpppsn.pdf. GPᴮɪʙ

A. Brabazon and M. O'Neill. *Biologically Inspired Algorithms for Financial Modelling*. Natural Computing Series. Springer, 2006. ISBN 3-540-26252-0. GPᴮɪʙ

M. Brameier and W. Banzhaf. A comparison of linear genetic programming and neural networks in medical data mining. *IEEE Transactions on Evolutionary Computation*, 5 (1):17–26, February 2001. URL http://web.cs.mun.ca/~banzhaf/papers/ieee_taec.pdf. GPᴮɪʙ

M. Brameier and W. Banzhaf. *Linear Genetic Programming*. Number XVI in Genetic and Evolutionary Computation. Springer, 2007. ISBN 0-387-31029-0. URL http://www.springer.com/west/home/default?SGWID=4-40356-22-173660820-0. GPᴮɪʙ

M. Brameier, J. Haan, A. Krings, and R. M. MacCallum. Automatic discovery of cross-family sequence features associated with protein function. *BMC bioinformatics [electronic resource]*, 7(16), January 12 2006. ISSN 1471-2105. URL http://www.biomedcentral.com/content/pdf/1471-2105-7-16.pdf. GPᴮɪʙ

S. Brave. Evolving recursive programs for tree search. In P. J. Angeline and K. E. Kinnear, Jr., editors, *Advances in Genetic Programming 2*, chapter 10, pages 203–220. MIT Press, Cambridge, MA, USA, 1996. ISBN 0-262-01158-1. GPᴮɪʙ

S. Brave and A. S. Wu, editors. *Late Breaking Papers at the 1999 Genetic and Evolutionary Computation Conference*, Orlando, Florida, USA, 13 July 1999. GPᴮɪʙ

M. Brezocnik. *Uporaba genetskega programiranja v inteligentnih proizvodnih sistemih*. University of Maribor, Faculty of mechanical engineering, Maribor, Slovenia, 2000. ISBN 86-435-0306-1. URL http://maja.uni-mb.si/slo/Knjige/2000-03-mon/index.htm. GPᴮɪʙ

M. Brezocnik, J. Balic, and L. Gusel. Artificial intelligence approach to determination of flow curve. *Journal for technology of plasticity*, 25(1-2):1–7, 2000. ISSN 0350-2368. GPᴮɪʙ

G. Buason, N. Bergfeldt, and T. Ziemke. Brains, bodies, and beyond: Competitive co-evolution of robot controllers, morphologies and environments. *Genetic Programming and Evolvable Machines*, 6(1):25–51, March 2005. ISSN 1389-2576.

E. K. Burke, M. R. Hyde, and G. Kendall. Evolving bin packing heuristics with genetic programming. In T. P. Runarsson, et al., editors, *Parallel Problem Solving from Nature - PPSN IX*, volume 4193 of *LNCS*, pages 860–869, Reykjavik, Iceland, 9-13 September 2006. Springer-Verlag. ISBN 3-540-38990-3. URL http://www.cs.nott.ac.uk/~mvh/ppsn2006.pdf. GPᴮɪʙ

E. K. Burke, G. Kendall, J. Newall, E. Hart, P. Ross, and S. Schulenburg. Hyper-heuristics: an emerging direction in modern search technology. In F. Glover and G. Kochenberger, editors, *Handbook of Metaheuristics*, pages 457–474. Kluwer Academic Publishers, 2003.

E. K. Burke, M. R. Hyde, G. Kendall, and J. Woodward. Automatic heuristic generation with genetic programming: evolving a jack-of-all-trades or a master of one. In D. Thierens, et al., editors, *GECCO '07: Proceedings of the 9th annual conference on*

Genetic and evolutionary computation, volume 2, pages 1559–1565, London, 7-11 July 2007. ACM Press. URL http://www.cs.bham.ac.uk/~wbl/biblio/gecco2007/docs/p1559.pdf. GP$_{BiB}$

B. F. Buxton, W. B. Langdon, and S. J. Barrett. Data fusion by intelligent classifier combination. *Measurement and Control*, 34(8):229–234, October 2001. URL http://www.cs.ucl.ac.uk/staff/W.Langdon/mc/. GP$_{BiB}$

W. Cai, A. Pacheco-Vega, M. Sen, and K. T. Yang. Heat transfer correlations by symbolic regression. *International Journal of Heat and Mass Transfer*, 49(23-24):4352–4359, November 2006. GP$_{BiB}$

E. Cantú-Paz, J. A. Foster, K. Deb, L. Davis, R. Roy, U.-M. O'Reilly, H.-G. Beyer, R. K. Standish, G. Kendall, S. W. Wilson, M. Harman, J. Wegener, D. Dasgupta, M. A. Potter, A. C. Schultz, K. A. Dowsland, N. Jonoska, and J. F. Miller, editors. *Genetic and Evolutionary Computation – GECCO 2003, Part I*, volume 2723 of *Lecture Notes in Computer Science*, Chicago, IL, USA, 12-16 July 2003. Springer. ISBN 3-540-40602-6. GP$_{BiB}$

F. Castillo, A. Kordon, and G. Smits. Robust pareto front genetic programming parameter selection based on design of experiments and industrial data. In R. L. Riolo, et al., editors, *Genetic Programming Theory and Practice IV*, volume 5 of *Genetic and Evolutionary Computation*, chapter 2, pages –. Springer, Ann Arbor, 11-13 May 2006a. ISBN 0-387-33375-4. GP$_{BiB}$

F. Castillo, A. Kordon, G. Smits, B. Christenson, and D. Dickerson. Pareto front genetic programming parameter selection based on design of experiments and industrial data. In M. Keijzer, et al., editors, *GECCO 2006: Proceedings of the 8th annual conference on Genetic and evolutionary computation*, volume 2, pages 1613–1620, Seattle, Washington, USA, 8-12 July 2006b. ACM Press. ISBN 1-59593-186-4. URL http://www.cs.bham.ac.uk/~wbl/biblio/gecco2006/docs/p1613.pdf. GP$_{BiB}$

M. Chami and D. Robilliard. Inversion of oceanic constituents in case I and II waters with genetic programming algorithms. *Applied Optics*, 41(30):6260–6275, October 2002. URL http://ao.osa.org/ViewMedia.cfm?id=70258&seq=0. GP$_{BiB}$

A. Channon. Unbounded evolutionary dynamics in a system of agents that actively process and transform their environment. *Genetic Programming and Evolvable Machines*, 7(3):253–281, October 2006. ISSN 1389-2576.

D. L. Chao and S. Forrest. Information immune systems. *Genetic Programming and Evolvable Machines*, 4(4):311–331, December 2003. ISSN 1389-2576.

S. M. Cheang, K. S. Leung, and K. H. Lee. Genetic parallel programming: Design and implementation. *Evolutionary Computation*, 14(2):129–156, Summer 2006. ISSN 1063-6560. GP$_{BiB}$

K. Chellapilla. Evolving computer programs without subtree crossover. *IEEE Transactions on Evolutionary Computation*, 1(3):209–216, September 1997a. GP$_{BiB}$

K. Chellapilla. Evolutionary programming with tree mutations: Evolving computer programs without crossover. In J. R. Koza, et al., editors, *Genetic Programming 1997: Proceedings of the Second Annual Conference*, pages 431–438, Stanford University, CA, USA, 13-16 July 1997b. Morgan Kaufmann.

Generation 2
(see Sec. B.4)

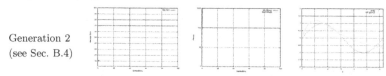

S.-H. Chen, editor. *Genetic Algorithms and Genetic Programming in Computational Finance.* Kluwer Academic Publishers, Dordrecht, July 2002. ISBN 0-7923-7601-3. URL http://www.springer.com/west/home/business?SGWID= 4-40517-22-33195998-detailsPage=ppmmedia|toc. GPBiB

S.-H. Chen, J. Duffy, and C.-H. Yeh. Equilibrium selection via adaptation: Using genetic programming to model learning in a coordination game. *The Electronic Journal of Evolutionary Modeling and Economic Dynamics,* 15 January 2002. ISSN 1298-0137. GPBiB

S.-H. Chen and C.-C. Liao. Agent-based computational modeling of the stock price-volume relation. *Information Sciences,* 170(1):75–100, 18 February 2005. URL http://www.sciencedirect.com/science/article/B6V0C-4B3JHTS-6/2/ 9e023835b1c70f176d1903dd3a8b638e. GPBiB

S.-H. Chen, H.-S. Wang, and B.-T. Zhang. Forecasting high-frequency financial time series with evolutionary neural trees: The case of heng-sheng stock index. In H. R. Arabnia, editor, *Proceedings of the International Conference on Artificial Intelligence, IC-AI '99,* volume 2, pages 437–443, Las Vegas, Nevada, USA, 28 June-1 July 1999. CSREA Press. ISBN 1-892512-17-3. URL http://bi.snu.ac.kr/Publications/Conferences/ International/ICAI99.ps. GPBiB

D. M. Chitty. A data parallel approach to genetic programming using programmable graphics hardware. In D. Thierens, et al., editors, *GECCO '07: Proceedings of the 9th annual conference on Genetic and evolutionary computation,* volume 2, pages 1566–1573, London, 7-11 July 2007. ACM Press. URL http://www.cs.bham.ac.uk/~wbl/ biblio/gecco2007/docs/p1566.pdf. GPBiB

S.-B. Cho, N. X. Hoai, and Y. Shan, editors. *Proceedings of The First Asian-Pacific Workshop on Genetic Programming,* Rydges (lakeside) Hotel, Canberra, Australia, 8 December 2003. ISBN 0-9751724-0-9. GPBiB

F. S. Chong and W. B. Langdon. Java based distributed genetic programming on the internet. In W. Banzhaf, et al., editors, *Proceedings of the Genetic and Evolutionary Computation Conference,* volume 2, page 1229, Orlando, Florida, USA, 13-17 July 1999. Morgan Kaufmann. ISBN 1-55860-611-4. URL http://www.cs.ucl.ac.uk/ staff/W.Langdon/ftp/papers/p.chong/DGPposter.pdf. Full text in technical report CSRP-99-7. GPBiB

V. Ciesielski and X. Li. Analysis of genetic programming runs. In R. I. Mckay and S.-B. Cho, editors, *Proceedings of The Second Asian-Pacific Workshop on Genetic Programming,* Cairns, Australia, 6-7 December 2004. URL http://goanna.cs.rmit. edu.au/~xiali/pub/ai04.vc.pdf. GPBiB

R. Cilibrasi, P. Vitanyi, and R. de Wolf. Algorithmic clustering of music based on string compression. *Computer Music Journal,* 28(4):49–67, Winter 2004. URL http://homepages.cwi.nl/~paulv/papers/music.pdf. GPBiB

R. Cilibrasi and P. M. B. Vitanyi. Clustering by compression. *IEEE Transactions on Information Theory,* 51(4):1523–1545, April 2005. URL http://homepages.cwi.nl/ ~paulv/papers/cluster.pdf. GPBiB

J. Clegg, J. A. Walker, and J. F. Miller. A new crossover technique for cartesian genetic programming. In D. Thierens, et al., editors, *GECCO '07: Proceedings of the 9th annual conference on Genetic and evolutionary computation,* volume 2, pages 1580–1587, London, 7-11 July 2007. ACM Press. URL http://www.cs.bham.ac.uk/~wbl/ biblio/gecco2007/docs/p1580.pdf. GPBiB

P. Collet. Genetic programming. In J.-P. Rennard, editor, *Handbook of Research on Nature-Inspired Computing for Economics and Management*, volume I, chapter V, pages 59–73. Idea Group Inc., 1200 E. Colton Ave, 2007. ISBN 1-59140-984-5. GP$_{\text{BiB}}$

P. Collet, M. Tomassini, M. Ebner, S. M. Gustafson, and A. Ekárt, editors. *Proceedings of the 9th European Conference on Genetic Programming*, volume 3905 of *Lecture Notes in Computer Science*, Budapest, Hungary, 10 - 12 April 2006. Springer. ISBN 3-540-33143-3. URL http://www.springerlink.com/openurl.asp?genre=issue&issn=0302-9743&volume=3905. GP$_{\text{BiB}}$

R. J. Collins. *Studies in Artificial Evolution*. PhD thesis, UCLA, Artificial Life Laboratory, Department of Computer Science, University of California, Los Angeles, LA CA 90024, USA, 1992.

O. Cordon, E. Herrera-Viedma, and M. Luque. Evolutionary learning of boolean queries by multiobjective genetic programming. In J. J. Merelo-Guervos, et al., editors, *Parallel Problem Solving from Nature - PPSN VII*, number 2439 in Lecture Notes in Computer Science, LNCS, pages 710–719, Granada, Spain, 7-11 September 2002. Springer-Verlag. ISBN 3-540-44139-5. URL http://link.springer.de/link/service/series/0558/bibs/2439/24390710.htm. GP$_{\text{BiB}}$

F. Corno, E. Sanchez, and G. Squillero. Evolving assembly programs: how games help microprocessor validation. *Evolutionary Computation, IEEE Transactions on*, 9(6): 695–706, 2005.

D. Costelloe and C. Ryan. Towards models of user preferences in interactive musical evolution. In D. Thierens, et al., editors, *GECCO '07: Proceedings of the 9th annual conference on Genetic and evolutionary computation*, volume 2, pages 2254–2254, London, 7-11 July 2007. ACM Press. URL http://www.cs.bham.ac.uk/~wbl/biblio/gecco2007/docs/p2254.pdf. GP$_{\text{BiB}}$

N. L. Cramer. A representation for the adaptive generation of simple sequential programs. In J. J. Grefenstette, editor, *Proceedings of an International Conference on Genetic Algorithms and the Applications*, pages 183–187, Carnegie-Mellon University, Pittsburgh, PA, USA, 24-26 July 1985. URL http://www.sover.net/~nichael/nlc-publications/icga85/index.html. GP$_{\text{BiB}}$

E. F. Crane and N. F. McPhee. The effects of size and depth limits on tree based genetic programming. In T. Yu, et al., editors, *Genetic Programming Theory and Practice III*, volume 9 of *Genetic Programming*, chapter 15, pages 223–240. Springer, Ann Arbor, 12-14 May 2005. ISBN 0-387-28110-X. GP$_{\text{BiB}}$

R. Crawford-Marks and L. Spector. Size control via size fair genetic operators in the PushGP genetic programming system. In W. B. Langdon, et al., editors, *GECCO 2002: Proceedings of the Genetic and Evolutionary Computation Conference*, pages 733–739, New York, 9-13 July 2002. Morgan Kaufmann Publishers. ISBN 1-55860-878-8. URL http://alum.hampshire.edu/~rpc01/gp234.pdf. GP$_{\text{BiB}}$

R. L. Crepeau. Genetic evolution of machine language software. In J. P. Rosca, editor, *Proceedings of the Workshop on Genetic Programming: From Theory to Real-World Applications*, pages 121–134, Tahoe City, California, USA, 9 July 1995. URL http://www.cs.ucl.ac.uk/staff/W.Langdon/ftp/papers/GEMS_Article.pdf. GP$_{\text{BiB}}$

R. Curry, P. Lichodzijewski, and M. I. Heywood. Scaling genetic programming to large datasets using hierarchical dynamic subset selection. *IEEE Transactions on Systems, Man, and Cybernetics: Part B - Cybernetics*, 37(4):1065–1073, August 2007. ISSN 1083-4419. URL http://www.cs.dal.ca/~mheywood/X-files/GradPubs.html#curry. GP$_{\text{BiB}}$

Generation 3
(see Sec. B.4)

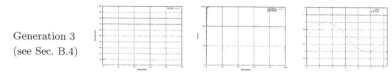

J. M. Daida, A. M. Hilss, D. J. Ward, and S. L. Long. Visualizing tree structures in genetic programming. *Genetic Programming and Evolvable Machines*, 6(1):79–110, March 2005. ISSN 1389-2576. GP$_{\text{BiB}}$

J. M. Daida, J. D. Hommes, T. F. Bersano-Begey, S. J. Ross, and J. F. Vesecky. Algorithm discovery using the genetic programming paradigm: Extracting low-contrast curvilinear features from SAR images of arctic ice. In P. J. Angeline and K. E. Kinnear, Jr., editors, *Advances in Genetic Programming 2*, chapter 21, pages 417–442. MIT Press, Cambridge, MA, USA, 1996. ISBN 0-262-01158-1. URL http://sitemaker.umich.edu/daida/files/GP2_cha21.pdf. GP$_{\text{BiB}}$

C. Darwin. *The Origin of Species*. John Murray, penguin classics, 1985 edition, 1859. ISBN 0-14-043205-1.

E. Dassau, B. Grosman, and D. R. Lewin. Modeling and temperature control of rapid thermal processing. *Computers and Chemical Engineering*, 30(4):686–697, 15 February 2006. URL http://tx.technion.ac.il/~dlewin/publications/rtp_paper_v9.pdf. GP$_{\text{BiB}}$

T. E. Davis and J. C. Principe. A Markov chain framework for the simple genetic algorithm. *Evolutionary Computation*, 1(3):269–288, 1993.

J. P. Day, D. B. Kell, and G. W. Griffith. Differentiation of phytophthora infestans sporangia from other airborne biological particles by flow cytometry. *Applied and Environmental Microbiology*, 68(1):37–45, January 2002. URL http://intl-aem.asm.org/cgi/reprint/68/1/37.pdf. GP$_{\text{BiB}}$

J. S. de Bonet, C. L. Isbell, Jr., and P. Viola. MIMIC: Finding optima by estimating probability densities. In M. C. M. et. al., editor, *Advances in Neural Information Processing Systems*, volume 9, page 424. MIT Press, 1997. URL http://citeseer.ist.psu.edu/debonet96mimic.html.

E. D. de Jong and J. B. Pollack. Multi-objective methods for tree size control. *Genetic Programming and Evolvable Machines*, 4(3):211–233, September 2003. ISSN 1389-2576. URL http://www.cs.uu.nl/~dejong/publications/bloat.ps. GP$_{\text{BiB}}$

E. D. de Jong, R. A. Watson, and J. B. Pollack. Reducing bloat and promoting diversity using multi-objective methods. In L. Spector, et al., editors, *Proceedings of the Genetic and Evolutionary Computation Conference (GECCO-2001)*, pages 11–18, San Francisco, California, USA, 7-11 July 2001. Morgan Kaufmann. ISBN 1-55860-774-9. URL http://www.demo.cs.brandeis.edu/papers/rbpd_gecco01.pdf. GP$_{\text{BiB}}$

J. S. de Sousa, L. de C. T. Gomes, G. B. Bezerra, L. N. de Castro, and F. J. Von Zuben. An immune-evolutionary algorithm for multiple rearrangements of gene expression data. *Genetic Programming and Evolvable Machines*, 5(2):157–179, June 2004. ISSN 1389-2576. GP$_{\text{BiB}}$

C. De Stefano, A. D. Cioppa, and A. Marcelli. Character preclassification based on genetic programming. *Pattern Recognition Letters*, 23(12):1439–1448, 2002. URL http://www.sciencedirect.com/science/article/B6V15-45J91MV-4/2/3e5c2ac0c51428d0f7ea9fc0142f6790. GP$_{\text{BiB}}$

K. Deb. *Multi-objective optimization using evolutionary algorithms*. Wiley, 2001.

K. Deb, S. Agrawal, A. Pratap, and T. Meyarivan. A fast elitist non-dominated sorting genetic algorithm for multi-objective optimisation: Nsga-ii. In *PPSN VI: Proceedings of the 6th International Conference on Parallel Problem Solving from Nature*, pages 849–858, London, UK, 2000. Springer-Verlag. ISBN 3-540-41056-2.

K. Deb, R. Poli, W. Banzhaf, H.-G. Beyer, E. Burke, P. Darwen, D. Dasgupta, D. Floreano, J. Foster, M. Harman, O. Holland, P. L. Lanzi, L. Spector, A. Tettamanzi, D. Thierens, and A. Tyrrell, editors. *Genetic and Evolutionary Computation – GECCO-2004, Part I*, volume 3102 of *Lecture Notes in Computer Science*, Seattle, WA, USA, 26-30 June 2004. Springer-Verlag. ISBN 3-540-22344-4. URL http://www.springerlink.com/content/978-3-540-22344-3. GP$_{\text{BiB}}$

M. Defoin Platel, M. Clergue, and P. Collard. Maximum homologous crossover for linear genetic programming. In C. Ryan, et al., editors, *Genetic Programming, Proceedings of EuroGP'2003*, volume 2610 of *LNCS*, pages 194–203, Essex, 14-16 April 2003. Springer-Verlag. ISBN 3-540-00971-X. URL http://www.i3s.unice.fr/~defoin/publications/eurogp_03.pdf. GP$_{\text{BiB}}$

M. A. H. Dempster and C. M. Jones. A real-time adaptive trading system using genetic programming. *Quantitative Finance*, 1:397–413, 2000. URL http://mahd-pc.jbs.cam.ac.uk/archive/PAPERS/2000/geneticprogramming.pdf. GP$_{\text{BiB}}$

M. A. H. Dempster, T. W. Payne, Y. Romahi, and G. W. P. Thompson. Computational learning techniques for intraday FX trading using popular technical indicators. *IEEE Transactions on Neural Networks*, 12(4):744–754, July 2001. ISSN 1045-9227. URL http://mahd-pc.jbs.cam.ac.uk/archive/PAPERS/2000/ieeetrading.pdf. GP$_{\text{BiB}}$

L. Deschaine. Using information fusion, machine learning, and global optimisation to increase the accuracy of finding and understanding items interest in the subsurface. *GeoDrilling International*, (122):30–32, May 2006. URL http://www.mining-journal.com/gdi_magazine/pdf/GDI0605scr.pdf. GP$_{\text{BiB}}$

L. M. Deschaine, R. A. Hoover, J. N. Skibinski, J. J. Patel, F. Francone, P. Nordin, and M. J. Ades. Using machine learning to compliment and extend the accuracy of UXO discrimination beyond the best reported results of the jefferson proving ground technology demonstration. In *2002 Advanced Technology Simulation Conference*, San Diego, CA, USA, 14-18 April 2002. URL http://www.cs.ucl.ac.uk/staff/W.Langdon/ftp/papers/deschaine/ASTC_2002_UXOFinder_Invention_Paper.pdf. GP$_{\text{BiB}}$

L. M. Deschaine, J. J. Patel, R. D. Guthrie, J. T. Grimski, and M. J. Ades. Using linear genetic programming to develop a C/C++ simulation model of a waste incinerator. In M. Ades, editor, *Advanced Technology Simulation Conference*, Seattle, 22-26 April 2001. URL http://www.aimlearning.com/Environmental.Engineering.pdf. GP$_{\text{BiB}}$

P. D'haeseleer. Context preserving crossover in genetic programming. In *Proceedings of the 1994 IEEE World Congress on Computational Intelligence*, volume 1, pages 256–261, Orlando, Florida, USA, 27-29 June 1994. IEEE Press. URL http://www.cs.ucl.ac.uk/staff/W.Langdon/ftp/ftp.io.com/papers/WCCI94_CPC.ps.Z. GP$_{\text{BiB}}$

P. D'haeseleer and J. Bluming. Effects of locality in individual and population evolution. In K. E. Kinnear, Jr., editor, *Advances in Genetic Programming*, chapter 8, pages 177–198. MIT Press, 1994. URL http://cognet.mit.edu/library/books/view?isbn=0262111888. GP$_{\text{BiB}}$

S. Dignum and R. Poli. Generalisation of the limiting distribution of program sizes in tree-based genetic programming and analysis of its effects on bloat. In D. Thierens, et al., editors, *GECCO '07: Proceedings of the 9th annual conference on Genetic and evolutionary computation*, volume 2, pages 1588–1595, London, 7-11 July 2007. ACM Press. URL http://www.cs.bham.ac.uk/~wbl/biblio/gecco2007/docs/p1588.pdf. GP$_{\text{BiB}}$

Generation 4
(see Sec. B.4)

C. Dimopoulos. A genetic programming methodology for the solution of the multi-objective cell-formation problem. In H.-D. Cheng, editor, *Proceedings of the 8th Joint Conference in Information Systems (JCIS 2005)*, pages 1487–1494, Salt Lake City, USA, 21-25 July 2005.   GPBiB

J. U. Dolinsky, I. D. Jenkinson, and G. J. Colquhoun. Application of genetic programming to the calibration of industrial robots. *Computers in Industry*, 58(3):255–264, April 2007. ISSN 0166-3615.   GPBiB

R. P. Domingos, R. Schirru, and A. S. Martinez. Soft computing systems applied to PWR's xenon. *Progress in Nuclear Energy*, 46(3-4):297–308, 2005.   GPBiB

M. Dorigo and T. Stützle. *Ant Colony Optimization*. MIT Press (Bradford Books), 2004.

D. C. Dracopoulos. *Evolutionary Learning Algorithms for Neural Adaptive Control*. Perspectives in Neural Computing. Springer Verlag, P.O. Box 31 13 40, D-10643 Berlin, Germany, August 1997. ISBN 3-540-76161-6. URL http://www.springer.de/catalog/html-files/deutsch/comp/3540761616.html.   GPBiB

S. Draves. The electric sheep. *SIGEVOlution*, 1(2):10–16, 2006. ISSN 1931-8499.

S. Droste, T. Jansen, G. Rudolph, H.-P. Schwefel, K. Tinnefeld, and I. Wegener. Theory of evolutionary algorithms and genetic programming. In H.-P. Schwefel, et al., editors, *Advances in Computational Intelligence: Theory and Practice*, Natural Computing Series, chapter 5, pages 107–144. Springer, 2003. ISBN 3-540-43269-8.   GPBiB

M. Ebner, M. Reinhardt, and J. Albert. Evolution of vertex and pixel shaders. In M. Keijzer, et al., editors, *Proceedings of the 8th European Conference on Genetic Programming*, volume 3447 of *Lecture Notes in Computer Science*, pages 261–270, Lausanne, Switzerland, 30 March - 1 April 2005. Springer. ISBN 3-540-25436-6. URL http://springerlink.metapress.com/openurl.asp?genre=article&issn=0302-9743&volume=3447&spage=261.   GPBiB

M. Ebner, M. O'Neill, A. Ekárt, L. Vanneschi, and A. I. Esparcia-Alcázar, editors. *Proceedings of the 10th European Conference on Genetic Programming*, volume 4445 of *Lecture Notes in Computer Science*, Valencia, Spain, 11 - 13 April 2007. Springer. ISBN 3-540-71602-5. URL http://www.springerlink.com/content/978-3-540-71602-0/. GPBiB

EC-Digest, 1985-2008. URL http://ec-digest.research.ucf.edu/.

A. E. Eiben and J. E. Smith. *Introduction to Evolutionary Computing*. Springer, 2003. ISBN 3-540-40184-9.   GPBiB

A. Ekart and S. Z. Nemeth. Selection based on the pareto nondomination criterion for controlling code growth in genetic programming. *Genetic Programming and Evolvable Machines*, 2(1):61–73, March 2001. ISSN 1389-2576.   GPBiB

S. E. Eklund. A massively parallel architecture for linear machine code genetic programming. In Y. Liu, et al., editors, *Evolvable Systems: From Biology to Hardware: Proceedings of 4th International Conference, ICES 2001*, volume 2210 of *Lecture Notes in Computer Science*, pages 216–224, Tokyo, Japan, October 3-5 2001. Springer-Verlag. URL http://www.springerlink.com/openurl.asp?genre=article&issn=0302-9743&volume=2210&spage=216.   GPBiB

S. E. Eklund. A massively parallel GP engine in VLSI. In D. B. Fogel, et al., editors, *Proceedings of the 2002 Congress on Evolutionary Computation CEC2002*, pages 629–633. IEEE Press, 2002. ISBN 0-7803-7278-6.   GPBiB

S. E. Eklund. A massively parallel architecture for distributed genetic algorithms. *Parallel Computing*, 30(5-6):647–676, 2004. URL http://www.sciencedirect.com/science/article/B6V12-4CDS49V-1/2/5ba1531eae2c9d8b336f1e90cc0ba5e9. GP BiB

D. I. Ellis, D. Broadhurst, and R. Goodacre. Rapid and quantitative detection of the microbial spoilage of beef by fourier transform infrared spectroscopy and machine learning. *Analytica Chimica Acta*, 514(2):193–201, 2004. URL http://dbkgroup.org/dave_files/ACAbeef04.pdf. GP BiB

D. I. Ellis, D. Broadhurst, D. B. Kell, J. J. Rowland, and R. Goodacre. Rapid and quantitative detection of the microbial spoilage of meat by fourier transform infrared spectroscopy and machine learning. *Applied and Environmental Microbiology*, 68(6): 2822–2828, June 2002. URL http://dbkgroup.org/Papers/app_%20env_microbiol_68_(2822).pdf. GP BiB

R. Eriksson and B. Olsson. Adapting genetic regulatory models by genetic programming. *Biosystems*, 76(1-3):217–227, 2004. URL http://www.sciencedirect.com/science/article/B6T2K-4D09KY2-7/2/1abfe196bb4afc60afc3311cadb75d66. GP BiB

A. I. Esparcia-Alcazar and K. C. Sharman. Genetic programming techniques that evolve recurrent neural networks architectures for signal processing. In *IEEE Workshop on Neural Networks for Signal Processing*, Seiko, Kyoto, Japan, September 1996. GP BiB

C. Evans, P. J. Fleming, D. C. Hill, J. P. Norton, I. Pratt, D. Rees, and K. Rodriguez-Vazquez. Application of system identification techniques to aircraft gas turbine engines. *Control Engineering Practice*, 9(2):135–148, 2001. URL http://www.sciencedirect.com/science/article/B6V2H-4280YP2-3/1/24d44180070f91dea854032d98f9187a. GP BiB

F. Federman, G. Sparkman, and S. Watt. Representation of music in a learning classifier system utilizing bach chorales. In W. Banzhaf, et al., editors, *Proceedings of the Genetic and Evolutionary Computation Conference*, volume 1, page 785, Orlando, Florida, USA, 13-17 July 1999. Morgan Kaufmann. ISBN 1-55860-611-4.

M. J. Felton. Survival of the fittest in drug design. *Modern Drug Discovery*, 3(9):49–50, November/December 2000. ISSN 1532-4486. URL http://pubs.acs.org/subscribe/journals/mdd/v03/i09/html/felton.html. GP BiB

F. Fernandez, J. M. Sanchez, M. Tomassini, and J. A. Gomez. A parallel genetic programming tool based on PVM. In J. Dongarra, et al., editors, *Recent Advances in Parallel Virtual Machine and Message Passing Interface, Proceedings of the 6th European PVM/MPI Users' Group Meeting*, volume 1697 of *Lecture Notes in Computer Science*, pages 241–248, Barcelona, Spain, September 1999. Springer-Verlag. ISBN 3-540-66549-8. GP BiB

F. Fernandez, M. Tomassini, and L. Vanneschi. An empirical study of multipopulation genetic programming. *Genetic Programming and Evolvable Machines*, 4(1):21–51, March 2003. ISSN 1389-2576. GP BiB

G. Folino, C. Pizzuti, and G. Spezzano. A scalable cellular implementation of parallel genetic programming. *IEEE Transactions on Evolutionary Computation*, 7(1):37–53, February 2003. GP BiB

J. A. Foster. Review: Discipulus: A commercial genetic programming system. *Genetic Programming and Evolvable Machines*, 2(2):201–203, June 2001. ISSN 1389-2576. GP BiB

Generation 5
(see Sec. B.4)

J. A. Foster, E. Lutton, J. Miller, C. Ryan, and A. G. B. Tettamanzi, editors. *Genetic Programming, Proceedings of the 5th European Conference, EuroGP 2002*, volume 2278 of *LNCS*, Kinsale, Ireland, 3-5 April 2002. Springer-Verlag. ISBN 3-540-43378-3. GPBiB

F. D. Francone, M. Conrads, W. Banzhaf, and P. Nordin. Homologous crossover in genetic programming. In W. Banzhaf, et al., editors, *Proceedings of the Genetic and Evolutionary Computation Conference*, volume 2, pages 1021–1026, Orlando, Florida, USA, 13-17 July 1999. Morgan Kaufmann. ISBN 1-55860-611-4. URL http://www.cs. bham.ac.uk/~wbl/biblio/gecco1999/GP-463.pdf.   GPBiB

F. D. Francone and L. M. Deschaine. Getting it right at the very start – building project models where data is expensive by combining human expertise, machine learning and information theory. In *2004 Business and Industry Symposium*, Washington, DC, April 2004. URL http://www.cs.ucl.ac.uk/staff/W.Langdon/ftp/papers/ deschaine/ASTC_2004_Getting_It_Right_from_the_Very_Start.pdf.   GPBiB

A. Fraser and T. Weinbrenner. GPC++ Genetic Programming C++ Class Library, 1993-1997. URL http://www.cs.ucl.ac.uk/staff/W.Langdon/ftp/weinbenner/gp.html.

C. Fujiki and J. Dickinson. Using the genetic algorithm to generate lisp source code to solve the prisoner's dilemma. In J. J. Grefenstette, editor, *Genetic Algorithms and their Applications: Proceedings of the second international conference on Genetic Algorithms*, pages 236–240, MIT, Cambridge, MA, USA, 28-31 July 1987. Lawrence Erlbaum Associates.

A. Fukunaga. Automated discovery of composite SAT variable selection heuristics. In *Proceedings of the National Conference on Artificial Intelligence (AAAI)*, pages 641–648, 2002.   GPBiB

A. Fukunaga and A. Stechert. Evolving nonlinear predictive models for lossless image compression with genetic programming. In J. R. Koza, et al., editors, *Genetic Programming 1998: Proceedings of the Third Annual Conference*, pages 95–102, University of Wisconsin, Madison, Wisconsin, USA, 22-25 July 1998. Morgan Kaufmann. ISBN 1-55860-548-7. URL http://citeseer.ist.psu.edu/507773.html.   GPBiB

A. S. Fukunaga. Evolving local search heuristics for SAT using genetic programming. In K. Deb, et al., editors, *Genetic and Evolutionary Computation – GECCO-2004, Part II*, volume 3103 of *Lecture Notes in Computer Science*, pages 483–494, Seattle, WA, USA, 26-30 June 2004. Springer-Verlag. ISBN 3-540-22343-6. URL http://alexf04. maclisp.org/gecco2004.pdf.   GPBiB

P. Funes, E. Sklar, H. Juille, and J. Pollack. Animal-animat coevolution: Using the animal population as fitness function. In R. Pfeifer, et al., editors, *From Animals to Animats 5: Proceedings of the Fifth International Conference on Simulation of Adaptive Behavior*, pages 525–533, Zurich, Switzerland, August 17-21 1998a. MIT Press. ISBN 0-262-66144-6. URL http://www.demo.cs.brandeis.edu/papers/tronsab98.pdf.   GPBiB

P. Funes, E. Sklar, H. Juille, and J. Pollack. Animal-animat coevolution: Using the animal population as fitness function. In R. Pfeifer, et al., editors, *From Animals to Animats 5: Proceedings of the Fifth International Conference on Simulation of Adaptive Behavior.*, pages 525–533, Zurich, Switzerland, August 17-21 1998b. MIT Press. ISBN 0-262-66144-6. URL http://www.demo.cs.brandeis.edu/papers/tronsab98.html.

C. Gagné and M. Parizeau. Open BEAGLE: A new C++ evolutionary computation framework. In W. B. Langdon, et al., editors, *GECCO 2002: Proceedings of the Genetic and Evolutionary Computation Conference*, page 888, New York, 9-13 July

2002. Morgan Kaufmann Publishers. ISBN 1-55860-878-8. URL http://www.cs.bham.ac.uk/~wbl/biblio/gecco2002/GP272.pdf. GPBiB

C. Gagne and M. Parizeau. Genetic engineering of hierarchical fuzzy regional representations for handwritten character recognition. *International Journal on Document Analysis and Recognition*, 8(4):223–231, September 2006. URL http://vision.gel.ulaval.ca/fr/publications/Id_607/PublDetails.php. GPBiB

C. Gagné and M. Parizeau. Co-evolution of nearest neighbor classifiers. *International Journal of Pattern Recognition and Artificial Intelligence*, 21(5):921–946, August 2007. ISSN 0218-0014. URL http://vision.gel.ulaval.ca/en/publications/Id_692/PublDetails.php. GPBiB

A. L. Garcia-Almanza and E. P. K. Tsang. Simplifying decision trees learned by genetic programming. In *Proceedings of the 2006 IEEE Congress on Evolutionary Computation*, pages 7906–7912, Vancouver, 6-21 July 2006. IEEE Press. ISBN 0-7803-9487-9. URL http://privatewww.essex.ac.uk/~algarc/Publications/WCCI2006.pdf. GPBiB

A. L. Garcia-Almanza and E. P. K. Tsang. Repository method to suit different investment strategies. In D. Srinivasan and L. Wang, editors, *2007 IEEE Congress on Evolutionary Computation*, pages 790–797, Singapore, 25-28 September 2007. IEEE Computational Intelligence Society, IEEE Press. ISBN 1-4244-1340-0. GPBiB

C. Gathercole and P. Ross. Dynamic training subset selection for supervised learning in genetic programming. In Y. Davidor, et al., editors, *Parallel Problem Solving from Nature III*, volume 866 of *LNCS*, pages 312–321, Jerusalem, 9-14 October 1994. Springer-Verlag. ISBN 3-540-58484-6. URL http://citeseer.ist.psu.edu/gathercole94dynamic.html. GPBiB

C. Gathercole and P. Ross. The MAX problem for genetic programming - highlighting an adverse interaction between the crossover operator and a restriction on tree depth. Technical report, Department of Artificial Intelligence, University of Edinburgh, 80 South Bridge, Edinburgh, EH1 1HN, UK, 1995. URL http://citeseer.ist.psu.edu/gathercole95max.html. GPBiB

C. Gathercole and P. Ross. Tackling the boolean even N parity problem with genetic programming and limited-error fitness. In J. R. Koza, et al., editors, *Genetic Programming 1997: Proceedings of the Second Annual Conference*, pages 119–127, Stanford University, CA, USA, 13-16 July 1997. Morgan Kaufmann. URL http://citeseer.ist.psu.edu/79389.html. GPBiB

S. Gelly, O. Teytaud, N. Bredeche, and M. Schoenauer. Universal consistency and bloat in GP. *Revue d'Intelligence Artificielle*, 20(6):805–827, 2006. ISSN 0992-499X. URL http://hal.inria.fr/docs/00/11/28/40/PDF/riabloat.pdf. Issue on New Methods in Machine Learning. Theory and Applications. GPBiB

Genetic Programming mailing list, 2001-2008. URL http://tech.groups.yahoo.com/group/genetic_programming/.

R. J. Gilbert, R. Goodacre, A. M. Woodward, and D. B. Kell. Genetic programming: A novel method for the quantitative analysis of pyrolysis mass spectral data. *ANALYTICAL CHEMISTRY*, 69(21):4381–4389, 1997. URL http://pubs.acs.org/journals/ancham/article.cgi/ancham/1997/69/i21/pdf/ac970460j.pdf. GPBiB

A. Globus, J. Lawton, and T. Wipke. Automatic molecular design using evolutionary techniques. In A. Globus and D. Srivastava, editors, *The Sixth Foresight Conference*

Generation 6
(see Sec. B.4)

on Molecular Nanotechnology, Westin Hotel in Santa Clara, CA, USA, November 12-15, 1998 1998. URL http://www.foresight.org/Conferences/MNT6/Papers/Globus/index.html. GPBiB

D. E. Goldberg. *Genetic Algorithms in Search Optimization and Machine Learning.* Addison-Wesley, 1989.

R. Goodacre and R. J. Gilbert. The detection of caffeine in a variety of beverages using curie-point pyrolysis mass spectrometry and genetic programming. *The Analyst*, 124: 1069–1074, 1999. GPBiB

R. Goodacre. Explanatory analysis of spectroscopic data using machine learning of simple, interpretable rules. *Vibrational Spectroscopy*, 32(1):33–45, 5 August 2003. URL http://www.biospec.net/learning/Metab06/Goodacre-FTIRmaps.pdf. A collection of Papers Presented at Shedding New Light on Disease: Optical Diagnostics for the New Millennium (SPEC 2002) Reims, France 23-27 June 2002. GPBiB

R. Goodacre, B. Shann, R. J. Gilbert, E. M. Timmins, A. C. McGovern, B. K. Alsberg, D. B. Kell, and N. A. Logan. The detection of the dipicolinic acid biomarker in bacillus spores using curie-point pyrolysis mass spectrometry and fourier-transform infrared spectroscopy. *Analytical Chemistry*, 72(1):119–127, 1 January 2000. URL http://pubs.acs.org/cgi-bin/article.cgi/ancham/2000/72/i01/html/ac990661i.html. GPBiB

R. Goodacre, S. Vaidyanathan, W. B. Dunn, G. G. Harrigan, and D. B. Kell. Metabolomics by numbers: acquiring and understanding global metabolite data. *Trends in Biotechnology*, 22(5):245–252, 1 May 2004. URL http://dbkgroup.org/Papers/trends%20in%20biotechnology_22_(245).pdf. GPBiB

F. Gruau. *Neural Network Synthesis using Cellular Encoding and the Genetic Algorithm.* PhD thesis, Laboratoire de l'Informatique du Parallilisme, Ecole Normale Supirieure de Lyon, France, 1994. URL ftp://ftp.ens-lyon.fr/pub/LIP/Rapports/PhD/PhD1994/PhD1994-01-E.ps.Z. GPBiB

F. Gruau and D. Whitley. Adding learning to the cellular development process: a comparative study. *Evolutionary Computation*, 1(3):213–233, 1993. GPBiB

F. Gruau. Genetic micro programming of neural networks. In K. E. Kinnear, Jr., editor, *Advances in Genetic Programming*, chapter 24, pages 495–518. MIT Press, 1994. URL http://cognet.mit.edu/library/books/view?isbn=0262111888. GPBiB

F. Gruau. On using syntactic constraints with genetic programming. In P. J. Angeline and K. E. Kinnear, Jr., editors, *Advances in Genetic Programming 2*, chapter 19, pages 377–394. MIT Press, Cambridge, MA, USA, 1996. ISBN 0-262-01158-1. GPBiB

S. M. Gustafson. *An Analysis of Diversity in Genetic Programming.* PhD thesis, School of Computer Science and Information Technology, University of Nottingham, Nottingham, England, February 2004. URL http://www.cs.nott.ac.uk/~smg/research/publications/phdthesis-gustafson.pdf. GPBiB

S. M. Gustafson and E. K. Burke. The speciating island model: An alternative parallel evolutionary algorithm. *Journal of Parallel and Distributed Computing*, 66(8):1025–1036, August 2006. Parallel Bioinspired Algorithms. GPBiB

S. M. Gustafson, E. K. Burke, and N. Krasnogor. On improving genetic programming for symbolic regression. In D. Corne, et al., editors, *Proceedings of the 2005 IEEE Congress on Evolutionary Computation*, volume 1, pages 912–919, Edinburgh, UK, 2-5 September 2005. IEEE Press. ISBN 0-7803-9363-5. GPBiB

R. J. Hampo and K. A. Marko. Application of genetic programming to control of vehicle systems. In *Proceedings of the Intelligent Vehicles '92 Symposium*, 1992. June 29 - July 1, 1992, Detroit, Mi, USA.   GP$_{\text{BIB}}$

P. Han, S. Zhou, and D. Wang. A multi-objective genetic programming/ NARMAX approach to chaotic systems identification. In *The Sixth World Congress on Intelligent Control and Automation, WCICA 2006*, volume 1, pages 1735–1739, Dalian, 2006. IEEE. ISBN 1-4244-0332-4.   GP$_{\text{BIB}}$

S. Handley. On the use of a directed acyclic graph to represent a population of computer programs. In *Proceedings of the 1994 IEEE World Congress on Computational Intelligence*, volume 1, pages 154–159, Orlando, Florida, USA, 27-29 June 1994. IEEE Press.   GP$_{\text{BIB}}$

S. Handley. Automatic learning of a detector for alpha-helices in protein sequences via genetic programming. In S. Forrest, editor, *Proceedings of the 5th International Conference on Genetic Algorithms, ICGA-93*, pages 271–278, University of Illinois at Urbana-Champaign, 17-21 July 1993. Morgan Kaufmann.   GP$_{\text{BIB}}$

J. V. Hansen. Genetic programming experiments with standard and homologous crossover methods. *Genetic Programming and Evolvable Machines*, 4(1):53–66, March 2003. ISSN 1389-2576.   GP$_{\text{BIB}}$

J. V. Hansen, P. B. Lowry, R. D. Meservy, and D. M. McDonald. Genetic programming for prevention of cyberterrorism through dynamic and evolving intrusion detection. *Decision Support Systems*, 43(4):1362–1374, August 2007. Special Issue Clusters. GP$_{\text{BIB}}$

S. Harding and W. Banzhaf. Fast genetic programming on GPUs. In M. Ebner, et al., editors, *Proceedings of the 10th European Conference on Genetic Programming*, volume 4445 of *Lecture Notes in Computer Science*, pages 90–101, Valencia, Spain, 11 - 13 April 2007. Springer. ISBN 3-540-71602-5.   GP$_{\text{BIB}}$

G. Harik. Linkage learning via probabilistic modeling in the ECGA. IlliGAL Report 99010, University of Illinois at Urbana-Champaign, 1999.

K. Harries and P. Smith. Exploring alternative operators and search strategies in genetic programming. In J. R. Koza, et al., editors, *Genetic Programming 1997: Proceedings of the Second Annual Conference*, pages 147–155, Stanford University, CA, USA, 13-16 July 1997. Morgan Kaufmann. URL http://www.cs.ucl.ac.uk/staff/W.Langdon/ftp/papers/harries.gp97_paper.ps.gz.   GP$_{\text{BIB}}$

G. G. Harrigan, R. H. LaPlante, G. N. Cosma, G. Cockerell, R. Goodacre, J. F. Maddox, J. P. Luyendyk, P. E. Ganey, and R. A. Roth. Application of high-throughput fourier-transform infrared spectroscopy in toxicology studies: contribution to a study on the development of an animal model for idiosyncratic toxicity. *Toxicology Letters*, 146(3): 197–205, 2 February 2004.   GP$_{\text{BIB}}$

C. Harris and B. Buxton. GP-COM: A distributed, component-based genetic programming system in C++. In J. R. Koza, et al., editors, *Genetic Programming 1996: Proceedings of the First Annual Conference*, page 425, Stanford University, CA, USA, 28–31 July 1996. MIT Press. URL http://www.cs.ucl.ac.uk/staff/W.Langdon/ftp/papers/gp96com.ps.gz.   GP$_{\text{BIB}}$

B. Harvey, J. Foster, and D. Frincke. Towards byte code genetic programming. In W. Banzhaf, et al., editors, *Proceedings of the Genetic and Evolutionary Computation Conference*, volume 2, page 1234, Orlando, Florida, USA, 13-17 July 1999. Morgan Kaufmann. ISBN 1-55860-611-4. URL http://citeseer.ist.psu.edu/468509.html. GP$_{\text{BIB}}$

Generation 7
(see Sec. B.4)

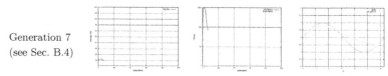

S. Hasan, S. Daugelat, P. S. S. Rao, and M. Schreiber. Prioritizing genomic drug targets in pathogens: Application to mycobacterium tuberculosis. *PLoS Computational Biology*, 2(6):e61, June 2006. URL http://compbiol.plosjournals.org/archive/1553-7358/2/6/pdf/10.1371_journal.pcbi.0020061-L.pdf.

T. Hastie, R. Tibshirani, and J. Friedman. *The elements of statistical learning: Data mining, inference, and prediction*. Springer, 2001.

A. Hauptman and M. Sipper. GP-endchess: Using genetic programming to evolve chess endgame players. In M. Keijzer, et al., editors, *Proceedings of the 8th European Conference on Genetic Programming*, volume 3447 of *Lecture Notes in Computer Science*, pages 120–131, Lausanne, Switzerland, 30 March - 1 April 2005. Springer. ISBN 3-540-25436-6. URL http://www.cs.bgu.ac.il/~sipper/papabs/eurogpchess-final.pdf. GP$_{\text{BiB}}$

A. Hauptman and M. Sipper. Evolution of an efficient search algorithm for the mate-in-N problem in chess. In M. Ebner, et al., editors, *Proceedings of the 10th European Conference on Genetic Programming*, volume 4445 of *Lecture Notes in Computer Science*, pages 78–89, Valencia, Spain, 11 - 13 April 2007. Springer. ISBN 3-540-71602-5. GP$_{\text{BiB}}$

T. Haynes, R. Wainwright, S. Sen, and D. Schoenefeld. Strongly typed genetic programming in evolving cooperation strategies. In L. Eshelman, editor, *Genetic Algorithms: Proceedings of the Sixth International Conference (ICGA95)*, pages 271–278, Pittsburgh, PA, USA, 15-19 July 1995. Morgan Kaufmann. ISBN 1-55860-370-0. URL http://www.mcs.utulsa.edu/~rogerw/papers/Haynes-icga95.pdf.   GP$_{\text{BiB}}$

T. D. Haynes, D. A. Schoenefeld, and R. L. Wainwright. Type inheritance in strongly typed genetic programming. In P. J. Angeline and K. E. Kinnear, Jr., editors, *Advances in Genetic Programming 2*, chapter 18, pages 359–376. MIT Press, Cambridge, MA, USA, 1996. ISBN 0-262-01158-1. URL http://www.mcs.utulsa.edu/~rogerw/papers/Haynes-hier.pdf.   GP$_{\text{BiB}}$

J. He, X. Wang, M. Zhang, J. Wang, and Q. Fang. New research on scalability of lossless image compression by GP engine. In J. Lohn, et al., editors, *Proceedings of the 2005 NASA/DoD Conference on Evolvable Hardware*, pages 160–164, Washington, DC, USA, 29 June-1 July 2005. IEEE Press. ISBN 0-7695-2399-4. URL http://doi.ieeecomputersociety.org/10.1109/EH.2005.35.   GP$_{\text{BiB}}$

A. G. Heidema, J. M. A. Boer, N. Nagelkerke, E. C. M. Mariman, D. L. van der A, and E. J. M. Feskens. The challenge for genetic epidemiologists: how to analyze large numbers of SNPs in relation to complex diseases. *BMC Genetics*, 7(23), April 21 2006. ISSN 1471-2156. URL http://www.biomedcentral.com/content/pdf/1471-2156-7-23.pdf. GP$_{\text{BiB}}$

M. I. Heywood and A. N. Zincir-Heywood. Register based genetic programming on FPGA computing platforms. In R. Poli, et al., editors, *Genetic Programming, Proceedings of EuroGP'2000*, volume 1802 of *LNCS*, pages 44–59, Edinburgh, 15-16 April 2000. Springer-Verlag. ISBN 3-540-67339-3. URL http://www.springerlink.com/openurl.asp?genre=article&issn=0302-9743&volume=1802&spage=44.   GP$_{\text{BiB}}$

W. D. Hillis. Co-evolving parasites improve simulated evolution as an optimization procedure. In C. G. Langton, et al., editors, *Artificial Life II*, volume X of *Santa Fe Institute Studies in the Sciences of Complexity*, pages 313–324. Addison-Wesley, Santa Fe Institute, New Mexico, USA, February 1990 1992.

M. Hinchliffe, M. Willis, and M. Tham. Chemical process sytems modelling using multi-objective genetic programming. In J. R. Koza, et al., editors, *Genetic Programming 1998: Proceedings of the Third Annual Conference*, pages 134–139, University of Wisconsin, Madison, Wisconsin, USA, 22-25 July 1998. Morgan Kaufmann. ISBN 1-55860-548-7. GP_{BiB}

M. P. Hinchliffe and M. J. Willis. Dynamic systems modelling using genetic programming. *Computers & Chemical Engineering*, 27(12):1841–1854, 2003. URL `http://www.sciencedirect.com/science/article/B6TFT-49MDYGW-2/2/742bcc7f22240c7a0381027aa5ff7e73`. GP_{BiB}

S.-Y. Ho, C.-H. Hsieh, H.-M. Chen, and H.-L. Huang. Interpretable gene expression classifier with an accurate and compact fuzzy rule base for microarray data analysis. *Biosystems*, 85(3):165–176, September 2006. GP_{BiB}

N. X. Hoai and R. I. McKay. Softening the structural difficulty in genetic programming with TAG-based representation and insertion/deletion operators. In K. Deb, et al., editors, *Genetic and Evolutionary Computation – GECCO-2004, Part II*, volume 3103 of *Lecture Notes in Computer Science*, pages 605–616, Seattle, WA, USA, 26-30 June 2004. Springer-Verlag. ISBN 3-540-22343-6. URL `http://link.springer.de/link/service/series/0558/bibs/3103/31030605.htm`. GP_{BiB}

N. X. Hoai, R. I. McKay, and H. A. Abbass. Tree adjoining grammars, language bias, and genetic programming. In C. Ryan, et al., editors, *Genetic Programming, Proceedings of EuroGP'2003*, volume 2610 of *LNCS*, pages 335–344, Essex, 14-16 April 2003. Springer-Verlag. ISBN 3-540-00971-X. URL `http://www.cs.adfa.edu.au/~abbass/publications/hardcopies/TAG3P-EuroGp-03.pdf`. GP_{BiB}

N. X. Hoai, R. I. B. McKay, and D. Essam. Representation and structural difficulty in genetic programming. *IEEE Transactions on Evolutionary Computation*, 10(2):157–166, April 2006. URL `http://sc.snu.ac.kr/courses/2006/fall/pg/aai/GP/nguyen/Structdiff.pdf`. GP_{BiB}

N. X. Hoai, R. I. McKay, D. Essam, and H. T. Hao. Genetic transposition in tree-adjoining grammar guided genetic programming: The duplication operator. In M. Keijzer, et al., editors, *Proceedings of the 8th European Conference on Genetic Programming*, volume 3447 of *Lecture Notes in Computer Science*, pages 108–119, Lausanne, Switzerland, 30 March - 1 April 2005. Springer. ISBN 3-540-25436-6. URL `http://springerlink.metapress.com/openurl.asp?genre=article&issn=0302-9743&volume=3447&spage=108`. GP_{BiB}

T.-H. Hoang, D. Essam, R. I. B. McKay, and X. H. Nguyen. Building on success in genetic programming:adaptive variation & developmental evaluation. In *Proceedings of the 2007 International Symposium on Intelligent Computation and Applications (ISICA)*, Wuhan, China, September 21-23 2007. China University of Geosciences Press. URL `http://sc.snu.ac.kr/PAPERS/dtag.pdf`. GP_{BiB}

J. H. Holland. *Adaptation in Natural and Artificial Systems: An Introductory Analysis with Applications to Biology, Control and Artificial Intelligence*. MIT Press, 1992. First Published by University of Michigan Press 1975.

P. Holmes. The odin genetic programming system. Tech Report RR-95-3, Computer Studies, Napier University, Craiglockhart, 216 Colinton Road, Edinburgh, EH14 1DJ, 1995. URL `http://citeseer.ist.psu.edu/holmes95odin.html`. GP_{BiB}

Generation 8
(see Sec. B.4)

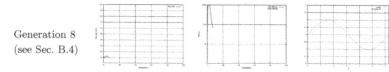

P. Holmes and P. J. Barclay. Functional languages on linear chromosomes. In J. R. Koza, et al., editors, *Genetic Programming 1996: Proceedings of the First Annual Conference*, page 427, Stanford University, CA, USA, 28–31 July 1996. MIT Press. GP_{BiB}

J.-H. Hong and S.-B. Cho. The classification of cancer based on DNA microarray data that uses diverse ensemble genetic programming. *Artificial Intelligence In Medicine*, 36(1):43–58, January 2006.   GP_{BiB}

G. S. Hornby and J. B. Pollack. Body-brain co-evolution using L-systems as a generative encoding. In L. Spector, et al., editors, *Proceedings of the Genetic and Evolutionary Computation Conference (GECCO-2001)*, pages 868–875, San Francisco, California, USA, 7-11 July 2001. Morgan Kaufmann. ISBN 1-55860-774-9. URL http://www.demo.cs.brandeis.edu/papers/hornby_gecco01.pdf.   GP_{BiB}

D. Howard and S. C. Roberts. Incident detection on highways. In U.-M. O'Reilly, et al., editors, *Genetic Programming Theory and Practice II*, chapter 16, pages 263–282. Springer, Ann Arbor, 13-15 May 2004. ISBN 0-387-23253-2.   GP_{BiB}

D. Howard, S. C. Roberts, and R. Brankin. Target detection in imagery by genetic programming. *Advances in Engineering Software*, 30(5):303–311, 1999. URL http://www.sciencedirect.com/science/article/B6V1P-3W1XV4H-1/1/6e7aee809f33757d0326c62a21824411.   GP_{BiB}

D. Howard, S. C. Roberts, and C. Ryan. Pragmatic genetic programming strategy for the problem of vehicle detection in airborne reconnaissance. *Pattern Recognition Letters*, 27(11):1275–1288, August 2006. Evolutionary Computer Vision and Image Understanding.   GP_{BiB}

W. H. Hsu and S. M. Gustafson. Wrappers for automatic parameter tuning in multi-agent optimization by genetic programming. In *IJCAI-2001 Workshop on Wrappers for Performance Enhancement in Knowledge Discovery in Databases (KDD)*, Seattle, Washington, USA, 4 August 2001.   GP_{BiB}

H. Iba. Random tree generation for genetic programming. In H.-M. Voigt, et al., editors, *Parallel Problem Solving from Nature IV, Proceedings of the International Conference on Evolutionary Computation*, volume 1141 of *LNCS*, pages 144–153, Berlin, Germany, 22-26 September 1996a. Springer Verlag. ISBN 3-540-61723-X.   GP_{BiB}

H. Iba. *Genetic Programming*. Tokyo Denki University Press, 1996b.   GP_{BiB}

H. Iba. Complexity-based fitness evaluation for variable length representation. Position paper at the Workshop on Evolutionary Computation with Variable Size Representation at ICGA-97, 20 July 1997. URL http://coblitz.codeen.org:3125/citeseer.ist.psu.edu/cache/papers/cs/16452/http:zSzzSzwww.miv.t.u-tokyo.ac.jpzSz~ibazSztmpzSzagp94.pdf/iba94genetic.pdf. GP_{BiB}

H. Iba, H. de Garis, and T. Sato. Genetic programming using a minimum description length principle. In K. E. Kinnear, Jr., editor, *Advances in Genetic Programming*, chapter 12, pages 265–284. MIT Press, 1994. URL http://citeseer.ist.psu.edu/327857.html.   GP_{BiB}

H. Iba, H. de Garis, and T. Sato. Temporal data processing using genetic programming. In L. Eshelman, editor, *Genetic Algorithms: Proceedings of the Sixth International Conference (ICGA95)*, pages 279–286, Pittsburgh, PA, USA, 15-19 July 1995a. Morgan Kaufmann. ISBN 1-55860-370-0.   GP_{BiB}

H. Iba, T. Sato, and H. de Garis. Recombination guidance for numerical genetic programming. In *1995 IEEE Conference on Evolutionary Computation*, volume 1, pages 97–102, Perth, Australia, 29 November - 1 December 1995b. IEEE Press.   GP_{BiB}

Y. Inagaki. On synchronized evolution of the network of automata. *IEEE Transactions on Evolutionary Computation*, 6(2):147–158, April 2002. ISSN 1089-778X. URL http://ieeexplore.ieee.org/iel5/4235/21497/00996014.pdf?tp=&arnumber= 996014&isnumber=21497&arSt=147&ared=158&arAuthor=Inagaki%2C+Y.%3B.   GP_{BiB}

C. Jacob. *Principia Evolvica – Simulierte Evolution mit Mathematica.* dpunkt.verlag, Heidelberg, Germany, August 1997. ISBN 3-920993-48-9.   GP_{BiB}

C. Jacob. The art of genetic programming. *IEEE Intelligent Systems*, 15(3):83–84, May-June 2000. ISSN 1094-7167. URL http://ieeexplore.ieee.org/iel5/5254/18363/ 00846288.pdf.   GP_{BiB}

C. Jacob. *Illustrating Evolutionary Computation with Mathematica.* Morgan Kaufmann, 2001. ISBN 1-55860-637-8. URL http://www.mkp.com/books_catalog/catalog.asp? ISBN=1-55860-637-8.   GP_{BiB}

N. Jin. Equilibrium selection by co-evolution for bargaining problems under incomplete information about time preferences. In *Proceedings of the IEEE Congress on Evolutionary Computation (CEC)*, pages 2661–2668, Edinburgh, 2–5 September 2005.

N. Jin and E. P. K. Tsang. Co-adaptive strategies for sequential bargaining problems with discount factors and outside options. In *Proceedings of the 2006 IEEE Congress on Evolutionary Computation*, pages 7913–7920, Vancouver, 6-21 July 2006. IEEE Press. ISBN 0-7803-9487-9.   GP_{BiB}

H. E. Johnson, R. J. Gilbert, M. K. Winson, R. Goodacre, A. R. Smith, J. J. Rowland, M. A. Hall, and D. B. Kell. Explanatory analysis of the metabolome using genetic programming of simple, interpretable rules. *Genetic Programming and Evolvable Machines*, 1(3):243–258, July 2000. ISSN 1389-2576.   GP_{BiB}

A. Jones, D. Young, J. Taylor, D. B. Kell, and J. J. Rowland. Quantification of microbial productivity via multi-angle light scattering and supervised learning. *Biotechnology and Bioengineering*, 59(2):131–143, 20 July 1998. ISSN 0006-3592.   GP_{BiB}

Jong-Wan Kim. *Proceedings of the 2001 Congress on Evolutionary Computation CEC2001*, COEX, World Trade Center, 159 Samseong-dong, Gangnam-gu, Seoul, Korea, 27-30 May 2001. IEEE Press. ISBN 0-7803-6658-1.   GP_{BiB}

E. Jordaan, J. den Doelder, and G. Smits. Novel approach to develop structure-property relationships using genetic programming. In T. P. Runarsson, et al., editors, *Parallel Problem Solving from Nature - PPSN IX*, volume 4193 of *LNCS*, pages 322–331, Reykjavik, Iceland, 9-13 September 2006. Springer-Verlag. ISBN 3-540-38990-3. GP_{BiB}

E. Jordaan, A. Kordon, L. Chiang, and G. Smits. Robust inferential sensors based on ensemble of predictors generated by genetic programming. In X. Yao, et al., editors, *Parallel Problem Solving from Nature - PPSN VIII*, volume 3242 of *LNCS*, pages 522–531, Birmingham, UK, 18-22 September 2004. Springer-Verlag. ISBN 3-540-23092-0. URL http://www.springerlink.com/openurl.asp?genre=article&issn= 0302-9743&volume=3242&spage=522.   GP_{BiB}

A. K. Joshi and Y. Schabes. Tree adjoining grammars. In G. Rozenber and A. Saloma, editors, *Handbook of of Formal Languages*, pages 69–123. Springer-Verlag, 1997.

Generation 9
(see Sec. B.4)

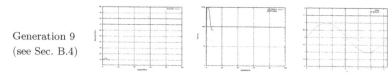

H. Juille and J. B. Pollack. Massively parallel genetic programming. In P. J. Angeline and K. E. Kinnear, Jr., editors, *Advances in Genetic Programming 2*, chapter 17, pages 339–358. MIT Press, Cambridge, MA, USA, 1996. ISBN 0-262-01158-1. URL http://www.demo.cs.brandeis.edu/papers/gp2.pdf.   GPBiB

M. Kaboudan. A measure of time series predictability using genetic programming applied to stock returns. *Journal of Forecasting*, 18:345–357, 1999.   GPBiB

M. A. Kaboudan. Genetic programming prediction of stock prices. *Computational Economics*, 6(3):207–236, December 2000.   GPBiB

M. Kaboudan. Extended daily exchange rates forecasts using wavelet temporal resolutions. *New Mathematics and Natural Computing*, 1:79–107, 2005.   GPBiB

T. Kalganova and J. Miller. Evolving more efficient digital circuits by allowing circuit layout evolution and multi-objective fitness. In A. Stoica, et al., editors, *The First NASA/DoD Workshop on Evolvable Hardware*, pages 54–63, Pasadena, California, 19-21 July 1999. IEEE Computer Society. ISBN 0-7695-0256-3.   GPBiB

A. Kattan and R. Poli. Evolutionary lossless compression with GP-ZIP. In *Proceedings of the IEEE World Congress on Computational Intelligence*, 2008.

C. Keber and M. G. Schuster. Option valuation with generalized ant programming. In W. B. Langdon, et al., editors, *GECCO 2002: Proceedings of the Genetic and Evolutionary Computation Conference*, pages 74–81, New York, 9-13 July 2002. Morgan Kaufmann Publishers. ISBN 1-55860-878-8. URL http://www.cs.bham.ac.uk/~wbl/biblio/gecco2002/aaaa075.ps.   GPBiB

M. Keijzer. Efficiently representing populations in genetic programming. In P. J. Angeline and K. E. Kinnear, Jr., editors, *Advances in Genetic Programming 2*, chapter 13, pages 259–278. MIT Press, Cambridge, MA, USA, 1996. ISBN 0-262-01158-1.   GPBiB

M. Keijzer. Scaled symbolic regression. *Genetic Programming and Evolvable Machines*, 5(3):259–269, September 2004. ISSN 1389-2576.   GPBiB

M. Keijzer, U.-M. O'Reilly, S. M. Lucas, E. Costa, and T. Soule, editors. *Genetic Programming 7th European Conference, EuroGP 2004, Proceedings*, volume 3003 of *LNCS*, Coimbra, Portugal, 5-7 April 2004. Springer-Verlag. ISBN 3-540-21346-5. URL http://www.springerlink.com/openurl.asp?genre=issue&issn=0302-9743&volume=3003.   GPBiB

M. Keijzer, A. Tettamanzi, P. Collet, J. I. van Hemert, and M. Tomassini, editors. *Proceedings of the 8th European Conference on Genetic Programming*, volume 3447 of *Lecture Notes in Computer Science*, Lausanne, Switzerland, 30 March - 1 April 2005. Springer. ISBN 3-540-25436-6. URL http://www.springerlink.com/openurl.asp?genre=issue&issn=0302-9743&volume=3447.   GPBiB

M. Keijzer, M. Cattolico, D. Arnold, V. Babovic, C. Blum, P. Bosman, M. V. Butz, C. Coello Coello, D. Dasgupta, S. G. Ficici, J. Foster, A. Hernandez-Aguirre, G. Hornby, H. Lipson, P. McMinn, J. Moore, G. Raidl, F. Rothlauf, C. Ryan, and D. Thierens, editors. *GECCO 2006: Proceedings of the 8th annual conference on Genetic and evolutionary computation*, Seattle, Washington, USA, 8-12 July 2006. ACM Press. ISBN 1-59593-010-8. URL http://portal.acm.org/citation.cfm?id=1143997. GPBiB

D. B. Kell. Defence against the flood. *Bioinformatics World*, pages 16–18, January/February 2002a. URL http://dbkgroup.org/Papers/biwpp16-18_as_publ.pdf.   GPBiB

D. B. Kell. Metabolomics and machine learning: Explanatory analysis of complex metabolome data using genetic programming to produce simple, robust rules. *Molecular Biology Reports*, 29(1-2):237–241, 2002b. URL http://dbkgroup.org/Papers/btk2002_dbk.pdf. GPBiB

D. B. Kell. Genotype-phenotype mapping: genes as computer programs. *Trends in Genetics*, 18(11):555–559, November 2002c. URL http://dbkgroup.org/Papers/trends_genet_18_(555).pdf. GPBiB

D. B. Kell, R. M. Darby, and J. Draper. Genomic computing. explanatory analysis of plant expression profiling data using machine learning. *Plant Physiology*, 126(3):943–951, July 2001. URL http://www.plantphysiol.org/cgi/content/full/126/3/943. GPBiB

R. E. Keller and R. Poli. Linear genetic programming of metaheuristics. In D. Thierens, et al., editors, *GECCO '07: Proceedings of the 9th annual conference on Genetic and evolutionary computation*, volume 2, pages 1753–1753, London, 7-11 July 2007a. ACM Press. URL http://www.cs.bham.ac.uk/~wbl/biblio/gecco2007/docs/p1753.pdf. GPBiB

R. E. Keller and R. Poli. Cost-benefit investigation of a genetic-programming hyper-heuristic. In *Proceedings of Evolution Artificielle*, October 2007b.

R. E. Keller and R. Poli. Linear genetic programming of parsimonious metaheuristics. In *Proceedings of IEEE Congress on Evolutionary Computation (CEC)*, September 2007c.

D. Keymeulen, A. Stoica, J. Lohn, and R. S. Zebulum, editors. *The Third NASA/DoD workshop on Evolvable Hardware*, Long Beach, California, 12-14 July 2001. IEEE Computer Society. ISBN 0-7695-1180-5. URL http://cism.jpl.nasa.gov/ehw/events/nasaeh01/.

A. Khan. *Intelligent Perceptual Shaping of a Digital Watermark*. PhD thesis, Computer Science and Engineering, Ghulam Ishaq Khan Institute of Engineering Sciences and Technology, Topi, Pakistan, May 2006. URL http://www.cs.ucl.ac.uk/staff/W.Langdon/ftp/papers/Intelligent_perceptual_shaping_WM_asif.pdf. GPBiB

A. Khan and A. M. Mirza. Genetic perceptual shaping: Utilizing cover image and conceivable attack information during watermark embedding. *Information Fusion*, 8(4):354–365, October 2007. ISSN 1566-2535. GPBiB

B. KHosraviani. Organization design optimization using genetic programming. In J. R. Koza, editor, *Genetic Algorithms and Genetic Programming at Stanford 2003*, pages 109–117. Stanford Bookstore, Stanford, California, 94305-3079 USA, 4 December 2003. URL http://www.genetic-programming.org/sp2003/KHosraviani.pdf. GPBiB

B. KHosraviani, R. E. Levitt, and J. R. Koza. Organization design optimization using genetic programming. In M. Keijzer, editor, *Late Breaking Papers at the 2004 Genetic and Evolutionary Computation Conference*, Seattle, Washington, USA, 26 July 2004. URL http://www.cs.bham.ac.uk/~wbl/biblio/gecco2004/LBP056.pdf. GPBiB

R. H. Kibria and Y. Li. Optimizing the initialization of dynamic decision heuristics in DPLL SAT solvers using genetic programming. In P. Collet, et al., editors, *Proceedings of the 9th European Conference on Genetic Programming*, volume 3905 of *Lecture Notes in Computer Science*, pages 331–340, Budapest, Hungary, 10 - 12 April 2006. Springer. ISBN 3-540-33143-3. URL http://link.springer.de/link/service/series/0558/papers/3905/39050331.pdf. GPBiB

Generation 11
(see Sec. B.4)

K. E. Kinnear, Jr. Evolving a sort: Lessons in genetic programming. In *Proceedings of the 1993 International Conference on Neural Networks*, volume 2, pages 881–888, San Francisco, USA, 28 March-1 April 1993. IEEE Press. ISBN 0-7803-0999-5. URL http://www.cs.ucl.ac.uk/staff/W.Langdon/ftp/ftp.io.com/papers/kinnear.icnn93.ps.Z.   GPBiB

K. E. Kinnear, Jr. Fitness landscapes and difficulty in genetic programming. In *Proceedings of the 1994 IEEE World Conference on Computational Intelligence*, volume 1, pages 142–147, Orlando, Florida, USA, 27-29 June 1994a. IEEE Press. ISBN 0-7803-1899-4. URL http://www.cs.ucl.ac.uk/staff/W.Langdon/ftp/ftp.io.com/papers/kinnear.wcci.ps.Z.   GPBiB

K. E. Kinnear, Jr. A perspective on the work in this book. In K. E. Kinnear, Jr., editor, *Advances in Genetic Programming*, chapter 1, pages 3–19. MIT Press, 1994b. URL http://cognet.mit.edu/library/books/view?isbn=0262111888.   GPBiB

K. E. Kinnear, Jr., editor. *Advances in Genetic Programming*. MIT Press, Cambridge, MA, 1994c. URL http://mitpress.mit.edu/book-home.tcl?isbn=0262111888. GPBiB

A. Klappenecker and F. U. May. Evolving better wavelet compression schemes. In A. F. Laine, et al., editors, *Wavelet Applications in Signal and Image Processing III*, volume 2569, San Diego, CA, USA, 9-14 July 1995. SPIE. ISBN 0-8194-1928-1. URL http://citeseer.ist.psu.edu/334994.html.   GPBiB

T. J. Klassen and M. I. Heywood. Towards the on-line recognition of arabic characters. In *Proceedings of the 2002 International Joint Conference on Neural Networks IJCNN'02*, pages 1900–1905, Hilton Hawaiian Village Hotel, Honolulu, Hawaii, 12-17 May 2002. IEEE Press. ISBN 0-7803-7278-6. URL http://users.cs.dal.ca/~mheywood/X-files/Publications/IEEEarabic.pdf.   GPBiB

J. Klein and L. Spector. Unwitting distributed genetic programming via asynchronous javascript and XML. In D. Thierens, et al., editors, *GECCO '07: Proceedings of the 9th annual conference on Genetic and evolutionary computation*, volume 2, pages 1628–1635, London, 7-11 July 2007. ACM Press. URL http://www.cs.bham.ac.uk/~wbl/biblio/gecco2007/docs/p1628.pdf.   GPBiB

A. Kordon. Evolutionary computation at dow chemical. *SIGEVOlution*, 1(3):4–9, September 2006. URL http://www.sigevolution.org/2006/03/issue.pdf.   GPBiB

A. Kordon, F. Castillo, G. Smits, and M. Kotanchek. Application issues of genetic programming in industry. In T. Yu, et al., editors, *Genetic Programming Theory and Practice III*, volume 9 of *Genetic Programming*, chapter 16, pages 241–258. Springer, Ann Arbor, 12-14 May 2005. ISBN 0-387-28110-X.   GPBiB

M. Kotanchek, G. Smits, and E. Vladislavleva. Pursuing the pareto paradigm tournaments, algorithm variations & ordinal optimization. In R. L. Riolo, et al., editors, *Genetic Programming Theory and Practice IV*, volume 5 of *Genetic and Evolutionary Computation*, chapter 3, pages –. Springer, Ann Arbor, 11-13 May 2006. ISBN 0-387-33375-4.   GPBiB

M. Kovacic and J. Balic. Evolutionary programming of a CNC cutting machine. *International journal for advanced manufacturing technology*, 22(1-2):118–124, September 2003. ISSN 0268-3768. URL http://www.springerlink.com/openurl.asp?genre=article&eissn=1433-3015&volume=22&issue=1&spage=118.   GPBiB

J. R. Koza. Hierarchical genetic algorithms operating on populations of computer programs. In N. S. Sridharan, editor, *Proceedings of the Eleventh International Joint Conference on Artificial Intelligence IJCAI-89*, volume 1, pages 768–774, Detroit, MI, USA, 20-25 August 1989. Morgan Kaufmann. URL http://www.genetic-programming.com/jkpdf/ijcai1989.pdf. GPBiB

J. R. Koza. Genetic programming: A paradigm for genetically breeding populations of computer programs to solve problems. Technical Report STAN-CS-90-1314, Dept. of Computer Science, Stanford University, June 1990. URL http://www.genetic-programming.com/jkpdf/tr1314.pdf. GPBiB

J. R. Koza. A genetic approach to econometric modeling. In *Sixth World Congress of the Econometric Society*, Barcelona, Spain, 1990. URL http://www.genetic-programming.com/jkpdf/wces1990.pdf. GPBiB

J. R. Koza. *Genetic Programming: On the Programming of Computers by Means of Natural Selection*. MIT Press, Cambridge, MA, USA, 1992. ISBN 0-262-11170-5. GPBiB

J. R. Koza. *Genetic Programming II: Automatic Discovery of Reusable Programs*. MIT Press, Cambridge Massachusetts, May 1994. ISBN 0-262-11189-6. GPBiB

J. R. Koza. Two ways of discovering the size and shape of a computer program to solve a problem. In L. Eshelman, editor, *Genetic Algorithms: Proceedings of the Sixth International Conference (ICGA95)*, pages 287–294, Pittsburgh, PA, USA, 15-19 July 1995. Morgan Kaufmann. ISBN 1-55860-370-0. URL http://www.genetic-programming.com/jkpdf/icga1995.pdf. GPBiB

J. R. Koza, editor. *Late Breaking Papers at the Genetic Programming 1996 Conference Stanford University July 28-31, 1996*, Stanford University, CA, USA, 28–31 July 1996. Stanford Bookstore. ISBN 0-18-201031-7. URL http://www.genetic-programming.org/gp96latebreaking.html. GPBiB

J. R. Koza, editor. *Late Breaking Papers at the 1997 Genetic Programming Conference*, Stanford University, CA, USA, 13–16 July 1997. Stanford Bookstore. ISBN 0-18-206995-8. URL http://www.genetic-programming.org/gp97latebreaking.html. GPBiB

J. R. Koza, editor. *Late Breaking Papers at the 1998 Genetic Programming Conference*, University of Wisconsin, Madison, WI, USA, 22-25 July 1998. Omni Press. GPBiB

J. R. Koza, S. H. Al-Sakran, and L. W. Jones. Automated re-invention of six patented optical lens systems using genetic programming. In H.-G. Beyer, et al., editors, *GECCO 2005: Proceedings of the 2005 conference on Genetic and evolutionary computation*, volume 2, pages 1953–1960, Washington DC, USA, 25-29 June 2005. ACM Press. ISBN 1-59593-010-8. URL http://www.cs.bham.ac.uk/~wbl/biblio/gecco2005/docs/p1953.pdf. GPBiB

J. R. Koza and D. Andre. Classifying protein segments as transmembrane domains using architecture-altering operations in genetic programming. In P. J. Angeline and K. E. Kinnear, Jr., editors, *Advances in Genetic Programming 2*, chapter 8, pages 155–176. MIT Press, Cambridge, MA, USA, 1996. ISBN 0-262-01158-1. URL http://www.genetic-programming.com/jkpdf/aigp2aatmjk1996.pdf. GPBiB

J. R. Koza, D. Andre, F. H. Bennet, III, and M. Keane. *Genetic Programming 3: Darwinian Invention and Problem Solving*. Morgan Kaufman, April 1999. ISBN 1-55860-543-6. URL http://www.genetic-programming.org/gpbook3toc.html. GPBiB

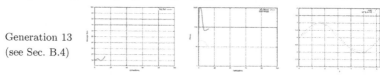

Generation 13
(see Sec. B.4)

J. R. Koza, D. Andre, F. H. Bennett, III, and M. A. Keane. Use of automatically defined functions and architecture-altering operations in automated circuit synthesis using genetic programming. In J. R. Koza, et al., editors, *Genetic Programming 1996: Proceedings of the First Annual Conference*, pages 132–149, Stanford University, CA, USA, 28–31 July 1996a. MIT Press. URL http://www.genetic-programming.com/ jkpdf/gp1996adfaa.pdf.   GPBiB

J. R. Koza, F. H. Bennett, III, D. Andre, and M. A. Keane. Four problems for which a computer program evolved by genetic programming is competitive with human performance. In *Proceedings of the 1996 IEEE International Conference on Evolutionary Computation*, volume 1, pages 1–10. IEEE Press, 1996b. URL http://www.genetic-programming.com/jkpdf/icec1996.pdf.   GPBiB

J. R. Koza, F. H. Bennett, III, D. Andre, and M. A. Keane. Automated WYWIWYG design of both the topology and component values of electrical circuits using genetic programming. In J. R. Koza, et al., editors, *Genetic Programming 1996: Proceedings of the First Annual Conference*, pages 123–131, Stanford University, CA, USA, 28–31 July 1996c. MIT Press. URL http://www.genetic-programming.com/jkpdf/ gp1996nielsen.pdf.   GPBiB

J. R. Koza, F. H. Bennett, III, D. Andre, and M. A. Keane. The design of analog circuits by means of genetic programming. In P. Bentley, editor, *Evolutionary Design by Computers*, chapter 16, pages 365–385. Morgan Kaufmann, San Francisco, USA, 1999. ISBN 1-55860-605-X. URL http://www.genetic-programming.com/jkpdf/edc1999. pdf.   GPBiB

J. R. Koza, F. H. Bennett, III, J. L. Hutchings, S. L. Bade, M. A. Keane, and D. Andre. Evolving sorting networks using genetic programming and the rapidly reconfigurable xilinx 6216 field-programmable gate array. In *Proceedings of the 31st Asilomar Conference on Signals, Systems, and Computers*. IEEE Press, 1997. URL http://www.genetic-programming.com/jkpdf/ieeeasilmoar1997.pdf.   GPBiB

J. R. Koza, F. H. Bennett, III, and O. Stiffelman. Genetic programming as a Darwinian invention machine. In R. Poli, et al., editors, *Genetic Programming, Proceedings of EuroGP'99*, volume 1598 of *LNCS*, pages 93–108, Goteborg, Sweden, 26-27 May 1999. Springer-Verlag. ISBN 3-540-65899-8. URL http://www.genetic-programming.com/ jkpdf/eurogp1999.pdf.   GPBiB

J. R. Koza, L. W. Jones, M. A. Keane, and M. J. Streeter. Towards industrial strength automated design of analog electrical circuits by means of genetic programming. In U.-M. O'Reilly, et al., editors, *Genetic Programming Theory and Practice II*, chapter 8, pages 120–?? Springer, Ann Arbor, 13-15 May 2004. ISBN 0-387-23253-2. URL http://www.genetic-programming.com/gptp2004.pdf. pages missing?   GPBiB

J. R. Koza, M. A. Keane, M. J. Streeter, W. Mydlowec, J. Yu, and G. Lanza. *Genetic Programming IV: Routine Human-Competitive Machine Intelligence*. Kluwer Academic Publishers, 2003. ISBN 1-4020-7446-8. URL http://www.genetic-programming.org/ gpbook4toc.html.   GPBiB

J. R. Koza and R. Poli. Genetic programming. In E. K. Burke and G. Kendall, editors, *Search Methodologies: Introductory Tutorials in Optimization and Decision Support Techniques*, chapter 5. Springer, 2005. ISBN 0-387-23460-8. URL http:// www.springer.com/sgw/cda/frontpage/0,11855,4-10045-22-67933962-0,00.html. GPBiB

J. R. Koza, D. E. Goldberg, D. B. Fogel, and R. L. Riolo, editors. *Genetic Program-ming 1996: Proceedings of the First Annual Conference*, Stanford University, CA, USA, 28–31 July 1996. MIT Press. URL http://www.genetic-programming.org/gp96proceedings.html. GPBiB

J. R. Koza, K. Deb, M. Dorigo, D. B. Fogel, M. Garzon, H. Iba, and R. L. Riolo, editors. *Genetic Programming 1997: Proceedings of the Second Annual Conference*, Stanford University, CA, USA, 13-16 July 1997. Morgan Kaufmann. URL http://www.mkp.com/books_catalog/1-55860-483-9.asp. GPBiB

J. R. Koza, W. Banzhaf, K. Chellapilla, K. Deb, M. Dorigo, D. B. Fogel, M. H. Garzon, D. E. Goldberg, H. Iba, and R. Riolo, editors. *Genetic Programming 1998: Proceedings of the Third Annual Conference*, University of Wisconsin, Madison, WI, USA, 22-25 July 1998. Morgan Kaufmann. ISBN 1-55860-548-7. GPBiB

D. H. Kraft, F. E. Petry, W. P. Buckles, and T. Sadasivan. The use of genetic programming to build queries for information retrieval. In *Proceedings of the 1994 IEEE World Congress on Computational Intelligence*, pages 468–473, Orlando, Florida, USA, 27-29 June 1994. IEEE Press. GPBiB

T. Krantz, O. Lindberg, G. Thorburn, and P. Nordin. Programmatic compression of natural video. In E. Cantú-Paz, editor, *Late Breaking Papers at the Genetic and Evolutionary Computation Conference (GECCO-2002)*, pages 301–307, New York, NY, July 2002. AAAI. URL http://thomas.krantz.com/paper.pdf. GPBiB

N. Krasnogor. Self generating metaheuristics in bioinformatics: The proteins structure comparison case. *Genetic Programming and Evolvable Machines*, 5(2):181–201, June 2004. ISSN 1389-2576.

K. Krawiec. *Evolutionary Feature Programming: Cooperative learning for knowledge discovery and computer vision*. Number 385. Wydawnictwo Politechniki Poznanskiej, Poznan University of Technology, Poznan, Poland, 2004. URL http://idss.cs.put.poznan.pl/~krawiec/pubs/hab/krawiec_hab.pdf. GPBiB

W. B. Langdon. The evolution of size in variable length representations. In *1998 IEEE International Conference on Evolutionary Computation*, pages 633–638, Anchorage, Alaska, USA, 5-9 May 1998. IEEE Press. URL http://www.cs.bham.ac.uk/~wbl/ftp/papers/WBL.wcci98_bloat.pdf. GPBiB

W. B. Langdon. Size fair and homologous tree genetic programming crossovers. In W. Banzhaf, et al., editors, *Proceedings of the Genetic and Evolutionary Computation Conference*, volume 2, pages 1092–1097, Orlando, Florida, USA, 13-17 July 1999a. Morgan Kaufmann. ISBN 1-55860-611-4. URL http://www.cs.ucl.ac.uk/staff/W.Langdon/ftp/papers/WBL.gecco99.fairxo.ps.gz. GPBiB

W. B. Langdon. Scaling of program tree fitness spaces. *Evolutionary Computation*, 7(4): 399–428, Winter 1999b. ISSN 1063-6560. URL http://www.mitpressjournals.org/doi/pdf/10.1162/evco.1999.7.4.399. GPBiB

W. B. Langdon. Convergence rates for the distribution of program outputs. In W. B. Langdon, et al., editors, *GECCO 2002: Proceedings of the Genetic and Evolutionary Computation Conference*, pages 812–819, New York, 9-13 July 2002a. Morgan Kaufmann Publishers. ISBN 1-55860-878-8. URL http://www.cs.ucl.ac.uk/staff/W.Langdon/ftp/papers/wbl_gecco2002.pdf. GPBiB

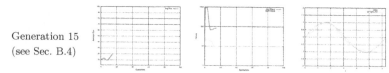

Generation 15
(see Sec. B.4)

W. B. Langdon. How many good programs are there? How long are they? In K. A. De Jong, et al., editors, *Foundations of Genetic Algorithms VII*, pages 183–202, Torremolinos, Spain, 4-6 September 2002b. Morgan Kaufmann. ISBN 0-12-208155-2. URL http://www.cs.ucl.ac.uk/staff/W.Langdon/ftp/papers/wbl_foga2002.pdf. Published 2003.   GPBiB

W. B. Langdon. Convergence of program fitness landscapes. In E. Cantú-Paz, et al., editors, *Genetic and Evolutionary Computation – GECCO-2003*, volume 2724 of *LNCS*, pages 1702–1714, Chicago, 12-16 July 2003a. Springer-Verlag. ISBN 3-540-40603-4. URL http://www.cs.ucl.ac.uk/staff/W.Langdon/ftp/papers/wbl_gecco2003. pdf.   GPBiB

W. B. Langdon. The distribution of reversible functions is Normal. In R. L. Riolo and B. Worzel, editors, *Genetic Programming Theory and Practise*, chapter 11, pages 173–188. Kluwer, 2003b. ISBN 1-4020-7581-2. URL http://www.cs.ucl.ac.uk/staff/W. Langdon/ftp/papers/wbl_reversible.pdf.   GPBiB

W. B. Langdon. Global distributed evolution of L-systems fractals. In M. Keijzer, et al., editors, *Genetic Programming, Proceedings of EuroGP'2004*, volume 3003 of *LNCS*, pages 349–358, Coimbra, Portugal, 5-7 April 2004. Springer-Verlag. ISBN 3-540-21346-5. URL http://www.cs.ucl.ac.uk/staff/W.Langdon/ftp/papers/egp2004_pfeiffer. pdf.   GPBiB

W. B. Langdon. Pfeiffer – A distributed open-ended evolutionary system. In B. Edmonds, et al., editors, *AISB'05: Proceedings of the Joint Symposium on Socially Inspired Computing (METAS 2005)*, pages 7–13, University of Hertfordshire, Hatfield, UK, 12-15 April 2005a. URL http://www.cs.ucl.ac.uk/staff/W.Langdon/ftp/papers/wbl_metas2005.pdf. SSAISB 2005 Convention.   GPBiB

W. B. Langdon. The distribution of amorphous computer outputs. In S. Stepney and S. Emmott, editors, *The Grand Challenge in Non-Classical Computation: International Workshop*, York, UK, 18-19 April 2005b. URL http://www.cs.ucl.ac.uk/staff/W.Langdon/ftp/papers/grand_2005.pdf.   GPBiB

W. B. Langdon. Mapping non-conventional extensions of genetic programming. In C. S. Calude, et al., editors, *Unconventional Computing 2006*, volume 4135 of *LNCS*, pages 166–180, York, 4-8 September 2006. Springer-Verlag. ISBN 3-540-38593-2. URL http://www.cs.ucl.ac.uk/staff/W.Langdon/ftp/papers/wbl_uc2002.pdf.   GPBiB

W. B. Langdon and W. Banzhaf. A SIMD interpreter for genetic programming on GPU graphics cards. In *EuroGP*, LNCS, Naples, 26-28 March 2008. Springer. URL http://www.cs.ucl.ac.uk/staff/W.Langdon/ftp/papers/langdon_2008_eurogp.pdf. Forthcoming.

W. B. Langdon, S. J. Barrett, and B. F. Buxton. Predicting biochemical interactions – human P450 2D6 enzyme inhibition. In R. Sarker, et al., editors, *Proceedings of the 2003 Congress on Evolutionary Computation CEC2003*, pages 807–814, Canberra, 8-12 December 2003. IEEE Press. ISBN 0-7803-7804-0. URL http://www.cs.ucl.ac. uk/staff/W.Langdon/ftp/papers/wbl_cec2003.pdf.   GPBiB

W. B. Langdon and B. F. Buxton. Genetic programming for mining DNA chip data from cancer patients. *Genetic Programming and Evolvable Machines*, 5(3):251–257, September 2004. ISSN 1389-2576. URL http://www.cs.ucl.ac.uk/staff/W.Langdon/ftp/papers/wbl_dnachip.pdf.   GPBiB

W. B. Langdon and A. P. Harrison. GP on SPMD parallel graphics hardware for mega bioinformatics data mining. 2008. In preparation.

W. B. Langdon and J. P. Nordin. Seeding GP populations. In R. Poli, et al., editors, *Genetic Programming, Proceedings of EuroGP'2000*, volume 1802 of *LNCS*, pages 304–315, Edinburgh, 15-16 April 2000. Springer-Verlag. ISBN 3-540-67339-3. URL http://www.cs.ucl.ac.uk/staff/W.Langdon/ftp/papers/WBL_eurogp2000_seed.pdf. GP$_{\text{BiB}}$

W. B. Langdon and R. Poli. Fitness causes bloat. In P. K. Chawdhry, et al., editors, *Soft Computing in Engineering Design and Manufacturing*, pages 13–22. Springer-Verlag London, 23-27 June 1997. ISBN 3-540-76214-0. URL http://www.cs.bham.ac.uk/~wbl/ftp/papers/WBL.bloat_wsc2.ps.gz. GP$_{\text{BiB}}$

W. B. Langdon and R. Poli. Why ants are hard. In J. R. Koza, et al., editors, *Genetic Programming 1998: Proceedings of the Third Annual Conference*, pages 193–201, University of Wisconsin, Madison, Wisconsin, USA, 22-25 July 1998a. Morgan Kaufmann. ISBN 1-55860-548-7. URL http://www.cs.ucl.ac.uk/staff/W.Langdon/ftp/papers/WBL.antspace_gp98.pdf. GP$_{\text{BiB}}$

W. B. Langdon and R. Poli. Better trained ants for genetic programming. Technical Report CSRP-98-12, University of Birmingham, School of Computer Science, April 1998b. URL ftp://ftp.cs.bham.ac.uk/pub/tech-reports/1998/CSRP-98-12.ps.gz. GP$_{\text{BiB}}$

W. B. Langdon and R. Poli. The halting probability in von Neumann architectures. In P. Collet, et al., editors, *Proceedings of the 9th European Conference on Genetic Programming*, volume 3905 of *Lecture Notes in Computer Science*, pages 225–237, Budapest, Hungary, 10 - 12 April 2006. Springer. ISBN 3-540-33143-3. URL http://www.cs.ucl.ac.uk/staff/W.Langdon/ftp/papers/wbl_egp2006.pdf. GP$_{\text{BiB}}$

W. B. Langdon and R. Poli. *Foundations of Genetic Programming*. Springer-Verlag, 2002. ISBN 3-540-42451-2. URL http://www.cs.ucl.ac.uk/staff/W.Langdon/FOGP/. GP$_{\text{BiB}}$

W. B. Langdon and P. C. Treleaven. Scheduling maintenance of electrical power transmission networks using genetic programming. In K. Warwick, et al., editors, *Artificial Intelligence Techniques in Power Systems*, chapter 10, pages 220–237. IEE, 1997. ISBN 0-85296-897-3. URL http://www.iee.org/Publish/Books/Power/Po022c.cfm#10.Scheduling. GP$_{\text{BiB}}$

W. B. Langdon, R. Poli, P. Nordin, and T. Fogarty, editors. *Late-Breaking Papers of EuroGP-99*, Goteborg, Sweden, 26-27 May 1999. URL ftp://ftp.cwi.nl/pub/CWIreports/SEN/SEN-R9913.pdf. GP$_{\text{BiB}}$

W. B. Langdon, E. Cantú-Paz, K. Mathias, R. Roy, D. Davis, R. Poli, K. Balakrishnan, V. Honavar, G. Rudolph, J. Wegener, L. Bull, M. A. Potter, A. C. Schultz, J. F. Miller, E. Burke, and N. Jonoska, editors. *GECCO 2002: Proceedings of the Genetic and Evolutionary Computation Conference*, New York, 9-13 July 2002. Morgan Kaufmann Publishers. ISBN 1-55860-878-8. URL http://www.isgec.org/GECCO-2002. GP$_{\text{BiB}}$

W. B. Langdon. A bibliography for genetic programming. In P. J. Angeline and K. E. Kinnear, Jr., editors, *Advances in Genetic Programming 2*, chapter B, pages 507–532. MIT Press, Cambridge, MA, USA, 1996. ISBN 0-262-01158-1. URL http://www.cs.ucl.ac.uk/staff/W.Langdon/ftp/papers/WBL.aigp2.appx.ps.gz. GP$_{\text{BiB}}$

W. B. Langdon. *Genetic Programming and Data Structures*. Kluwer, Boston, 1998. ISBN 0-7923-8135-1. URL http://www.cs.ucl.ac.uk/staff/W.Langdon/gpdata. GP$_{\text{BiB}}$

Generation 17
(see Sec. B.4)

W. B. Langdon. Size fair and homologous tree genetic programming crossovers. *Genetic Programming and Evolvable Machines*, 1(1/2):95–119, April 2000. ISSN 1389-2576. URL http://www.cs.ucl.ac.uk/staff/W.Langdon/ftp/papers/WBL_fairxo.pdf.   GP<small>BiB</small>

W. B. Langdon and W. Banzhaf. Repeated sequences in linear genetic programming genomes. *Complex Systems*, 15(4):285–306, 2005. ISSN 0891-2513. URL http://www.cs.ucl.ac.uk/staff/W.Langdon/ftp/papers/wbl_repeat_linear.pdf.   GP<small>BiB</small>

W. B. Langdon, S. M. Gustafson, and J. Koza. The Genetic Programming Bibliography, 1995-2008. URL http://www.cs.bham.ac.uk/~wbl/biblio/.

W. B. Langdon and P. Nordin. Evolving hand-eye coordination for a humanoid robot with machine code genetic programming. In J. F. Miller, et al., editors, *Genetic Programming, Proceedings of EuroGP'2001*, volume 2038 of *LNCS*, pages 313–324, Lake Como, Italy, 18-20 April 2001. Springer-Verlag. ISBN 3-540-41899-7. URL http://www.cs.ucl.ac.uk/staff/W.Langdon/ftp/papers/wbl_handeye.ps.gz.   GP<small>BiB</small>

W. B. Langdon and R. Poli. Evolutionary solo pong players. In D. Corne, et al., editors, *Proceedings of the 2005 IEEE Congress on Evolutionary Computation*, volume 3, pages 2621–2628, Edinburgh, UK, 2-5 September 2005. IEEE Press. ISBN 0-7803-9363-5. URL http://www.cs.ucl.ac.uk/staff/W.Langdon/ftp/papers/pong_cec2005.pdf.
GP<small>BiB</small>

W. B. Langdon and R. Poli. On turing complete T7 and MISC F–4 program fitness landscapes. In D. V. Arnold, et al., editors, *Theory of Evolutionary Algorithms*, number 06061 in Dagstuhl Seminar Proceedings, Dagstuhl, Germany, 5-10 February 2006. Internationales Begegnungs- und Forschungszentrum fuer Informatik (IBFI), Schloss Dagstuhl, Germany. URL http://drops.dagstuhl.de/opus/volltexte/2006/595. <http://drops.dagstuhl.de/opus/volltexte/2006/595> [date of citation: 2006-01-01].
GP<small>BiB</small>

W. B. Langdon and R. Poli. Mapping non-conventional extensions of genetic programming. *Natural Computing*, 7:21–43, March 2008. Invited contribution to special issue on Unconventional computing.   GP<small>BiB</small>

W. B. Langdon, T. Soule, R. Poli, and J. A. Foster. The evolution of size and shape. In L. Spector, et al., editors, *Advances in Genetic Programming 3*, chapter 8, pages 163–190. MIT Press, Cambridge, MA, USA, June 1999. ISBN 0-262-19423-6. URL http://www.cs.bham.ac.uk/~wbl/aigp3/ch08.pdf.   GP<small>BiB</small>

P. Larrañaga. *A review on estimation of distribution algorithms*, chapter 3, pages 57–100. Kluwer Academic Publishers, 2002.

P. Larrañaga and J. A. Lozano. *Estimation of Distribution Algorithms, A New Tool for Evolutionary Computation*. Kluwer Academic Publishers, 2002.

S. Lavington, N. Dewhurst, E. Wilkins, and A. Freitas. Interfacing knowledge discovery algorithms to large database management systems. *Information and Software Technology*, 41(9):605–617, 25 June 1999. URL http://www.sciencedirect.com/science/article/B6V0B-3WN7DYN-8/1/cdabdda09c085c6a4536aa5e116366ee. special issue on data mining.   GP<small>BiB</small>

K. S. Leung, K. H. Lee, and S. M. Cheang. Genetic parallel programming - evolving linear machine codes on a multiple-ALU processor. In S. Yaacob, et al., editors, *Proceedings of International Conference on Artificial Intelligence in Engineering and Technology - ICAIET 2002*, pages 207–213. Universiti Malaysia Sabah, June 2002. ISBN 983-2188-92-X.   GP<small>BiB</small>

T. L. Lew, A. B. Spencer, F. Scarpa, K. Worden, A. Rutherford, and F. Hemez. Identification of response surface models using genetic programming. *Mechanical Systems and Signal Processing*, 20(8):1819–1831, November 2006. GPBiB

D. R. Lewin, S. Lachman-Shalem, and B. Grosman. The role of process system engineering (PSE) in integrated circuit (IC) manufacturing. *Control Engineering Practice*, 15(7): 793–802, July 2006. Special Issue on Award Winning Applications, 2005 IFAC World Congress. GPBiB

J. Li and E. P. K. Tsang. Investment decision making using FGP: A case study. In P. J. Angeline, et al., editors, *Proceedings of the Congress on Evolutionary Computation*, volume 2, pages 1253–1259, Mayflower Hotel, Washington D.C., USA, 6-9 July 1999. IEEE Press. ISBN 0-7803-5536-9 (softbound). URL http://www.cs.bham.ac.uk/~jxl/cercialink/web/publication/CEC99.pdf. GPBiB

L. Li, W. Jiang, X. Li, K. L. Moser, Z. Guo, L. Du, Q. Wang, E. J. Topol, Q. Wang, and S. Rao. A robust hybrid between genetic algorithm and support vector machine for extracting an optimal feature gene subset. *Genomics*, 85(1):16–23, January 2005. GPBiB

R. Linden and A. Bhaya. Evolving fuzzy rules to model gene expression. *Biosystems*, 88 (1-2):76–91, March 2007. GPBiB

A. Lindenmayer. Mathematic models for cellular interaction in development, parts I and II. *Journal of Theoretical Biology*, 18:280–299 and 300–315, 1968.

H. Lipson. How to draw a straight line using a GP: Benchmarking evolutionary design against 19th century kinematic synthesis. In M. Keijzer, editor, *Late Breaking Papers at the 2004 Genetic and Evolutionary Computation Conference*, Seattle, Washington, USA, 26 July 2004. URL http://www.cs.bham.ac.uk/~wbl/biblio/gecco2004/LBP063.pdf. GPBiB

J. Lohn, G. Hornby, and D. Linden. Evolutionary antenna design for a NASA spacecraft. In U.-M. O'Reilly, et al., editors, *Genetic Programming Theory and Practice II*, chapter 18, pages 301–315. Springer, Ann Arbor, 13-15 May 2004. ISBN 0-387-23253-2. GPBiB

J. Lohn, A. Stoica, and D. Keymeulen, editors. *The Second NASA/DoD Workshop on Evolvable Hardware*, Palo Alto, California, 13-15 July 2000. IEEE Computer Society. ISBN 0-7695-0762-X.

M. A. Lones. *Enzyme Genetic Programming: Modelling Biological Evolvability in Genetic Programming*. PhD thesis, The University of York, Heslington, York, YO10 5DD, UK, September 2003. URL http://www-users.york.ac.uk/~mal503/common/thesis/main.html. GPBiB

M. Looks. Scalable estimation-of-distribution program evolution. In H. Lipson, editor, *GECCO*, pages 539–546. ACM, 2007. ISBN 978-1-59593-697-4.

M. Looks, B. Goertzel, and C. Pennachin. Learning computer programs with the bayesian optimization algorithm. In H.-G. Beyer, et al., editors, *GECCO 2005: Proceedings of the 2005 conference on Genetic and evolutionary computation*, volume 1, pages 747–748, Washington DC, USA, 25-29 June 2005. ACM Press. ISBN 1-59593-010-8. URL http://www.cs.bham.ac.uk/~wbl/biblio/gecco2005/docs/p747.pdf. GPBiB

J. Louchet. Using an individual evolution strategy for stereovision. *Genetic Programming and Evolvable Machines*, 2(2):101–109, June 2001. ISSN 1389-2576. GPBiB

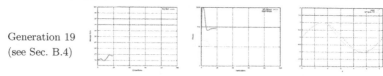

Generation 19
(see Sec. B.4)

J. Louchet, M. Guyon, M.-J. Lesot, and A. Boumaza. Dynamic flies: a new pattern recognition tool applied to stereo sequence processing. *Pattern Recognition Letters*, 23 (1-3):335–345, January 2002.   GP$_{\text{BiB}}$

J. Loviscach and J. Meyer-Spradow. Genetic programming of vertex shaders. In M. Chover, et al., editors, *Proceedings of EuroMedia 2003*, pages 29–31, 2003. GP$_{\text{BiB}}$

S. Luke. Evolving soccerbots: A retrospective. In *Proceedings of the 12th Annual Conference of the Japanese Society for Artificial Intelligence*, 1998. URL http://www.cs.gmu.edu/~sean/papers/robocupShort.pdf.   GP$_{\text{BiB}}$

S. Luke. Two fast tree-creation algorithms for genetic programming. *IEEE Transactions on Evolutionary Computation*, 4(3):274–283, September 2000. URL http://ieeexplore.ieee.org/iel5/4235/18897/00873237.pdf.   GP$_{\text{BiB}}$

S. Luke and L. Panait. Lexicographic parsimony pressure. In W. B. Langdon, et al., editors, *GECCO 2002: Proceedings of the Genetic and Evolutionary Computation Conference*, pages 829–836, New York, 9-13 July 2002. Morgan Kaufmann Publishers. ISBN 1-55860-878-8. URL http://cs.gmu.edu/~sean/papers/lexicographic.pdf.   GP$_{\text{BiB}}$

S. Luke, L. Panait, G. Balan, S. Paus, Z. Skolicki, E. Popovici, J. Harrison, J. Bassett, R. Hubley, and A. Chircop. ECJ: A Java-based Evolutionary Computation Research System , 2000-2007. URL http://www.cs.gmu.edu/~eclab/projects/ecj/.

S. Luke and L. Spector. A comparison of crossover and mutation in genetic programming. In J. R. Koza, et al., editors, *Genetic Programming 1997: Proceedings of the Second Annual Conference*, pages 240–248, Stanford University, CA, USA, 13-16 July 1997. Morgan Kaufmann. URL http://www.cs.gmu.edu/~sean/papers/comparison/comparison.pdf.   GP$_{\text{BiB}}$

E. Lukschandl, H. Borgvall, L. Nohle, M. Nordahl, and P. Nordin. Distributed java bytecode genetic programming. In R. Poli, et al., editors, *Genetic Programming, Proceedings of EuroGP'2000*, volume 1802 of *LNCS*, pages 316–325, Edinburgh, 15-16 April 2000. Springer-Verlag. ISBN 3-540-67339-3. URL http://www.springerlink.com/openurl.asp?genre=article&issn=0302-9743&volume=1802&spage=316.   GP$_{\text{BiB}}$

E. Lutton, J. Levy-Vehel, G. Cretin, P. Glevarec, and C. Roll. Mixed IFS: Resolution of the inverse problem using genetic programming. *Complex Systems*, 9:375–398, 1995a. GP$_{\text{BiB}}$

E. Lutton, J. Levy-Vehel, G. Cretin, P. Glevarec, and C. Roll. Mixed IFS: Resolution of the inverse problem using genetic programming. Research Report No 2631, Inria, 1995b. URL http://citeseer.ist.psu.edu/cretin95mixed.html.   GP$_{\text{BiB}}$

R. M. MacCallum. Introducing a perl genetic programming system: and can metaevolution solve the bloat problem? In C. Ryan, et al., editors, *Genetic Programming, Proceedings of EuroGP'2003*, volume 2610 of *LNCS*, pages 364–373, Essex, 14-16 April 2003. Springer-Verlag. ISBN 3-540-00971-X. URL http://www.sbc.su.se/~maccallr/publications/perlgp_eurogp2003.pdf.   GP$_{\text{BiB}}$

P. Machado and J. Romero, editors. *The Art of Artificial Evolution*. Springer, 2008.

A. J. Marek, W. D. Smart, and M. C. Martin. Learning visual feature detectors for obstacle avoidance using genetic programming. In E. Cantú-Paz, editor, *Late Breaking Papers at the Genetic and Evolutionary Computation Conference (GECCO-2002)*, pages 330–336, New York, NY, July 2002. AAAI. URL http://www.martincmartin.com/papers/LearingVisualFeatureDetectorsForObstAvoidGP_GECCO2002Marek.pdf. GP$_{\text{BiB}}$

P. Marenbach. Using prior knowledge and obtaining process insight in data based modelling of bioprocesses. *System Analysis Modelling Simulation*, 31:39–59, 1998. GP_{BiB}

J. P. Marney, D. Miller, C. Fyfe, and H. F. E. Tarbert. Risk adjusted returns to technical trading rules: a genetic programming approach. In *7th International Conference of Society of Computational Economics*, Yale, 28-29 June 2001. GP_{BiB}

M. C. Martin. Evolving visual sonar: Depth from monocular images. *Pattern Recognition Letters*, 27(11):1174–1180, August 2006. URL http://martincmartin.com/papers/EvolvingVisualSonarPatternRecognitionLetters2006.pdf. Evolutionary Computer Vision and Image Understanding. GP_{BiB}

P. Martin. A hardware implementation of a genetic programming system using FPGAs and Handel-C. *Genetic Programming and Evolvable Machines*, 2(4):317–343, December 2001. ISSN 1389-2576. URL http://www.naiadhome.com/gpem-d.pdf. GP_{BiB}

P. Martin. A pipelined hardware implementation of genetic programming using FPGAs and Handel-C. In J. A. Foster, et al., editors, *Genetic Programming, Proceedings of the 5th European Conference, EuroGP 2002*, volume 2278 of *LNCS*, pages 1–12, Kinsale, Ireland, 3-5 April 2002. Springer-Verlag. ISBN 3-540-43378-3. GP_{BiB}

P. Martin and R. Poli. Crossover operators for A hardware implementation of GP using FPGAs and Handel-C. In W. B. Langdon, et al., editors, *GECCO 2002: Proceedings of the Genetic and Evolutionary Computation Conference*, pages 845–852, New York, 9-13 July 2002. Morgan Kaufmann Publishers. ISBN 1-55860-878-8. URL http://www.cs.bham.ac.uk/~wbl/biblio/gecco2002/gp284.ps. GP_{BiB}

S. Martinez-Jaramillo and E. P. K. Tsang. An heterogeneous, endogenous and co-evolutionary GP-based financial market. *IEEE Transactions on Evolutionary Computation*, 2007. accepted for publication.

P. Massey, J. A. Clark, and S. Stepney. Evolution of a human-competitive quantum fourier transform algorithm using genetic programming. In H.-G. Beyer, et al., editors, *GECCO 2005: Proceedings of the 2005 conference on Genetic and evolutionary computation*, volume 2, pages 1657–1663, Washington DC, USA, 25-29 June 2005. ACM Press. ISBN 1-59593-010-8. URL http://www.cs.bham.ac.uk/~wbl/biblio/gecco2005/docs/p1657.pdf. GP_{BiB}

S. R. Maxwell, III. Why might some problems be difficult for genetic programming to find solutions? In J. R. Koza, editor, *Late Breaking Papers at the Genetic Programming 1996 Conference Stanford University July 28-31, 1996*, pages 125–128, Stanford University, CA, USA, 28–31 July 1996. Stanford Bookstore. ISBN 0-18-201031-7. GP_{BiB}

S. R. Maxwell, III. Experiments with a coroutine model for genetic programming. In *Proceedings of the 1994 IEEE World Congress on Computational Intelligence*, volume 1, pages 413–417a, Orlando, Florida, USA, 27-29 June 1994. IEEE Press. ISBN 0-7803-1899-4. URL http://ieeexplore.ieee.org/iel2/1125/8059/00349915.pdf?isNumber=8059. GP_{BiB}

J. McCormack. New challenges for evolutionary music and art. *SIGEvolution*, 1(1):5–11, April 2006. URL http://www.sigevolution.org/2006/01/issue.pdf. GP_{BiB}

A. C. McGovern, D. Broadhurst, J. Taylor, N. Kaderbhai, M. K. Winson, D. A. Small, J. J. Rowland, D. B. Kell, and R. Goodacre. Monitoring of complex industrial bioprocesses for metabolite concentrations using modern spectroscopies and machine learning: Application to gibberellic acid production. *Biotechnology and Bioengineering*, 78(5):527–538, 5 June 2002. URL http://dbkgroup.org/Papers/biotechnol_bioeng_78_(527).pdf. GP_{BiB}

Generation 21
(see Sec. B.4)

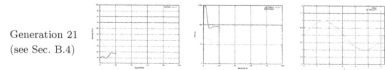

B. McKay, M. Willis, D. Searson, and G. Montague. Nonlinear continuum regression: an evolutionary approach. *Transactions of the Institute of Measurement and Control*, 22(2):125–140, 2000. URL http://www.ingentaconnect.com/content/arn/tm/2000/00000022/00000002/art00007.   GPBiB

B. McKay, M. J. Willis, and G. W. Barton. Using a tree structured genetic algorithm to perform symbolic regression. In A. M. S. Zalzala, editor, *First International Conference on Genetic Algorithms in Engineering Systems: Innovations and Applications, GALESIA*, volume 414, pages 487–492, Sheffield, UK, 12-14 September 1995. IEE. ISBN 0-85296-650-4. URL http://scitation.aip.org/getpdf/servlet/GetPDFServlet?filetype=pdf&id=IEECPS0019950CP414000487000001&idtype=cvips&prog=normal.   GPBiB

N. F. McPhee and N. J. Hopper. Analysis of genetic diversity through population history. In W. Banzhaf, et al., editors, *Proceedings of the Genetic and Evolutionary Computation Conference*, volume 2, pages 1112–1120, Orlando, Florida, USA, 13-17 July 1999. Morgan Kaufmann. ISBN 1-55860-611-4. URL http://www.cs.bham.ac.uk/~wbl/biblio/gecco1999/GP-421.pdf.   GPBiB

N. F. McPhee, N. J. Hopper, and M. L. Reierson. Sutherland: An extensible object-oriented software framework for evolutionary computation. In J. R. Koza, et al., editors, *Genetic Programming 1998: Proceedings of the Third Annual Conference*, page 241, University of Wisconsin, Madison, Wisconsin, USA, 22-25 July 1998. Morgan Kaufmann. ISBN 1-55860-548-7. URL http://www.mrs.umn.edu/~mcphee/Research/Sutherland/sutherland_gp98_announcement.ps.gz.   GPBiB

N. F. McPhee, A. Jarvis, and E. F. Crane. On the strength of size limits in linear genetic programming. In K. Deb, et al., editors, *Genetic and Evolutionary Computation – GECCO-2004, Part II*, volume 3103 of *Lecture Notes in Computer Science*, pages 593–604, Seattle, WA, USA, 26-30 June 2004. Springer-Verlag. ISBN 3-540-22343-6. URL http://link.springer.de/link/service/series/0558/bibs/3103/31030593.htm.   GPBiB

N. F. McPhee and J. D. Miller. Accurate replication in genetic programming. In L. Eshelman, editor, *Genetic Algorithms: Proceedings of the Sixth International Conference (ICGA95)*, pages 303–309, Pittsburgh, PA, USA, 15-19 July 1995. Morgan Kaufmann. ISBN 1-55860-370-0. URL http://www.mrs.umn.edu/~mcphee/Research/Accurate_replication.ps.   GPBiB

N. F. McPhee, B. Ohs, and T. Hutchison. Semantic building blocks in genetic programming. In *EurogGP 2008: Proceedings of the 2008 European Conference on Genetic Programming*, 2008.

N. F. McPhee and R. Poli. A schema theory analysis of the evolution of size in genetic programming with linear representations. In J. F. Miller, et al., editors, *Genetic Programming, Proceedings of EuroGP'2001*, volume 2038 of *LNCS*, pages 108–125, Lake Como, Italy, 18-20 April 2001. Springer-Verlag. ISBN 3-540-41899-7. URL http://cswww.essex.ac.uk/staff/poli/papers/McPhee-EUROGP2001-ST-Linear-Bloat.pdf. GPBiB

N. F. McPhee and R. Poli. Using schema theory to explore interactions of multiple operators. In W. B. Langdon, et al., editors, *GECCO 2002: Proceedings of the Genetic and Evolutionary Computation Conference*, pages 853–860, New York, 9-13 July 2002. Morgan Kaufmann Publishers. ISBN 1-55860-878-8. URL http://www.cs.bham.ac.uk/~wbl/biblio/gecco2002/GP139.pdf.   GPBiB

R. R. F. Mendes, F. de B. Voznika, J. C. Nievola, and A. A. Freitas. Discovering fuzzy classification rules with genetic programming and co-evolution. In L. Spector, et al., editors, *Proceedings of the Genetic and Evolutionary Computation Conference (GECCO-2001)*, page 183, San Francisco, California, USA, 7-11 July 2001. Morgan Kaufmann. ISBN 1-55860-774-9. URL http://www.cs.bham.ac.uk/~wbl/biblio/gecco2001/d02. pdf. GPBIB

P. K. Mercure, G. F. Smits, and A. Kordon. Empirical emulators for first principle models. In *AIChE Fall Annual Meeting*, Reno Hilton, 6 November 2001. URL http://www.aiche.org/conferences/techprogram/paperdetail.asp? PaperID=2373&DSN=annual01. GPBIB

J. Meyer-Spradow and J. Loviscach. Evolutionary design of BRDFs. In M. Chover, et al., editors, *Eurographics 2003 Short Paper Proceedings*, pages 301–306, 2003. URL http: //viscg.uni-muenster.de/publications/2003/ML03/evolutionary_web.pdf. GPBIB

J. Miller, M. Tomassini, P. L. Lanzi, C. Ryan, A. G. B. Tettamanzi, and W. B. Langdon, editors. *Genetic Programming, Proceedings of EuroGP'2001*, volume 2038 of *LNCS*, Lake Como, Italy, 18-20 April 2001. Springer-Verlag. ISBN 3-540-41899-7. URL http: //link.springer.de/link/service/series/0558/tocs/t2038.htm. GPBIB

J. F. Miller. An empirical study of the efficiency of learning boolean functions using a cartesian genetic programming approach. In W. Banzhaf, et al., editors, *Proceedings of the Genetic and Evolutionary Computation Conference*, volume 2, pages 1135–1142, Orlando, Florida, USA, 13-17 July 1999. Morgan Kaufmann. ISBN 1-55860-611-4. URL http://citeseer.ist.psu.edu/153431.html. GPBIB

J. F. Miller and S. L. Smith. Redundancy and computational efficiency in cartesian genetic programming. *IEEE Transactions on Evolutionary Computation*, 10(2):167–174, April 2006. GPBIB

J. F. Miller, A. Thompson, P. Thomson, and T. C. Fogarty, editors. *Proceedings of the Third International Conference on Evolvable Systems, ICES 2000*, volume 1801 of *LNCS*, Edinburgh, Scotland, UK, 17-19 April 2000. Springer-Verlag. ISBN 3-540-67338-5.

B. Mitavskiy and J. Rowe. Some results about the markov chains associated to GPs and to general EAs. *Theoretical Computer Science*, 361(1):72–110, 28 August 2006. GPBIB

D. J. Montana. Strongly typed genetic programming. *Evolutionary Computation*, 3(2): 199–230, 1995. URL http://vishnu.bbn.com/papers/stgp.pdf. GPBIB

G. E. Moore. Cramming more components onto integrated circuits. *Electronics*, 38(8):114–117, 1965. URL ftp://download.intel.com/museum/Moores_Law/ Articles-Press_Releases/Gordon_Moore_1965_Article.pdf.

J. H. Moore, J. S. Parker, N. J. Olsen, and T. M. Aune. Symbolic discriminant analysis of microarray data in autommimune disease. *Genetic Epidemiology*, 23:57–69, 2002. GPBIB

A. A. Motsinger, S. L. Lee, G. Mellick, and M. D. Ritchie. GPNN: Power studies and applications of a neural network method for detecting gene-gene interactions in studies of human disease. *BMC bioinformatics [electronic resource]*, 7(1):39–39, January 25 2006. ISSN 1471-2105. URL http://www.biomedcentral.com/1471-2105/7/39. GPBIB

H. Mühlenbein and T. Mahnig. Convergence theory and application of the factorized distribution algorithm. *Journal of Computing and Information Technology*, 7(1):19–32, 1999a.

Generation 23
(see Sec. B.4)

H. Mühlenbein and T. Mahnig. FDA – a scalable evolutionary algorithm for the optimization of additively decomposed functions. *Evolutionary Computation*, 7(4):353–376, 1999b.

C. J. Neely. Risk-adjusted, ex ante, optimal technical trading rules in equity markets. *International Review of Economics and Finance*, 12(1):69–87, Spring 2003. URL `http://research.stlouisfed.org/wp/1999/1999-015.pdf`. GPBiB

C. J. Neely and P. A. Weller. Technical trading rules in the european monetary system. *Journal of International Money and Finance*, 18(3):429–458, 1999. URL `http://research.stlouisfed.org/wp/1997/97-015.pdf`. GPBiB

C. J. Neely and P. A. Weller. Technical analysis and central bank intervention. *Journal of International Money and Finance*, 20(7):949–970, December 2001. URL `http://research.stlouisfed.org/wp/1997/97-002.pdf`. GPBiB

C. J. Neely, P. A. Weller, and R. Dittmar. Is technical analysis in the foreign exchange market profitable? A genetic programming approach. *The Journal of Financial and Quantitative Analysis*, 32(4):405–426, December 1997. ISSN 00221090. URL `http://links.jstor.org/sici?sici=0022-1090%28199712%2932%3A4%3C405%3AITAITF%3E2.0.CO%3B2-T`. GPBiB

C. J. Neely, P. A. Weller, and J. M. Ulrich. The adaptive markets hypothesis: evidence from the foreign exchange market. Working Paper 2006-046B, Federal Reserve Bank of St. Louis, Research Division, P.O. Box 442, St. Louis, MO 63166, USA, August 2006. URL `http://research.stlouisfed.org/wp/2006/2006-046.pdf`. Revised March 2007. GPBiB

O. Nicolotti, V. J. Gillet, P. J. Fleming, and D. V. S. Green. Multiobjective optimization in quantitative structure-activity relationships: Deriving accurate and interpretable QSARs. *Journal of Medicinal Chemistry*, 45(23):5069–5080, November 7 2002. ISSN 0022-2623. URL `http://pubs3.acs.org/acs/journals/doilookup?in_doi=10.1021/jm020919o`. GPBiB

N. Nikolaev and H. Iba. *Adaptive Learning of Polynomial Networks Genetic Programming, Backpropagation and Bayesian Methods.* Number 4 in Genetic and Evolutionary Computation. Springer, 2006. ISBN 0-387-31239-0. June. GPBiB

N. Y. Nikolaev and H. Iba. Genetic programming of polynomial models for financial forecasting. In S.-H. Chen, editor, *Genetic Algorithms and Genetic Programming in Computational Finance*, chapter 5, pages 103–123. Kluwer Academic Press, 2002. ISBN 0-7923-7601-3. GPBiB

A. E. Nix and M. D. Vose. Modeling genetic algorithms with Markov chains. *Annals of Mathematics and Artificial Intelligence*, 5:79–88, 1992.

P. Nordin. A compiling genetic programming system that directly manipulates the machine code. In K. E. Kinnear, Jr., editor, *Advances in Genetic Programming*, chapter 14, pages 311–331. MIT Press, 1994. URL `http://cognet.mit.edu/library/books/view?isbn=0262111888`. GPBiB

P. Nordin. *Evolutionary Program Induction of Binary Machine Code and its Applications.* PhD thesis, der Universitat Dortmund am Fachereich Informatik, 1997. GPBiB

P. Nordin and W. Banzhaf. Programmatic compression of images and sound. In J. R. Koza, et al., editors, *Genetic Programming 1996: Proceedings of the First Annual Conference*, pages 345–350, Stanford University, CA, USA, 28–31 July 1996. MIT Press. URL `http://www.cs.mun.ca/~banzhaf/papers/gp96.pdf`. GPBiB

P. Nordin, W. Banzhaf, and F. D. Francone. Efficient evolution of machine code for CISC architectures using instruction blocks and homologous crossover. In L. Spector, et al., editors, *Advances in Genetic Programming 3*, chapter 12, pages 275–299. MIT Press, Cambridge, MA, USA, June 1999. ISBN 0-262-19423-6. URL http://www. aimlearning.com/aigp31.pdf. GP_BiB

P. Nordin and W. Johanna. *Humanoider: Sjavlarande robotar och artificiell intelligens.* Liber, 2003. GP_BiB

nVidia. NVIDIA CUDA Compute Unified Device Architecture, programming guide. Technical Report version 0.8, NVIDIA, 12 Feb 2007.

H. Oakley. Two scientific applications of genetic programming: Stack filters and nonlinear equation fitting to chaotic data. In K. E. Kinnear, Jr., editor, *Advances in Genetic Programming*, chapter 17, pages 369–389. MIT Press, 1994. URL http://cognet.mit.edu/library/books/view?isbn=0262111888. GP_BiB

J. R. Olsson. *Inductive functional programming using incremental program transformation and Execution of logic programs by iterative-deepening A* SLD-tree search.* Dr scient thesis, University of Oslo, Norway, 1994.

J. R. Olsson. How to invent functions. In R. Poli, et al., editors, *Genetic Programming, Proceedings of EuroGP'99*, volume 1598 of *LNCS*, pages 232–243, Goteborg, Sweden, 26-27 May 1999. Springer-Verlag. ISBN 3-540-65899-8. URL http://www.ia-stud. hiof.no/~rolando/abstract1.ps. GP_BiB

R. R. Olsson. Inductive functional programming using incremental program transformation. *Artificial Intelligence*, 74(1):55–81, March 1995. URL http://www.sciencedirect.com/science?_ob=MImg&_imagekey= B6TYF-4002FJH-9-1&_cdi=5617&_orig=browse&_coverDate=03%2F31%2F1995&_ sk=999259998&wchp=dGLbVlb-lSzBV&_acct=C000010182&_version=1&_userid= 125795&md5=ba5db57b3fa83d990440da8dfd8afcd7&ie=f.pdf. GP_BiB

M. Oltean. Evolving evolutionary algorithms using linear genetic programming. *Evolutionary Computation*, 13(3):387–410, Fall 2005. ISSN 1063-6560. GP_BiB

M. Oltean and D. Dumitrescu. Evolving TSP heuristics using multi expression programming. In M. Bubak, et al., editors, *Computational Science - ICCS 2004: 4th International Conference, Part II*, volume 3037 of *Lecture Notes in Computer Science*, pages 670–673, Krakow, Poland, 6-9 June 2004. Springer-Verlag. ISBN 3-540-22115-8. URL http://springerlink.metapress.com/openurl.asp?genre=article&issn= 0302-9743&volume=3037&spage=670. GP_BiB

R. Ondas, M. Pelikan, and K. Sastry. Genetic programming, probabilistic incremental program evolution, and scalability. In J. Knowles, editor, *WSC10: 10th Online World Conference on Soft Computing in Industrial Applications*, pages 363–372, On the World Wide Web, 19 September - 7 October 2005. ISBN 3-540-29123-7. URL http://isxp1010c.sims.cranfield.ac.uk/Papers/paper122.pdf. GP_BiB

M. O'Neill and C. Ryan. *Grammatical Evolution: Evolutionary Automatic Programming in a Arbitrary Language*, volume 4 of *Genetic programming*. Kluwer Academic Publishers, 2003. ISBN 1-4020-7444-1. URL http://www.wkap.nl/prod/b/1-4020-7444-1. GP_BiB

M. O'Neill, C. Ryan, M. Keijzer, and M. Cattolico. Crossover in grammatical evolution. *Genetic Programming and Evolvable Machines*, 4(1):67–93, March 2003. ISSN 1389-2576. GP_BiB

Generation 25
(see Sec. B.4)

S. Openshaw and I. Turton. Building new spatial interaction models using genetic programming. In T. C. Fogarty, editor, *Evolutionary Computing*, Lecture Notes in Computer Science, Leeds, UK, 11-13 April 1994. Springer-Verlag. URL http://www.geog.leeds.ac.uk/papers/94-1/94-1.pdf. GPBiB

U.-M. O'Reilly. *An Analysis of Genetic Programming*. PhD thesis, Carleton University, Ottawa-Carleton Institute for Computer Science, Ottawa, Ontario, Canada, 22 September 1995. URL http://www.cs.ucl.ac.uk/staff/W.Langdon/ftp/papers/oreilly/abstract.ps.gz. GPBiB

U.-M. O'Reilly. Investigating the generality of automatically defined functions. In J. R. Koza, et al., editors, *Genetic Programming 1996: Proceedings of the First Annual Conference*, pages 351–356, Stanford University, CA, USA, 28–31 July 1996. MIT Press. URL http://citeseer.ist.psu.edu/24128.html. GPBiB

U.-M. O'Reilly and M. Hemberg. Integrating generative growth and evolutionary computation for form exploration. *Genetic Programming and Evolvable Machines*, 8(2): 163–186, June 2007. ISSN 1389-2576. Special issue on developmental systems. GPBiB

U.-M. O'Reilly and F. Oppacher. Program search with a hierarchical variable length representation: Genetic programming, simulated annealing and hill climbing. In Y. Davidor, et al., editors, *Parallel Problem Solving from Nature – PPSN III*, number 866 in Lecture Notes in Computer Science, pages 397–406, Jerusalem, 9-14 October 1994a. Springer-Verlag. ISBN 3-540-58484-6. URL http://www.cs.ucl.ac.uk/staff/W.Langdon/ftp/papers/ppsn-94.ps.gz. GPBiB

U.-M. O'Reilly and F. Oppacher. The troubling aspects of a building block hypothesis for genetic programming. In L. D. Whitley and M. D. Vose, editors, *Foundations of Genetic Algorithms 3*, pages 73–88, Estes Park, Colorado, USA, 31 July–2 August 1994b. Morgan Kaufmann. ISBN 1-55860-356-5. URL http://citeseer.ist.psu.edu/cache/papers/cs/163/http:zSzzSzwww.ai.mit.eduzSzpeoplezSzunamayzSzpaperszSzfoga.pdf/oreilly92troubling.pdf. Published 1995. GPBiB

U.-M. O'Reilly, T. Yu, R. L. Riolo, and B. Worzel, editors. *Genetic Programming Theory and Practice II*, volume 8 of *Genetic Programming*, Ann Arbor, MI, USA, 13-15 May 2004. Springer. ISBN 0-387-23253-2. URL http://www.springeronline.com/sgw/cda/frontpage/0,11855,5-40356-22-34954683-0,00.html. GPBiB

M. Oussaidène, B. Chopard, O. V. Pictet, and M. Tomassini. Parallel genetic programming and its application to trading model induction. *Parallel Computing*, 23(8):1183–1198, August 1997. URL http://citeseer.ist.psu.edu/cache/papers/cs/166/http:zSzzSzlslwww.epfl.chzSz~marcozSzparcomp.pdf/oussaidene97parallel.pdf. GPBiB

J. D. Owens, D. Luebke, N. Govindaraju, M. Harris, J. Kruger, A. E. Lefohn, and T. J. Purcell. A survey of general-purpose computation on graphics hardware. *Computer Graphics Forum*, 26(1):80–113, March 2007.

L. Panait and S. Luke. Alternative bloat control methods. In K. Deb, et al., editors, *Genetic and Evolutionary Computation – GECCO-2004, Part II*, volume 3103 of *Lecture Notes in Computer Science*, pages 630–641, Seattle, WA, USA, 26-30 June 2004. Springer-Verlag. ISBN 3-540-22343-6. URL http://cs.gmu.edu/~lpanait/papers/panait04alternative.pdf. GPBiB

J. Parent and A. Nowe. Evolving compression preprocessors with genetic programming. In W. B. Langdon, et al., editors, *GECCO 2002: Proceedings of the Genetic and Evolutionary Computation Conference*, pages 861–867, New York, 9-13 July 2002.

Morgan Kaufmann Publishers. ISBN 1-55860-878-8. URL http://www.cs.bham.ac.uk/~wbl/biblio/gecco2002/gp256.ps. GPBiB

D. Parrott, X. Li, and V. Ciesielski. Multi-objective techniques in genetic programming for evolving classifiers. In D. Corne, et al., editors, *Proceedings of the 2005 IEEE Congress on Evolutionary Computation*, volume 2, pages 1141–1148, Edinburgh, UK, 2-5 September 2005. IEEE Press. ISBN 0-7803-9363-5. URL http://goanna.cs.rmit.edu.au/~xiaodong/publications/183.pdf. GPBiB

M. Pelikan, D. E. Goldberg, and E. Cantú-Paz. BOA: The Bayesian optimization algorithm. In W. Banzhaf, et al., editors, *Proc. of the Genetic and Evolutionary Computation Conference GECCO-99*, volume I, pages 525–532, Orlando, FL, 13-17 1999. Morgan Kaufmann Publishers, San Fransisco, CA. ISBN 1-55860-611-4.

T. Perkis. Stack-based genetic programming. In *Proceedings of the 1994 IEEE World Congress on Computational Intelligence*, volume 1, pages 148–153, Orlando, Florida, USA, 27-29 June 1994. IEEE Press. URL http://citeseer.ist.psu.edu/432690.html. GPBiB

W. Piaseczny, H. Suzuki, and H. Sawai. Chemical genetic programming – coevolution between genotypic strings and phenotypic trees. In K. Deb, et al., editors, *Genetic and Evolutionary Computation – GECCO-2004, Part II*, volume 3103 of *Lecture Notes in Computer Science*, pages 715–716, Seattle, WA, USA, 26-30 June 2004. Springer-Verlag. ISBN 3-540-22343-6. URL http://link.springer.de/link/service/series/0558/bibs/3103/31030715.htm. GPBiB

N. Pillay. Evolving solutions to ASCII graphics programming problems in intelligent programming tutors. In R. Akerkar, editor, *International Conference on Applied Artificial Intelligence (ICAAI'2003)*, pages 236–243, Fort Panhala, Kolhapur, India, 15-16 December 2003. TMRF. ISBN 81-901918-0-2. GPBiB

H. Pohlheim. Visualization of evolutionary algorithms - set of standard techniques and multidimensional visualization. In W. Banzhaf, et al., editors, *Proceedings of the Genetic and Evolutionary Computation Conference*, volume 1, pages 533–540, Orlando, Florida, USA, 13-17 July 1999. Morgan Kaufmann. ISBN 1-55860-611-4. URL http://www.cs.bham.ac.uk/~wbl/biblio/gecco1999/GA-820.pdf.

R. Poli. Discovery of symbolic, neuro-symbolic and neural networks with parallel distributed genetic programming. Technical Report CSRP-96-14, University of Birmingham, School of Computer Science, August 1996a. URL ftp://ftp.cs.bham.ac.uk/pub/tech-reports/1996/CSRP-96-14.ps.gz. Presented at 3rd International Conference on Artificial Neural Networks and Genetic Algorithms, ICANNGA'97. GPBiB

R. Poli. Genetic programming for image analysis. In J. R. Koza, et al., editors, *Genetic Programming 1996: Proceedings of the First Annual Conference*, pages 363–368, Stanford University, CA, USA, 28–31 July 1996b. MIT Press. URL http://cswww.essex.ac.uk/staff/rpoli/papers/Poli-GP1996.pdf. GPBiB

R. Poli. Parallel distributed genetic programming. In D. Corne, et al., editors, *New Ideas in Optimization*, Advanced Topics in Computer Science, chapter 27, pages 403–431. McGraw-Hill, Maidenhead, Berkshire, England, 1999a. ISBN 0-07-709506-5. URL http://citeseer.ist.psu.edu/328504.html. GPBiB

R. Poli. Sub-machine-code GP: New results and extensions. In R. Poli, et al., editors, *Genetic Programming, Proceedings of EuroGP'99*, volume 1598 of *LNCS*, pages 65–82, Goteborg, Sweden, 26-27 May 1999b. Springer-Verlag. ISBN 3-540-65899-8. URL http://www.cs.essex.ac.uk/staff/poli/papers/Poli-EUROGP1999.pdf. GPBiB

Generation 27
(see Sec. B.4)

R. Poli. Hyperschema theory for GP with one-point crossover, building blocks, and some new results in GA theory. In R. Poli, et al., editors, *Genetic Programming, Proceedings of EuroGP'2000*, volume 1802 of *LNCS*, pages 163–180, Edinburgh, 15-16 April 2000a. Springer-Verlag. ISBN 3-540-67339-3. URL http://www.springerlink.com/openurl.asp?genre=article&issn=0302-9743&volume=1802&spage=163.   GPBiB

R. Poli. Exact schema theorem and effective fitness for GP with one-point crossover. In D. Whitley, et al., editors, *Proceedings of the Genetic and Evolutionary Computation Conference*, pages 469–476, Las Vegas, July 2000b. Morgan Kaufmann.

R. Poli. Exact schema theory for genetic programming and variable-length genetic algorithms with one-point crossover. *Genetic Programming and Evolvable Machines*, 2(2): 123–163, 2001a.

R. Poli. General schema theory for genetic programming with subtree-swapping crossover. In *Genetic Programming, Proceedings of EuroGP 2001*, LNCS, Milan, 18-20 April 2001b. Springer-Verlag.

R. Poli. A simple but theoretically-motivated method to control bloat in genetic programming. In C. Ryan, et al., editors, *Genetic Programming, Proceedings of the 6th European Conference, EuroGP 2003*, LNCS, pages 211–223, Essex, UK, 14-16 April 2003. Springer-Verlag.

R. Poli. Tournament selection, iterated coupon-collection problem, and backward-chaining evolutionary algorithms. In A. H. Wright, et al., editors, *Foundations of Genetic Algorithms 8*, volume 3469 of *Lecture Notes in Computer Science*, pages 132–155, Aizu-Wakamatsu City, Japan, 5-9 January 2005. Springer-Verlag. ISBN 3-540-27237-2. URL http://www.cs.essex.ac.uk/staff/rpoli/papers/foga2005_Poli.pdf. GPBiB

R. Poli, C. Di Chio, and W. B. Langdon. Exploring extended particle swarms: a genetic programming approach. In H.-G. Beyer, et al., editors, *GECCO 2005: Proceedings of the 2005 conference on Genetic and evolutionary computation*, volume 1, pages 169–176, Washington DC, USA, 25-29 June 2005. ACM Press. ISBN 1-59593-010-8. URL http://www.cs.essex.ac.uk/staff/poli/papers/geccopso2005.pdf.   GPBiB

R. Poli and W. B. Langdon. A new schema theory for genetic programming with one-point crossover and point mutation. In J. R. Koza, et al., editors, *Genetic Programming 1997: Proceedings of the Second Annual Conference*, pages 278–285, Stanford University, CA, USA, 13-16 July 1997. Morgan Kaufmann. URL http://citeseer.ist.psu.edu/327495.html.   GPBiB

R. Poli and W. B. Langdon. Schema theory for genetic programming with one-point crossover and point mutation. *Evolutionary Computation*, 6(3):231–252, 1998a. URL http://cswww.essex.ac.uk/staff/poli/papers/Poli-ECJ1998.pdf.   GPBiB

R. Poli and W. B. Langdon. On the search properties of different crossover operators in genetic programming. In J. R. Koza, et al., editors, *Genetic Programming 1998: Proceedings of the Third Annual Conference*, pages 293–301, University of Wisconsin, Madison, Wisconsin, USA, 22-25 July 1998b. Morgan Kaufmann. ISBN 1-55860-548-7. URL http://www.cs.essex.ac.uk/staff/poli/papers/Poli-GP1998.pdf.   GPBiB

R. Poli and W. B. Langdon. Sub-machine-code genetic programming. In L. Spector, et al., editors, *Advances in Genetic Programming 3*, chapter 13, pages 301–323. MIT Press, Cambridge, MA, USA, June 1999. ISBN 0-262-19423-6. URL http://cswww.essex.ac.uk/staff/rpoli/papers/Poli-AIGP3-1999.pdf.   GPBiB

R. Poli and W. B. Langdon. Running genetic programming backward. In R. L. Riolo, et al., editors, *Genetic Programming Theory and Practice*. Kluwer, 2005a.

R. Poli and W. B. Langdon. Running genetic programming backward. In T. Yu, et al., editors, *Genetic Programming Theory and Practice III*, volume 9 of *Genetic Programming*, chapter 9, pages 125–140. Springer, Ann Arbor, 12-14 May 2005b. ISBN 0-387-28110-X. URL http://www.cs.essex.ac.uk/staff/poli/papers/GPTP2005.pdf. GP<small>BIB</small>

R. Poli and W. B. Langdon. Backward-chaining evolutionary algorithms. *Artificial Intelligence*, 170(11):953–982, August 2006a. URL http://www.cs.essex.ac.uk/staff/poli/papers/aijournal2006.pdf. GP<small>BIB</small>

R. Poli and W. B. Langdon. Efficient markov chain model of machine code program execution and halting. In R. L. Riolo, et al., editors, *Genetic Programming Theory and Practice IV*, volume 5 of *Genetic and Evolutionary Computation*, chapter 13. Springer, Ann Arbor, 11-13 May 2006b. ISBN 0-387-33375-4. URL http://www.cs.essex.ac.uk/staff/poli/papers/GPTP2006.pdf. GP<small>BIB</small>

R. Poli, W. B. Langdon, and S. Dignum. On the limiting distribution of program sizes in tree-based genetic programming. In M. Ebner, et al., editors, *Proceedings of the 10th European Conference on Genetic Programming*, volume 4445 of *Lecture Notes in Computer Science*, pages 193–204, Valencia, Spain, 11 - 13 April 2007. Springer. ISBN 3-540-71602-5. GP<small>BIB</small>

R. Poli, W. B. Langdon, and O. Holland. Extending particle swarm optimisation via genetic programming. In M. Keijzer, et al., editors, *Proceedings of the 8th European Conference on Genetic Programming*, volume 3447 of *Lecture Notes in Computer Science*, pages 291–300, Lausanne, Switzerland, 30 March - 1 April 2005. Springer. ISBN 3-540-25436-6. URL http://www.cs.essex.ac.uk/staff/poli/papers/eurogpPSO2005.pdf. GP<small>BIB</small>

R. Poli, W. B. Langdon, and N. F. McPhee. *A field guide to genetic programming*. Published via http://lulu.com and freely available at http://www.gp-field-guide.org.uk, 2008. (With contributions by J. R. Koza). GP<small>BIB</small>

R. Poli and N. F. McPhee. A linear estimation-of-distribution GP system. In *Proceedings of EuroGP 2008*, 2008a. GP<small>BIB</small>

R. Poli and N. F. McPhee. Covariant parsimony pressure in genetic programming. Technical Report CES-480, Department of Computing and Electronic Systems, University of Essex, January 2008b.

R. Poli and N. F. McPhee. Exact schema theorems for GP with one-point and standard crossover operating on linear structures and their application to the study of the evolution of size. In J. F. Miller, et al., editors, *Genetic Programming, Proceedings of EuroGP'2001*, volume 2038 of *LNCS*, pages 126–142, Lake Como, Italy, 18-20 April 2001. Springer-Verlag. ISBN 3-540-41899-7. URL http://www.springerlink.com/openurl.asp?genre=article&issn=0302-9743&volume=2038&spage=126. GP<small>BIB</small>

R. Poli and N. F. McPhee. General schema theory for genetic programming with subtree-swapping crossover: Part I. *Evolutionary Computation*, 11(1):53–66, March 2003a. URL http://cswww.essex.ac.uk/staff/rpoli/papers/ecj2003partI.pdf. GP<small>BIB</small>

R. Poli and N. F. McPhee. General schema theory for genetic programming with subtree-swapping crossover: Part II. *Evolutionary Computation*, 11(2):169–206, June 2003b. URL http://cswww.essex.ac.uk/staff/rpoli/papers/ecj2003partII.pdf. GP<small>BIB</small>

Generation 29
(see Sec. B.4)

R. Poli, N. F. McPhee, and J. E. Rowe. Exact schema theory and markov chain models for genetic programming and variable-length genetic algorithms with homologous crossover. *Genetic Programming and Evolvable Machines*, 5(1):31–70, March 2004. ISSN 1389-2576. URL http://cswww.essex.ac.uk/staff/rpoli/papers/GPEM2004. pdf.   GPBiB

R. Poli and J. Page. Solving high-order boolean parity problems with smooth uniform crossover, sub-machine code GP and demes. *Genetic Programming and Evolvable Machines*, 1(1/2):37–56, April 2000. ISSN 1389-2576. URL http://citeseer.ist. psu.edu/335584.html.   GPBiB

R. Poli, J. Page, and W. B. Langdon. Smooth uniform crossover, sub-machine code GP and demes: A recipe for solving high-order boolean parity problems. In W. Banzhaf, et al., editors, *Proceedings of the Genetic and Evolutionary Computation Conference*, volume 2, pages 1162–1169, Orlando, Florida, USA, 13-17 July 1999. Morgan Kaufmann. ISBN 1-55860-611-4. URL http://www.cs.bham.ac.uk/~wbl/biblio/ gecco1999/GP-466.pdf.   GPBiB

R. Poli, J. E. Rowe, and N. F. McPhee. Markov chain models for GP and variable-length GAs with homologous crossover. In L. Spector, et al., editors, *Proceedings of the Genetic and Evolutionary Computation Conference (GECCO-2001)*, pages 112–119, San Francisco, California, USA, 7-11 July 2001. Morgan Kaufmann. ISBN 1-55860-774-9. URL http://www.cs.bham.ac.uk/~wbl/biblio/gecco2001/d01.pdf.   GPBiB

R. Poli, J. Woodward, and E. K. Burke. A histogram-matching approach to the evolution of bin-packing strategies. In *Proceedings of the IEEE Congress on Evolutionary Computation*, Singapore, 2007. accepted.

R. Poli, W. B. Langdon, M. Schoenauer, T. Fogarty, and W. Banzhaf, editors. *Late Breaking Papers at EuroGP'98: the First European Workshop on Genetic Programming*, Paris, France, 14-15 April 1998. URL http://www.cs.ucl.ac.uk/staff/W.Langdon/ ftp/papers/csrp-98-10.pdf.   GPBiB

R. Poli, P. Nordin, W. B. Langdon, and T. C. Fogarty, editors. *Genetic Programming, Proceedings of EuroGP'99*, volume 1598 of *LNCS*, Goteborg, Sweden, 26-27 May 1999. Springer-Verlag. URL http://www.springerlink.com/openurl.asp?genre= article&issn=0302-9743&volume=1598.   GPBiB

R. Poli, W. Banzhaf, W. B. Langdon, J. F. Miller, P. Nordin, and T. C. Fogarty, editors. *Genetic Programming, Proceedings of EuroGP'2000*, volume 1802 of *LNCS*, Edinburgh, 15-16 April 2000. Springer-Verlag. ISBN 3-540-67339-3.   GPBiB

E. Popovici and K. De Jong. The effects of interaction frequency on the optimization performance of cooperative coevolution. In M. Keijzer, et al., editors, *GECCO 2006: Proceedings of the 8th annual conference on Genetic and evolutionary computation*, volume 1, pages 353–360, Seattle, Washington, USA, 8-12 July 2006. ACM Press. ISBN 1-59593-186-4. URL http://www.cs.bham.ac.uk/~wbl/biblio/gecco2006/docs/p353. pdf.

M. A. Potter. *The Design and Analysis of a Computational Model of Cooperative Coevolution*. PhD thesis, George Mason University, Washington, DC, spring 1997. URL http://www.cs.gmu.edu/~mpotter/dissertation.html.

S. Priesterjahn, O. Kramer, A. Weimer, and A. Goebels. Evolution of human-competitive agents in modern computer games. In G. G. Yen, et al., editors, *Proceedings of the 2006 IEEE Congress on Evolutionary Computation*, pages 777–784, Vancouver, BC, Canada, 16-21 July 2006. IEEE Press. ISBN 0-7803-9487-9. URL http://ieeexplore. ieee.org/servlet/opac?punumber=11108.

A. Prügel-Bennett and J. L. Shapiro. An analysis of genetic algorithms using statistical mechanics. *Physical Review Letters*, 72:1305–1309, 1994.

J. C. F. Pujol. *Evolution of Artificial Neural Networks Using a Two-dimensional Representation*. PhD thesis, School of Computer Science, University of Birmingham, UK, April 1999.   GP BiB

J. C. F. Pujol and R. Poli. Evolution of the topology and the weights of neural networks using genetic programming with a dual representation. Technical Report CSRP-97-7, University of Birmingham, School of Computer Science, February 1997. URL `ftp://ftp.cs.bham.ac.uk/pub/tech-reports/1997/CSRP-97-07.ps.gz`.   GP BiB

B. Punch and D. Zongker. lil-gp Genetic Programming System, 1998. URL `http://garage.cse.msu.edu/software/lil-gp/index.html`.

M. I. Quintana, R. Poli, and E. Claridge. On two approaches to image processing algorithm design for binary images using GP. In G. R. Raidl, et al., editors, *Applications of Evolutionary Computing, EvoWorkshops2003: EvoBIO, EvoCOP, EvoIASP, Evo-MUSART, EvoROB, EvoSTIM*, volume 2611 of *LNCS*, pages 422–431, University of Essex, England, UK, 14-16 April 2003. Springer-Verlag.   GP BiB

M. I. Quintana, R. Poli, and E. Claridge. Morphological algorithm design for binary images using genetic programming. *Genetic Programming and Evolvable Machines*, 7(1):81–102, March 2006. ISSN 1389-2576. URL `http://cswww.essex.ac.uk/staff/rpoli/papers/gpem2005.pdf`.   GP BiB

A. Ratle and M. Sebag. Genetic programming and domain knowledge: Beyond the limitations of grammar-guided machine discovery. In M. Schoenauer, et al., editors, *Parallel Problem Solving from Nature - PPSN VI 6th International Conference*, volume 1917 of *LNCS*, pages 211–220, Paris, France, 16-20 September 2000. Springer Verlag. URL `http://www.lri.fr/~sebag/REF/PPSN00.ps`.   GP BiB

A. Ratle and M. Sebag. Avoiding the bloat with probabilistic grammar-guided genetic programming. In P. Collet, et al., editors, *Artificial Evolution 5th International Conference, Evolution Artificielle, EA 2001*, volume 2310 of *LNCS*, pages 255–266, Creusot, France, October 29-31 2001. Springer Verlag. ISBN 3-540-43544-1. URL `http://link.springer.de/link/service/series/0558/papers/2310/23100255.pdf`. GP BiB

J. Reggia, M. Tagamets, J. Contreras-Vidal, D. Jacobs, S. Weems, W. Naqvi, R. Winder, T. Chabuk, J. Jung, and C. Yang. Development of a large-scale integrated neurocognitive architecture - part 2: Design and architecture. Technical Report TR-CS-4827, UMIACS-TR-2006-43, University of Maryland, USA, October 2006. URL `https://drum.umd.edu/dspace/bitstream/1903/3957/1/MarylandPart2.pdf`. GP BiB

E. N. Regolin and A. T. R. Pozo. Bayesian automatic programming. In M. Keijzer, et al., editors, *Proceedings of the 8th European Conference on Genetic Programming*, volume 3447 of *Lecture Notes in Computer Science*, pages 38–49, Lausanne, Switzerland, 30 March - 1 April 2005. Springer. ISBN 3-540-25436-6. URL `http://springerlink.metapress.com/openurl.asp?genre=article&issn=0302-9743&volume=3447&spage=38`.   GP BiB

D. M. Reif, B. C. White, and J. H. Moore. Integrated analysis of genetic, genomic, and proteomic data. *Expert Review of Proteomics*, 1(1):67–75, 2004. ISSN 1473-7159. URL `http://www.future-drugs.com/doi/abs/10.1586/14789450.1.1.67`.   GP BiB

C. W. Reynolds. Flocks, herds, and schools: A distributed behavioral model. *SIGGRAPH Computer Graphics*, 21(4):25–34, July 1987. ISSN 0097-8930. URL `http://www.red3d.com/cwr/papers/1987/boids.html`.

Generation 36
(see Sec. B.4)

R. L. Riolo and B. Worzel. *Genetic Programming Theory and Practice*, volume 6 of *Genetic Programming*. Kluwer, Boston, MA, USA, 2003. ISBN 1-4020-7581-2. URL http://www.wkap.nl/prod/b/1-4020-7581-2. Series Editor - John Koza.   GP<small>BIB</small>

R. L. Riolo, T. Soule, and B. Worzel, editors. *Genetic Programming Theory and Practice IV*, volume 5 of *Genetic and Evolutionary Computation*, Ann Arbor, 11-13 May 2007a. Springer. ISBN 0-387-33375-4. URL http://www.springer.com/west/home/computer/foundations?SGWID=4-156-22-173660377-0.   GP<small>BIB</small>

R. L. Riolo, T. Soule, and B. Worzel, editors. *Genetic Programming Theory and Practice V*, Genetic and Evolutionary Computation, Ann Arbor, 17-19 May 2007b. Springer. GP<small>BIB</small>

M. D. Ritchie, A. A. Motsinger, W. S. Bush, C. S. Coffey, and J. H. Moore. Genetic programming neural networks: A powerful bioinformatics tool for human genetics. *Applied Soft Computing*, 7(1):471–479, January 2007.   GP<small>BIB</small>

M. D. Ritchie, B. C. White, J. S. Parker, L. W. Hahn, and J. H. Moore. Optimization of neural network architecture using genetic programming improves detection and modeling of gene-gene interactions in studies of human diseases. *BMC Bioinformatics*, 4 (28), 7 July 2003. URL http://www.biomedcentral.com/1471-2105/4/28.   GP<small>BIB</small>

D. Rivero, J. R. R. nal, J. Dorado, and A. Pazos. Using genetic programming for character discrimination in damaged documents. In G. R. Raidl, et al., editors, *Applications of Evolutionary Computing, EvoWorkshops2004: EvoBIO, EvoCOMNET, EvoHOT, EvoIASP, EvoMUSART, EvoSTOC*, volume 3005 of *LNCS*, pages 349–358, Coimbra, Portugal, 5-7 April 2004. Springer Verlag. ISBN 3-540-21378-3.   GP<small>BIB</small>

RML Technologies. Discipulus Genetic-Programming Software, 1998-2007. URL http://www.rmltech.com/.

A. Robinson and L. Spector. Using genetic programming with multiple data types and automatic modularization to evolve decentralized and coordinated navigation in multi-agent systems. In E. Cantú-Paz, editor, *Late Breaking Papers at the Genetic and Evolutionary Computation Conference (GECCO-2002)*, pages 391–396, New York, NY, July 2002. AAAI.   GP<small>BIB</small>

K. Rodriguez-Vazquez, C. M. Fonseca, and P. J. Fleming. Multiobjective genetic programming: A nonlinear system identification application. In J. R. Koza, editor, *Late Breaking Papers at the 1997 Genetic Programming Conference*, pages 207–212, Stanford University, CA, USA, 13–16 July 1997. Stanford Bookstore. ISBN 0-18-206995-8. URL http://www.lania.mx/~ccoello/EMOO/katya97.ps.gz.   GP<small>BIB</small>

K. Rodriguez-Vazquez, C. M. Fonseca, and P. J. Fleming. Identifying the structure of nonlinear dynamic systems using multiobjective genetic programming. *IEEE Transactions on Systems, Man and Cybernetics, Part A*, 34(4):531–545, July 2004. ISSN 1083-4427.   GP<small>BIB</small>

J. P. Rosca. Generality versus size in genetic programming. In J. R. Koza, et al., editors, *Genetic Programming 1996: Proceedings of the First Annual Conference*, pages 381–387, Stanford University, CA, USA, 28–31 July 1996. MIT Press. URL ftp://ftp.cs.rochester.edu/pub/u/rosca/gp/96.gp.ps.gz.   GP<small>BIB</small>

J. P. Rosca. Analysis of complexity drift in genetic programming. In J. R. Koza, et al., editors, *Genetic Programming 1997: Proceedings of the Second Annual Conference*, pages 286–294, Stanford University, CA, USA, 13-16 July 1997. Morgan Kaufmann. URL ftp://ftp.cs.rochester.edu/pub/u/rosca/gp/97.gp.ps.gz.   GP<small>BIB</small>

J. P. Rosca. A probabilistic model of size drift. In R. L. Riolo and B. Worzel, editors, *Genetic Programming Theory and Practice*, chapter 8, pages 119–136. Kluwer, 2003. GPBiB

J. P. Rosca and D. H. Ballard. Discovery of subroutines in genetic programming. In P. J. Angeline and K. E. Kinnear, Jr., editors, *Advances in Genetic Programming 2*, chapter 9, pages 177–202. MIT Press, Cambridge, MA, USA, 1996a. ISBN 0-262-01158-1. URL ftp://ftp.cs.rochester.edu/pub/u/rosca/gp/96.aigp2.dsgp.ps.gz. GPBiB

J. P. Rosca and D. H. Ballard. Complexity drift in evolutionary computation with tree representations. Technical Report NRL5, University of Rochester, Computer Science Department, Rochester, NY, USA, December 1996b. URL ftp://ftp.cs.rochester. edu/pub/u/rosca/gp/96.drift.ps.gz.   GPBiB

J. P. Rosca and D. H. Ballard. Rooted-tree schemata in genetic programming. In L. Spector, et al., editors, *Advances in Genetic Programming 3*, chapter 11, pages 243–271. MIT Press, Cambridge, MA, USA, June 1999. ISBN 0-262-19423-6. URL http://www.cs.bham.ac.uk/~wbl/aigp3/ch11.pdf.   GPBiB

B. J. Ross, A. G. Gualtieri, F. Fueten, and P. Budkewitsch. Hyperspectral image analysis using genetic programming. *Applied Soft Computing*, 5(2):147–156, January 2005. URL http://www.cosc.brocku.ca/~bross/research/gp_hyper.pdf.   GPBiB

B. J. Ross and H. Zhu. Procedural texture evolution using multiobjective optimization. *New Generation Computing*, 22(3):271–293, 2004. URL http://www.cosc.brocku.ca/ files/downloads/research/cs0218.pdf.   GPBiB

R. Rossi, V. Liberali, and A. G. B. Tettamanzi. An application of genetic programming to electronic design automation: from frequency specifications to VHDL code. In R. Roy, et al., editors, *Soft Computing and Industry Recent Applications*, pages 809–820. Springer-Verlag, 10–24 September 2001. ISBN 1-85233-539-4. URL http://mago. crema.unimi.it/pub/RossiLiberaliTettamanzi2001.pdf. Published 2002.   GPBiB

F. Rothlauf. *Representations for genetic and evolutionary algorithms*. Springer-Verlag, pub-SV:adr, second edition, 2006. ISBN 3-540-25059-X. URL http://download-ebook. org/index.php?target=desc&ebookid=5771. First published 2002, 2nd edition available electronically.

C. Ryan. Pygmies and civil servants. In K. E. Kinnear, Jr., editor, *Advances in Genetic Programming*, chapter 11, pages 243–263. MIT Press, 1994. URL http://cognet.mit. edu/library/books/view?isbn=0262111888.   GPBiB

C. Ryan. *Reducing Premature Convergence in Evolutionary Algorithms*. PhD thesis, University College, Cork, Ireland, 2 July 1996. URL http://citeseer.ist.psu.edu/ cache/papers/cs/6401/ftp:zSzzSzodyssey.ucc.iezSzpubzSzgeneticzSzthesis.pdf/ ryan96reducing.pdf.   GPBiB

C. Ryan. *Automatic Re-engineering of Software Using Genetic Programming*, volume 2 of *Genetic Programming*. Kluwer Academic Publishers, 1 November 1999. ISBN 0-7923-8653-1. URL http://www.wkap.nl/book.htm/0-7923-8653-1.   GPBiB

C. Ryan, J. J. Collins, and M. O'Neill. Grammatical evolution: Evolving programs for an arbitrary language. In W. Banzhaf, et al., editors, *Proceedings of the First European Workshop on Genetic Programming*, volume 1391 of *LNCS*, pages 83–95, Paris, 14-15 April 1998. Springer-Verlag. ISBN 3-540-64360-5. URL http://www.lania.mx/ ~ccoello/eurogp98.ps.gz.   GPBiB

Generation 43
(see Sec. B.4)

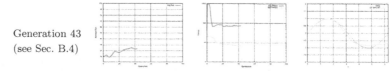

C. Ryan, T. Soule, M. Keijzer, E. P. K. Tsang, R. Poli, and E. Costa, editors. *Genetic Programming, Proceedings of the 6th European Conference, EuroGP 2003*, volume 2610 of *LNCS*, Essex, UK, 14-16 April 2003. Springer-Verlag. ISBN 3-540-00971-X. URL http://www.springerlink.com/openurl.asp?genre=article&issn=0302-9743&volume=2610.   GPBiB

R. P. Salustowicz and J. Schmidhuber. Probabilistic incremental program evolution. *Evolutionary Computation*, 5(2):123–141, 1997. URL ftp://ftp.idsia.ch/pub/rafal/PIPE.ps.gz.   GPBiB

R. P. Salustowicz, M. A. Wiering, and J. Schmidhuber. Learning team strategies: Soccer case studies. *Machine Learning*, 33(2-3):263–282, 12 November 1998. ISSN 0885-6125. URL ftp://ftp.idsia.ch/pub/rafal/soccer.ps.gz.

R. P. Salustowicz and J. Schmidhuber. From probabilities to programs with probabilistic incremental program evolution. In D. Corne, et al., editors, *New Ideas in Optimization*, Advanced Topics in Computer Science, chapter 28, pages 433–450. McGraw-Hill, Maidenhead, Berkshire, England, 1999. ISBN 0-07-709506-5.   GPBiB

A. L. Samuel. AI, where it has been and where it is going. In *IJCAI*, pages 1152–1157, 1983.

A. Sarafopoulos. Automatic generation of affine IFS and strongly typed genetic programming. In R. Poli, et al., editors, *Genetic Programming, Proceedings of EuroGP'99*, volume 1598 of *LNCS*, pages 149–160, Goteborg, Sweden, 26-27 May 1999. Springer-Verlag. ISBN 3-540-65899-8. URL http://www.springerlink.com/openurl.asp?genre=article&issn=0302-9743&volume=1598&spage=149.   GPBiB

K. Sastry and D. E. Goldberg. Probabilistic model building and competent genetic programming. In R. L. Riolo and B. Worzel, editors, *Genetic Programming Theory and Practise*, chapter 13, pages 205–220. Kluwer, 2003. ISBN 1-4020-7581-2.   GPBiB

M. D. Schmidt and H. Lipson. Co-evolving fitness predictors for accelerating and reducing evaluations. In R. L. Riolo, et al., editors, *Genetic Programming Theory and Practice IV*, volume 5 of *Genetic and Evolutionary Computation*, chapter 17, pages –. Springer, Ann Arbor, 11-13 May 2006. ISBN 0-387-33375-4.   GPBiB

F. Schmiedle, N. Drechsler, D. Grosse, and R. Drechsler. Priorities in multi-objective optimization for genetic programming. In L. Spector, et al., editors, *Proceedings of the Genetic and Evolutionary Computation Conference (GECCO-2001)*, pages 129–136, San Francisco, California, USA, 7-11 July 2001. Morgan Kaufmann. ISBN 1-55860-774-9. URL http://www.cs.bham.ac.uk/~wbl/biblio/gecco2001/d01.pdf.   GPBiB

M. Schoenauer, B. Lamy, and F. Jouve. Identification of mechanical behaviour by genetic programming part II: Energy formulation. Technical report, Ecole Polytechnique, 91128 Palaiseau, France, 1995.   GPBiB

M. Schoenauer and M. Sebag. Using domain knowledge in evolutionary system identification. In K. C. Giannakoglou, et al., editors, *Evolutionary Methods for Design, Optimization and Control with Applications to Industrial Problems*, Athens, 19-21 September 2001. URL http://arxiv.org/abs/cs/0602021.   GPBiB

M. Schoenauer, M. Sebag, F. Jouve, B. Lamy, and H. Maitournam. Evolutionary identification of macro-mechanical models. In P. J. Angeline and K. E. Kinnear, Jr., editors, *Advances in Genetic Programming 2*, chapter 23, pages 467–488. MIT Press, Cambridge, MA, USA, 1996. ISBN 0-262-01158-1. URL http://citeseer.ist.psu.edu/cache/papers/cs/902/http:zSzzSzwww.eeaax.

polytechnique.frzSzpaperszSzmarczSzAGP2.pdf/schoenauer96evolutionary.pdf.
GP_{BIB}

M. Schoenauer, K. Deb, G. Rudolph, X. Yao, E. Lutton, J. J. Merelo, and H.-P. Schwefel, editors. *Parallel Problem Solving from Nature - PPSN VI 6th International Conference*, volume 1917 of *LNCS*, Paris, France, 16-20 September 2000. Springer Verlag. ISBN 3-540-41056-2. URL http://www.springer.de/cgi-bin/search_book.pl?isbn= 3-540-41056-2. GP_{BIB}

D. P. Searson, G. A. Montague, and M. J. Willis. Evolutionary design of process controllers. In *In Proceedings of the 1998 United Kingdom Automatic Control Council International Conference on Control (UKACC International Conference on Control '98)*, volume 455 of *IEE Conference Publications*, University of Wales, Swansea, UK, 1-4 September 1998. Institution of Electrical Engineers (IEE). URL http: //www.staff.ncl.ac.uk/d.p.searson/docs/Searsoncontrol98.pdf. GP_{BIB}

L. Sekanina. *Evolvable Components: From Theory to Hardware Implementations*. Natural Computing. Springer-Verlag, 2003. ISBN 3-540-40377-9. URL http://www.fit.vutbr. cz/~sekanina/ehw/books.html.en.

H.-S. Seok, K.-J. Lee, and B.-T. Zhang. An on-line learning method for object-locating robots using genetic programming on evolvable hardware. In M. Sugisaka and H. Tanaka, editors, *Proceedings of the Fifth International Symposium on Artificial Life and Robotics*, volume 1, pages 321–324, Oita, Japan, 26-28 January 2000. URL http://bi.snu.ac.kr/Publications/Conferences/International/AROB00.ps. GP_{BIB}

C. Setzkorn. *On The Use Of Multi-Objective Evolutionary Algorithms For Classification Rule Induction*. PhD thesis, University of Liverpool, UK, March 2005. GP_{BIB}

S. C. Shah and A. Kusiak. Data mining and genetic algorithm based gene/SNP selection. *Artificial Intelligence in Medicine*, 31(3):183–196, July 2004. URL http://www.icaen. uiowa.edu/~ankusiak/Journal-papers/Gen_Shital.pdf. GP_{BIB}

Y. Shan, H. Abbass, R. I. McKay, and D. Essam. AntTAG: a further study. In R. Sarker and B. McKay, editors, *Proceedings of the Sixth Australia-Japan Joint Workshop on Intelligent and Evolutionary Systems*, Australian National University, Canberra, Australia, 30 November 2002. GP_{BIB}

Y. Shan, R. I. McKay, H. A. Abbass, and D. Essam. Program evolution with explicit learning: a new framework for program automatic synthesis. In R. Sarker, et al., editors, *Proceedings of the 2003 Congress on Evolutionary Computation CEC2003*, pages 1639–1646, Canberra, 8-12 December 2003. IEEE Press. ISBN 0-7803-7804-0. URL http://citeseer.ist.psu.edu/560804.html. GP_{BIB}

Y. Shan, R. I. McKay, R. Baxter, H. Abbass, D. Essam, and N. X. Hoai. Grammar model-based program evolution. In *Proceedings of the 2004 IEEE Congress on Evolutionary Computation*, pages 478–485, Portland, Oregon, 20-23 June 2004. IEEE Press. ISBN 0-7803-8515-2. URL http://sc.snu.ac.kr/courses/2006/fall/pg/aai/ GP/shan/scfgcec04.pdf. GP_{BIB}

Y. Shan, R. I. McKay, D. Essam, and H. A. Abbass. A survey of probabilistic model building genetic programming. In M. Pelikan, et al., editors, *Scalable Optimization via Probabilistic Modeling: From Algorithms to Applications*. Springer, 2006. ISBN 3-540-34953-7. GP_{BIB}

S. Sharabi and M. Sipper. GP-sumo: Using genetic programming to evolve sumobots. *Genetic Programming and Evolvable Machines*, 7(3):211–230, October 2006. ISSN 1389-2576. GP_{BIB}

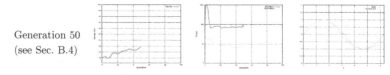

Generation 50
(see Sec. B.4)

K. C. Sharman and A. I. Esparcia-Alcazar. Genetic evolution of symbolic signal models. In *Proceedings of the Second International Conference on Natural Algorithms in Signal Processing, NASP'93*, Essex University, UK, 15-16 November 1993. URL http://www.iti.upv.es/~anna/papers/natalg93.ps. GPBiB

K. C. Sharman, A. I. Esparcia Alcazar, and Y. Li. Evolving signal processing algorithms by genetic programming. In A. M. S. Zalzala, editor, *First International Conference on Genetic Algorithms in Engineering Systems: Innovations and Applications, GALESIA*, volume 414, pages 473–480, Sheffield, UK, 12-14 September 1995. IEE. ISBN 0-85296-650-4. URL http://www.iti.upv.es/~anna/papers/galesi95.ps. GPBiB

A. D. Shaw, M. K. Winson, A. M. Woodward, A. C. McGovern, H. M. Davey, N. Kaderbhai, D. Broadhurst, R. J. Gilbert, J. Taylor, E. M. Timmins, R. Goodacre, D. B. Kell, B. K. Alsberg, and J. J. Rowland. Bioanalysis and biosensors for bioprocess monitoring rapid analysis of high-dimensional bioprocesses using multivariate spectroscopies and advanced chemometrics. *Advances in Biochemical Engineering/Biotechnology*, 66: 83–113, January 2000. ISSN 0724-6145. URL http://www.springerlink.com/link.asp?id=t8b4ya0bl42jnjj3. GPBiB

Y. Shichel, E. Ziserman, and M. Sipper. GP-robocode: Using genetic programming to evolve robocode players. In M. Keijzer, et al., editors, *Proceedings of the 8th European Conference on Genetic Programming*, volume 3447 of *Lecture Notes in Computer Science*, pages 143–154, Lausanne, Switzerland, 30 March - 1 April 2005. Springer. ISBN 3-540-25436-6. URL http://www.cs.bgu.ac.il/~sipper/papabs/eurogprobo-final.pdf. GPBiB

H. Z. Si, T. Wang, K. J. Zhang, Z. D. Hu, and B. T. Fan. QSAR study of 1,4-dihydropyridine calcium channel antagonists based on gene expression programming. *Bioorganic & Medicinal Chemistry*, 14(14):4834–4841, 15 July 2006. GPBiB

R. P. S. Sidhu, A. Mei, and V. K. Prasanna. Genetic programming using self-reconfigurable FPGAs. In *9th International Workshop on Field Programmable Logic and Applications*, volume 1673 of *LNCS*, pages 301–312, Glasgow, UK, 30 August - 1 September 1998. Springer-Verlag. ISBN 3-540-66457-2. URL http://ceng.usc.edu/~prasanna/papers/sidhuFPL99.ps. GPBiB

E. V. Siegel. Competitively evolving decision trees against fixed training cases for natural language processing. In K. E. Kinnear, Jr., editor, *Advances in Genetic Programming*, chapter 19, pages 409–423. MIT Press, 1994. URL http://www1.cs.columbia.edu/nlp/papers/1994/siegel_94.pdf. GPBiB

S. Silva and J. Almeida. Dynamic maximum tree depth. In E. Cantú-Paz, et al., editors, *Genetic and Evolutionary Computation – GECCO-2003*, volume 2724 of *LNCS*, pages 1776–1787, Chicago, 12-16 July 2003. Springer-Verlag. ISBN 3-540-40603-4. URL http://cisuc.dei.uc.pt/ecos/dlfile.php?fn=109_pub_27241776.pdf. GPBiB

S. Silva and E. Costa. Dynamic limits for bloat control: Variations on size and depth. In K. Deb, et al., editors, *Genetic and Evolutionary Computation – GECCO-2004, Part II*, volume 3103 of *Lecture Notes in Computer Science*, pages 666–677, Seattle, WA, USA, 26-30 June 2004. Springer-Verlag. ISBN 3-540-22343-6. URL http://cisuc.dei.uc.pt/ecos/dlfile.php?fn=714_pub_31030666.pdf&idp=714. GPBiB

S. Silva and E. Costa. Comparing tree depth limits and resource-limited GP. In D. Corne, et al., editors, *Proceedings of the 2005 IEEE Congress on Evolutionary Computation*, volume 1, pages 920–927, Edinburgh, UK, 2-5 September 2005a. IEEE Press. ISBN 0-7803-9363-5. GPBiB

S. Silva and E. Costa. Resource-limited genetic programming: the dynamic approach. In H.-G. Beyer, et al., editors, *GECCO 2005: Proceedings of the 2005 conference on Genetic and evolutionary computation*, volume 2, pages 1673–1680, Washington DC, USA, 25-29 June 2005b. ACM Press. ISBN 1-59593-010-8. URL http://www.cs.bham.ac.uk/~wbl/biblio/gecco2005/docs/p1673.pdf.   GPBiB

S. Silva, P. J. N. Silva, and E. Costa. Resource-limited genetic programming: Replacing tree depth limits. In B. Ribeiro, et al., editors, *Adaptive and Natural Computing Algorithms*, Springer Computer Series, pages 243–246, Coimbra, Portugal, 21-23 March 2005. Springer. ISBN 3-211-24934-6. URL http://www.lri.fr/~sebag/Examens/sara.icannga05.pdf.   GPBiB

K. Sims. Artificial evolution for computer graphics. *ACM Computer Graphics*, 25(4):319–328, July 1991. URL http://delivery.acm.org/10.1145/130000/122752/p319-sims.pdf. SIGGRAPH '91 Proceedings.   GPBiB

W. Smart and M. Zhang. Applying online gradient descent search to genetic programming for object recognition. In J. Hogan, et al., editors, *CRPIT '04: Proceedings of the second workshop on Australasian information security, Data Mining and Web Intelligence, and Software Internationalisation*, volume 32 no. 7, pages 133–138, Dunedin, New Zealand, January 2004. Australian Computer Society, Inc. ISBN 1-920682-14-7. URL http://crpit.com/confpapers/CRPITV32Smart.pdf.   GPBiB

T. Smith, S. Bullock, and J. Bird. Beyond fitness: Visualising evolution – workshop overview. In E. Bilotta, et al., editors, *ALife VIII: Workshop proceedings*, pages 100–102, 2002. URL http://www.alife.org/alife8/workshops/14.pdf.

T. Soule. *Code Growth in Genetic Programming*. PhD thesis, University of Idaho, Moscow, Idaho, USA, 15 May 1998. URL http://www.cs.uidaho.edu/~tsoule/research/the3.ps.   GPBiB

T. Soule. Cooperative evolution on the intertwined spirals problem. In C. Ryan, et al., editors, *Genetic Programming, Proceedings of EuroGP'2003*, volume 2610 of *LNCS*, pages 434–442, Essex, 14-16 April 2003. Springer-Verlag. ISBN 3-540-00971-X. URL http://www.springerlink.com/openurl.asp?genre=article&issn=0302-9743&volume=2610&spage=434.   GPBiB

T. Soule and J. A. Foster. Removal bias: a new cause of code growth in tree based evolutionary programming. In *1998 IEEE International Conference on Evolutionary Computation*, pages 781–186, Anchorage, Alaska, USA, 5-9 May 1998a. IEEE Press. URL http://citeseer.ist.psu.edu/313655.html.   GPBiB

T. Soule and J. A. Foster. Effects of code growth and parsimony pressure on populations in genetic programming. *Evolutionary Computation*, 6(4):293–309, Winter 1998b. URL http://mitpress.mit.edu/journals/EVCO/Soule.pdf.   GPBiB

T. Soule and P. Komireddy. Orthogonal evolution of teams: A class of algorithms for evolving teams with inversely correlated errors. In R. L. Riolo, et al., editors, *Genetic Programming Theory and Practice IV*, volume 5 of *Genetic and Evolutionary Computation*, chapter 8, pages –. Springer, Ann Arbor, 11-13 May 2006. ISBN 0-387-33375-4. GPBiB

L. Spector. Autoconstructive evolution: Push, pushGP, and pushpop. In L. Spector, et al., editors, *Proceedings of the Genetic and Evolutionary Computation Conference (GECCO-2001)*, pages 137–146, San Francisco, California, USA, 7-11 July 2001. Morgan Kaufmann. ISBN 1-55860-774-9. URL http://hampshire.edu/lspector/pubs/ace.pdf.   GPBiB

Generation 57
(see Sec. B.4)

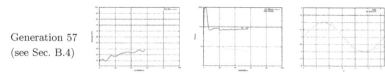

L. Spector. Adaptive populations of endogenously diversifying pushpop organisms are reliably diverse. In R. K. Standish, et al., editors, *Proceedings of Artificial Life VIII, the 8th International Conference on the Simulation and Synthesis of Living Systems*, pages 142–145, University of New South Wales, Sydney, NSW, Australia, 9th-13th December 2002. The MIT Press. URL http://hampshire.edu/lspector/pubs/spector-alife8.pdf.   GPBiB

L. Spector. *Automatic Quantum Computer Programming: A Genetic Programming Approach*, volume 7 of *Genetic Programming*. Kluwer Academic Publishers, Boston/Dordrecht/New York/London, June 2004. ISBN 1-4020-7894-3. URL http://www.wkap.nl/prod/b/1-4020-7894-3.   GPBiB

L. Spector and A. Alpern. Criticism, culture, and the automatic generation of artworks. In *Proceedings of Twelfth National Conference on Artificial Intelligence*, pages 3–8, Seattle, Washington, USA, 1994. AAAI Press/MIT Press.   GPBiB

L. Spector and A. Alpern. Induction and recapitulation of deep musical structure. In *Proceedings of International Joint Conference on Artificial Intelligence, IJCAI'95 Workshop on Music and AI*, Montreal, Quebec, Canada, 20-25 August 1995. URL http://hampshire.edu/lspector/pubs/IJCAI95mus-toappear.ps.   GPBiB

L. Spector, H. Barnum, and H. J. Bernstein. Genetic programming for quantum computers. In J. R. Koza, et al., editors, *Genetic Programming 1998: Proceedings of the Third Annual Conference*, pages 365–373, University of Wisconsin, Madison, Wisconsin, USA, 22-25 July 1998. Morgan Kaufmann. ISBN 1-55860-548-7.   GPBiB

L. Spector, H. Barnum, H. J. Bernstein, and N. Swamy. Finding a better-than-classical quantum AND/OR algorithm using genetic programming. In P. J. Angeline, et al., editors, *Proceedings of the Congress on Evolutionary Computation*, volume 3, pages 2239–2246, Mayflower Hotel, Washington D.C., USA, 6-9 July 1999. IEEE Press. ISBN 0-7803-5536-9 (softbound). URL http://hampshire.edu/~lasCCS/pubs/spector-cec99.ps.   GPBiB

L. Spector and J. Klein. Multidimensional tags, cooperative populations, and genetic programming. In R. L. Riolo, et al., editors, *Genetic Programming Theory and Practice IV*, volume 5 of *Genetic and Evolutionary Computation*, chapter 15, pages –. Springer, Ann Arbor, 11-13 May 2006. ISBN 0-387-33375-4.   GPBiB

L. Spector, J. Klein, and M. Keijzer. The push3 execution stack and the evolution of control. In H.-G. Beyer, et al., editors, *GECCO 2005: Proceedings of the 2005 conference on Genetic and evolutionary computation*, volume 2, pages 1689–1696, Washington DC, USA, 25-29 June 2005a. ACM Press. ISBN 1-59593-010-8. URL http://www.cs.bham.ac.uk/~wbl/biblio/gecco2005/docs/p1689.pdf.   GPBiB

L. Spector, J. Klein, C. Perry, and M. Feinstein. Emergence of collective behavior in evolving populations of flying agents. *Genetic Programming and Evolvable Machines*, 6(1):111–125, March 2005b. ISSN 1389-2576. URL http://hampshire.edu/lspector/pubs/emergence-collective-GPEM.pdf.   GPBiB

L. Spector, W. B. Langdon, U.-M. O'Reilly, and P. J. Angeline, editors. *Advances in Genetic Programming 3*. MIT Press, Cambridge, MA, USA, June 1999. ISBN 0-262-19423-6. URL http://www.cs.bham.ac.uk/~wbl/aigp3.   GPBiB

L. Spector, E. D. Goodman, A. Wu, W. B. Langdon, H.-M. Voigt, M. Gen, S. Sen, M. Dorigo, S. Pezeshk, M. H. Garzon, and E. Burke, editors. *Proceedings of the Genetic and Evolutionary Computation Conference, GECCO-2001*, San Francisco, California, USA, 7-11 July 2001. Morgan Kaufmann. ISBN 1-55860-774-9. URL http://www.cs.bham.ac.uk/~wbl/biblio/gecco2001/.   GPBiB

J. Stender, editor. *Parallel Genetic Algorithms: Theory and Applications.* IOS press, 1993.

C. R. Stephens and H. Waelbroeck. Effective degrees of freedom in genetic algorithms and the block hypothesis. In T. Bäck, editor, *Proceedings of the Seventh International Conference on Genetic Algorithms (ICGA97)*, pages 34–40, East Lansing, 1997. Morgan Kaufmann.

C. R. Stephens and H. Waelbroeck. Schemata evolution and building blocks. *Evolutionary Computation*, 7(2):109–124, 1999.

T. Sterling. Beowulf-class clustered computing: Harnessing the power of parallelism in a pile of PCs. In J. R. Koza, et al., editors, *Genetic Programming 1998: Proceedings of the Third Annual Conference*, page 883, University of Wisconsin, Madison, Wisconsin, USA, 22-25 July 1998. Morgan Kaufmann. ISBN 1-55860-548-7. Invited talk.

A. Stoica, J. Lohn, and D. Keymeulen, editors. *The First NASA/DoD Workshop on Evolvable Hardware*, Pasadena, California, 19-21 July 1999. IEEE Computer Society. URL http://cism.jpl.nasa.gov/ehw/events/nasa_eh/.

W. A. Tackett. Genetic generation of "dendritic" trees for image classification. In *Proceedings of WCNN93*, pages IV 646–649. IEEE Press, July 1993. URL http://www.cs.ucl.ac.uk/staff/W.Langdon/ftp/ftp.io.com/papers/GP.feature.discovery.ps.Z. GPBiB

H. Takagi. Interactive evolutionary computation: Fusion of the capabilities of EC optimization and human evaluation. *Proceedings of the IEEE*, 89(9):1275–1296, September 2001. ISSN 0018-9219. Invited Paper. GPBiB

I. Tanev, T. Uozumi, and D. Akhmetov. Component object based single system image for dependable implementation of genetic programming on clusters. *Cluster Computing Journal*, 7(4):347–356, October 2004. ISSN 1386-7857 (Paper) 1573-7543 (Online). URL http://www.kluweronline.com/issn/1386-7857. GPBiB

J. Taylor, R. Goodacre, W. G. Wade, J. J. Rowland, and D. B. Kell. The deconvolution of pyrolysis mass spectra using genetic programming: application to the identification of some eubacterium species. *FEMS Microbiology Letters*, 160:237–246, 1998. GPBiB

A. Teller. Genetic programming, indexed memory, the halting problem, and other curiosities. In *Proceedings of the 7th annual Florida Artificial Intelligence Research Symposium*, pages 270–274, Pensacola, Florida, USA, May 1994. IEEE Press. URL http://www.cs.cmu.edu/afs/cs/usr/astro/public/papers/Curiosities.ps. GPBiB

A. Teller. Evolving programmers: The co-evolution of intelligent recombination operators. In P. J. Angeline and K. E. Kinnear, Jr., editors, *Advances in Genetic Programming 2*, chapter 3, pages 45–68. MIT Press, Cambridge, MA, USA, 1996. ISBN 0-262-01158-1. URL http://www.cs.cmu.edu/afs/cs/usr/astro/public/papers/AiGPII.ps. GPBiB

A. Teller and D. Andre. Automatically choosing the number of fitness cases: The rational allocation of trials. In J. R. Koza, et al., editors, *Genetic Programming 1997: Proceedings of the Second Annual Conference*, pages 321–328, Stanford University, CA, USA, 13-16 July 1997. Morgan Kaufmann. URL http://www.cs.cmu.edu/afs/cs/usr/astro/public/papers/GR.ps. GPBiB

A. Teredesai and V. Govindaraju. GP-based secondary classifiers. *Pattern Recognition*, 38(4):505–512, April 2005. GPBiB

Generation 64
(see Sec. B.4)

J. P. Theiler, N. R. Harvey, S. P. Brumby, J. J. Szymanski, S. Alferink, S. J. Perkins, R. B. Porter, and J. J. Bloch. Evolving retrieval algorithms with a genetic programming scheme. In M. R. Descour and S. S. Shen, editors, *Proceedings of SPIE 3753 Imaging Spectrometry V*, pages 416–425, 1999. URL http://public.lanl.gov/jt/ Papers/ga-spie.ps.   GPBiB

D. Thierens, H.-G. Beyer, J. Bongard, J. Branke, J. A. Clark, D. Cliff, C. B. Congdon, K. Deb, B. Doerr, T. Kovacs, S. Kumar, J. F. Miller, J. Moore, F. Neumann, M. Pelikan, R. Poli, K. Sastry, K. O. Stanley, T. Stutzle, R. A. Watson, and I. Wegener, editors. *GECCO 2007: Proceedings of the 9th annual conference on Genetic and evolutionary computation*, London, UK, 7-11 July 2007. ACM Press.   GPBiB

S. Thompson. *Type theory and functional programming*. Addison Wesley Longman Publishing Co., Inc., Redwood City, CA, USA, 1991. ISBN 0-201-41667-0.

P. M. Todd and G. M. Werner. Frankensteinian approaches to evolutionary music composition. In N. Griffith and P. M. Todd, editors, *Musical Networks: Parallel Distributed Perception and Performance*, pages 313–340. MIT Press, 1999. ISBN 0-262-07181-9. URL http://www-abc.mpib-berlin.mpg.de/users/ptodd/publications/99evmus/ 99evmus.pdf.   GPBiB

M. Tomassini, L. Luthi, M. Giacobini, and W. B. Langdon. The structure of the genetic programming collaboration network. *Genetic Programming and Evolvable Machines*, 8(1):97–103, March 2007.   GPBiB

L. Trujillo and G. Olague. Using evolution to learn how to perform interest point detection. In X. Y. T. et al., editor, *ICPR 2006 18th International Conference on Pattern Recognition*, volume 1, pages 211–214. IEEE, 20-24 August 2006a. URL http: //www.genetic-programming.org/hc2006/Olague-Paper-2-ICPR-2006.pdf.   GPBiB

L. Trujillo and G. Olague. Synthesis of interest point detectors through genetic programming. In M. Keijzer, et al., editors, *GECCO 2006: Proceedings of the 8th annual conference on Genetic and evolutionary computation*, volume 1, pages 887–894, Seattle, Washington, USA, 8-12 July 2006b. ACM Press. ISBN 1-59593-186-4. URL http://www.cs.bham.ac.uk/~wbl/biblio/gecco2006/docs/p887.pdf.   GPBiB

E. P. K. Tsang, S. Markose, and H. Er. Chance discovery in stock index option and future arbitrage. *New Mathematics and Natural Computation*, 1(3):435–447, 2005.

E. P. K. Tsang and N. Jin. Incentive method to handle constraints in evolutionary. In P. Collet, et al., editors, *Proceedings of the 9th European Conference on Genetic Programming*, volume 3905 of *Lecture Notes in Computer Science*, pages 133–144, Budapest, Hungary, 10 - 12 April 2006. Springer. ISBN 3-540-33143-3. URL http: //link.springer.de/link/service/series/0558/papers/3905/39050133.pdf. GPBiB

E. P. K. Tsang and J. Li. EDDIE for financial forecasting. In S.-H. Chen, editor, *Genetic Algorithms and Genetic Programming in Computational Finance*, chapter 7, pages 161–174. Kluwer Academic Press, 2002. ISBN 0-7923-7601-3. URL http://cswww. essex.ac.uk/CSP/finance/papers/TsangLi-FGP-Chen_CompFinance.pdf.   GPBiB

E. P. K. Tsang, J. Li, and J. M. Butler. EDDIE beats the bookies. *Software: Practice and Experience*, 28(10):1033–1043, 1998. ISSN 0038-0644. URL http://cswww.essex. ac.uk/CSP/finance/papers/TsBuLi-Eddie-Software98.pdf.   GPBiB

E. P. K. Tsang, P. Yung, and J. Li. EDDIE-automation, a decision support tool for financial forecasting. *Decision Support Systems*, 37(4):559–565, 2004. URL http: //cswww.essex.ac.uk/CSP/finance/papers/TsYuLi-Eddie-Dss2004.pdf.   GPBiB

I. G. Tsoulos and I. E. Lagaris. Genanneal: Genetically modified simulated annealing. *Computer Physics Communications*, 174(10):846–851, 15 May 2006. GPBiB

A. M. Turing. Intelligent machinery. Report for National Physical Laboratory. Reprinted in Ince, D. C. (editor). 1992. Mechanical Intelligence: Collected Works of A. M. Turing. Amsterdam: North Holland. Pages 107127. Also reprinted in Meltzer, B. and Michie, D. (editors). 1969. Machine Intelligence 5. Edinburgh: Edinburgh University Press, 1948.

A. M. Turing. Computing machinery and intelligence. *Mind*, 49:433–460, January 01 1950. URL http://www.cs.umbc.edu/471/papers/turing.pdf. GPBiB

I. Usman, A. Khan, R. Chamlawi, and A. Majid. Image authenticity and perceptual optimization via genetic algorithm and a dependence neighborhood. *International Journal of Applied Mathematics and Computer Sciences*, 4(1):615–620, 2007. ISSN 1305-5313. URL http://www.waset.org/ijamcs/v4/v4-1-7.pdf. GPBiB

S. Vaidyanathan, D. I. Broadhurst, D. B. Kell, and R. Goodacre. Explanatory optimization of protein mass spectrometry via genetic search. *Analytical Chemistry*, 75(23): 6679–6686, 2003. URL http://dbkgroup.org/Papers/AnalChem75(6679-6686).pdf. GPBiB

J. J. Valdes and A. J. Barton. Virtual reality visual data mining via neural networks obtained from multi-objective evolutionary optimization: Application to geophysical prospecting. In *International Joint Conference on Neural Networks, IJCNN'06*, pages 4862–4869, Sheraton Vancouver Wall Centre Hotel, Vancouver, BC, Canada, 16-21 July 2006. IEEE. GPBiB

V. Venkatraman, A. R. Dalby, and Z. R. Yang. Evaluation of mutual information and genetic programming for feature selection in QSAR. *Journal of Chemical Information and Modeling*, 44(5):1686–1692, 2004. GPBiB

B. Vowk, A. S. Wait, and C. Schmidt. An evolutionary approach generates human competitive coreware programs. In M. Bedau, et al., editors, *Workshop and Tutorial Proceedings Ninth International Conference on the Simulation and Synthesis of Living Systems(Alife XI)*, pages 33–36, Boston, Massachusetts, 12 September 2004. Artificial Chemistry and its applications workshop. GPBiB

I. Vukusic, S. N. Grellscheid, and T. Wiehe. Applying genetic programming to the prediction of alternative mRNA splice variants. *Genomics*, 89(4):471–479, April 2007. GPBiB

R. L. Walker. Search engine case study: searching the web using genetic programming and MPI. *Parallel Computing*, 27(1-2):71–89, January 2001. URL http://www.sciencedirect.com/science/article/B6V12-42K5HNX-4/1/57eb870c72fb7768bb7d824557444b72. GPBiB

P. Walsh and C. Ryan. Paragen: A novel technique for the autoparallelisation of sequential programs using genetic programming. In J. R. Koza, et al., editors, *Genetic Programming 1996: Proceedings of the First Annual Conference*, pages 406–409, Stanford University, CA, USA, 28–31 July 1996. MIT Press. URL http://cognet.mit.edu/library/books/view?isbn=0262611279. GPBiB

D. C. Weaver. Applying data mining techniques to library design, lead generation and lead optimization. *Current Opinion in Chemical Biology*, 8(3):264–270, 2004. URL http://www.sciencedirect.com/science/article/B6VRX-4CB69R1-2/2/84a354cec9064ed07baab6a07998c942. GPBiB

Generation 71
(see Sec. B.4)

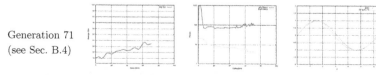

T. Weise and K. Geihs. Genetic programming techniques for sensor networks. In P. J. Marron, editor, *Proceedings of 5. GI/ITG KuVS Fachgesprach Drahtlose Sensornetze*, pages 21–25, University of Stuttgart, July 2006. URL http://dgpf.sourceforge.net/ documents/006-2006-07-17-kuvs_paper.pdf. Technical Report No. 2006/07. GPBiB

C. H. Westerberg and J. Levine. Investigations of different seeding strategies in a genetic planner. In E. J. W. Boers, et al., editors, *Applications of Evolutionary Computing*, volume 2037 of *LNCS*, pages 505–514, Lake Como, Italy, 18 April 2001. Springer-Verlag. ISBN 3-540-41920-9. URL http://www.aiai.ed.ac.uk/~johnl/ papers/westerberg-evostim01.ps.   GPBiB

P. A. Whigham. A schema theorem for context-free grammars. In *1995 IEEE Conference on Evolutionary Computation*, volume 1, pages 178–181, Perth, Australia, 29 November - 1 December 1995. IEEE Press. URL http://citeseer.ist.psu.edu/ whigham95schema.html.   GPBiB

P. A. Whigham. Search bias, language bias, and genetic programming. In J. R. Koza, et al., editors, *Genetic Programming 1996: Proceedings of the First Annual Conference*, pages 230–237, Stanford University, CA, USA, 28–31 July 1996. MIT Press. GPBiB

L. D. Whitley. A Genetic Algorithm Tutorial. *Statistics and Computing*, 4:65–85, 1994. URL http://www.cs.colostate.edu/~genitor/MiscPubs/tutorial.pdf.

L. D. Whitley. An overview of evolutionary algorithms: practical issues and common pitfalls. *Information and Software Technology*, 43(14):817–831, 2001. URL http: //www.cs.colostate.edu/~genitor/2001/overview.pdf.   GPBiB

L. D. Whitley, D. Goldberg, E. Cantu-Paz, L. Spector, I. Parmee, and H.-G. Beyer, editors. *Proceedings of the Genetic and Evolutionary Computation Conference (GECCO-2000)*, Las Vegas, Nevada, USA, 10-12 July 2000. Morgan Kaufmann. ISBN 1-55860-708-0. URL http://www.cs.colostate.edu/~genitor/GECCO-2000/ gecco2000mainpage.htm.   GPBiB

M. J. Willis, H. G. Hiden, and G. A. Montague. Developing inferential estimation algorithms using genetic programming. In *IFAC/ADCHEM International Symposium on Advanced Control of Chemical Processes*, pages 219–224, Banff, Canada, 1997a. GPBiB

M. Willis, H. Hiden, P. Marenbach, B. McKay, and G. A. Montague. Genetic programming: An introduction and survey of applications. In A. Zalzala, editor, *Second International Conference on Genetic Algorithms in Engineering Systems: Innovations and Applications, GALESIA*, University of Strathclyde, Glasgow, UK, 1-4 September 1997b. Institution of Electrical Engineers. ISBN 0-85296-693-8. URL http://www.staff.ncl.ac.uk/d.p.searson/docs/galesia97surveyofGP.pdf. GPBiB

G. Wilson and M. Heywood. Introducing probabilistic adaptive mapping developmental genetic programming with redundant mappings. *Genetic Programming and Evolvable Machines*, 8(2):187–220, June 2007. ISSN 1389-2576. Special issue on developmental systems.   GPBiB

M. L. Wong and K. S. Leung. Evolving recursive functions for the even-parity problem using genetic programming. In P. J. Angeline and K. E. Kinnear, Jr., editors, *Advances in Genetic Programming 2*, chapter 11, pages 221–240. MIT Press, Cambridge, MA, USA, 1996. ISBN 0-262-01158-1.   GPBiB

M. L. Wong and K. S. Leung. *Data Mining Using Grammar Based Genetic Programming and Applications*, volume 3 of *Genetic Programming*. Kluwer Academic Publishers, January 2000. ISBN 0-7923-7746-X.   GPBiB

M.-L. Wong, T.-T. Wong, and K.-L. Fok. Parallel evolutionary algorithms on graphics processing unit. In D. Corne, et al., editors, *Proceedings of the 2005 IEEE Congress on Evolutionary Computation*, volume 3, pages 2286–2293, Edinburgh, Scotland, UK, 2-5 September 2005. IEEE Press. ISBN 0-7803-9363-5. URL http://ieeexplore.ieee.org/servlet/opac?punumber=10417&isvol=3.

A. M. Woodward, R. J. Gilbert, and D. B. Kell. Genetic programming as an analytical tool for non-linear dielectric spectroscopy. *Bioelectrochemistry and Bioenergetics*, 48(2):389–396, 1999. URL http://www.sciencedirect.com/science/article/B6TF7-3WJ72RJ-T/2/19fd01a6eb6ae0b8e12b2bb2218fb6e9. GPBiB

S. Wright. The roles of mutation, inbreeding, crossbreeding and selection in evolution. In D. F. Jones, editor, *Proceedings of the Sixth International Congress on Genetics*, volume 1, pages 356–366, 1932.

H. Xie, M. Zhang, and P. Andreae. Genetic programming for automatic stress detection in spoken english. In F. Rothlauf, et al., editors, *Applications of Evolutionary Computing, EvoWorkshops2006: EvoBIO, EvoCOMNET, EvoHOT, EvoIASP, EvoInteraction, EvoMUSART, EvoSTOC*, volume 3907 of *LNCS*, pages 460–471, Budapest, 10-12 April 2006. Springer Verlag. ISBN 3-540-33237-5. URL http://www.springerlink.com/openurl.asp?genre=article&issn=0302-9743&volume=3907&spage=460. GPBiB

L. Yamamoto and C. F. Tschudin. Experiments on the automatic evolution of protocols using genetic programming. In I. Stavrakakis and M. Smirnov, editors, *Autonomic Communication, Second International IFIP Workshop, WAC 2005, Revised Selected Papers*, volume 3854 of *Lecture Notes in Computer Science*, pages 13–28, Athens, Greece, October 2-5 2005. Springer. ISBN 3-540-32992-7. URL http://cn.cs.unibas.ch/people/ly/doc/wac2005-lyct.pdf. GPBiB

D. Yamashiro, T. Yoshikawa, and T. Furuhashi. Visualization of search process and improvement of search performance in multi-objective genetic algorithm. In G. G. Yen, et al., editors, *Proceedings of the 2006 IEEE Congress on Evolutionary Computation*, pages 1151–1156, Vancouver, BC, Canada, 16-21 July 2006. IEEE Press. ISBN 0-7803-9487-9. URL http://ieeexplore.ieee.org/servlet/opac?punumber=11108.

K. Yanai and H. Iba. Estimation of distribution programming based on bayesian network. In R. Sarker, et al., editors, *Proceedings of the 2003 Congress on Evolutionary Computation CEC2003*, pages 1618–1625, Canberra, 8-12 December 2003. IEEE Press. ISBN 0-7803-7804-0. URL http://www.iba.k.u-tokyo.ac.jp/papers/2003/yanaiCEC2003.pdf. GPBiB

K. Yanai and H. Iba. Program evolution by integrating EDP and GP. In K. Deb, et al., editors, *Genetic and Evolutionary Computation – GECCO-2004, Part I*, volume 3102 of *Lecture Notes in Computer Science*, pages 774–785, Seattle, WA, USA, 26-30 June 2004. Springer-Verlag. ISBN 3-540-22344-4. URL http://www.iba.k.u-tokyo.ac.jp/papers/2004/yanaiGECCO2004.pdf. GPBiB

M. Yangiya. Efficient genetic programming based on binary decision diagrams. In *1995 IEEE Conference on Evolutionary Computation*, volume 1, pages 234–239, Perth, Australia, 29 November - 1 December 1995. IEEE Press. GPBiB

X. Yao, E. Burke, J. A. Lozano, J. Smith, J. J. Merelo-Guervós, J. A. Bullinaria, J. Rowe, P. T. A. Kabán, and H.-P. Schwefel, editors. *Parallel Problem Solving from Nature - PPSN VIII*, volume 3242 of *LNCS*, Birmingham, UK, 18-22 September 2004. Springer-Verlag. ISBN 3-540-23092-0. URL http://www.springerlink.com/openurl.asp?genre=issue&issn=0302-9743&volume=3242. GPBiB

Generation 78
(see Sec. B.4)

Yoshihara. *Proceedings of the 2000 Congress on Evolutionary Computation CEC00*, La Jolla Marriott Hotel La Jolla, California, USA, 6-9 July 2000. IEEE Press. ISBN 0-7803-6375-2.   GPBiB

J. Yu and B. Bhanu. Evolutionary feature synthesis for facial expression recognition. *Pattern Recognition Letters*, 27(11):1289–1298, August 2006. Evolutionary Computer Vision and Image Understanding.   GPBiB

J. Yu, J. Yu, A. A. Almal, S. M. Dhanasekaran, D. Ghosh, W. P. Worzel, and A. M. Chinnaiyan. Feature selection and molecular classification of cancer using genetic programming. *Neoplasia*, 9(4):292–303, April 2007.   GPBiB

T. Yu. Hierachical processing for evolving recursive and modular programs using higher order functions and lambda abstractions. *Genetic Programming and Evolvable Machines*, 2(4):345–380, December 2001. ISSN 1389-2576.   GPBiB

T. Yu and S.-H. Chen. Using genetic programming with lambda abstraction to find technical trading rules. In *Computing in Economics and Finance*, University of Amsterdam, 8-10 July 2004.   GPBiB

T. Yu, R. L. Riolo, and B. Worzel, editors. *Genetic Programming Theory and Practice III*, volume 9 of *Genetic Programming*, Ann Arbor, 12-14 May 2005. Springer. ISBN 0-387-28110-X.   GPBiB

B.-T. Zhang and D.-Y. Cho. Coevolutionary fitness switching: Learning complex collective behaviors using genetic programming. In L. Spector, et al., editors, *Advances in Genetic Programming 3*, chapter 18, pages 425–445. MIT Press, Cambridge, MA, USA, June 1999. ISBN 0-262-19423-6. URL http://bi.snu.ac.kr/Publications/Books/aigp3.ps.   GPBiB

B.-T. Zhang and H. Mühlenbein. Evolving optimal neural networks using genetic algorithms with Occam's razor. *Complex Systems*, 7:199–220, 1993. URL http://citeseer.ist.psu.edu/zhang93evolving.html.   GPBiB

B.-T. Zhang and H. Mühlenbein. Balancing accuracy and parsimony in genetic programming. *Evolutionary Computation*, 3(1):17–38, 1995. URL http://www.ais.fraunhofer.de/~muehlen/publications/gmd_as_ga-94_09.ps.   GPBiB

B.-T. Zhang, P. Ohm, and H. Mühlenbein. Evolutionary induction of sparse neural trees. *Evolutionary Computation*, 5(2):213–236, 1997. URL http://bi.snu.ac.kr/Publications/Journals/International/EC5-2.ps.   GPBiB

M. Zhang and U. Bhowan. Pixel statistics and program size in genetic programming for object detection. Technical Report CS-TR-04-3, Computer Science, Victoria University of Wellington, New Zealand, 2004.   GPBiB

M. Zhang and W. Smart. Using gaussian distribution to construct fitness functions in genetic programming for multiclass object classification. *Pattern Recognition Letters*, 27 (11):1266–1274, August 2006. Evolutionary Computer Vision and Image Understanding.   GPBiB

Q. Zhang, J. Sun, and E. P. K. Tsang. An Evolutionary Algorithm With Guided Mutation for the Maximum Clique Problem. *IEEE Transactions on Evolutionary Computation*, 9(2):192–200, 2005.

Y. Zhang and P. I. Rockett. Evolving optimal feature extraction using multi-objective genetic programming: a methodology and preliminary study on edge detection. In H.-G. Beyer, et al., editors, *GECCO 2005: Proceedings of the 2005 conference on Genetic and evolutionary computation*, volume 1, pages 795–802, Washington DC, USA, 25-29 June 2005. ACM Press. ISBN 1-59593-010-8. URL http://www.cs.bham.ac.uk/~wbl/biblio/gecco2005/docs/p795.pdf. GPBiB

Y. Zhang and P. I. Rockett. Feature extraction using multi-objective genetic programming. In Y. Jin, editor, *Multi-Objective Machine Learning*, volume 16 of *Studies in Computational Intelligence*, chapter 4, pages 79–106. Springer, 2006. ISBN 3-540-30676-5. Invited chapter. GPBiB

E. Zitzler, M. Laumanns, and L. Thiele. SPEA2: Improving the Strength Pareto Evolutionary Algorithm. Technical Report 103, Gloriastrasse 35, CH-8092 Zurich, Switzerland, 2001. URL http://citeseer.ist.psu.edu/article/zitzler01spea.html.

Generation 85
(see Sec. B.4)

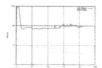
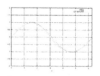

Index

Generation 92
(see Sec. B.4)

Generation 99
(see Sec. B.4)

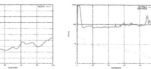

Colophon

This book was primarily written using the LaTeX document preparation system, along with BibTeX, pdflatex and makeindex. Most of the editing was done using the emacs and xemacs editors, along with extensions such as RefTeX; some was done with TeXShop as well. Most of the data plots were generated using gnuplot and the R statistics package. Diagrams were generated with a variety of tools, including the Graphviz package, tgif and xfig. A whole host of programming and scripting languages were used to automate various processes in both the initial scientific research and in the production of this book; they are too numerous to list here, but were crucial nonetheless. The cover was created with Adobe Photoshop[1] and gimp.

Coordinating the work of three busy, opinionated authors is not trivial, and would have been much more difficult without the use of revision control systems such as Subversion. Around 500 commits were made in a six month period, averaging around 10 commits per day in the final weeks. The actual files were hosted as a project at http://assembla.com; we didn't realise until several months into the project that Assembla's president is in fact Andy Singleton, who did some cool early work in GP in the mid-90's.

The "reviews" and "summaries" on the back cover were generated stochastically using the idea of N-grams from linguistics. For the "reviews" we collected a number of reviews of previous books on GP and EAs, and tabulated the frequency of different triples of adjacent words. These frequencies of triples in the source text were then used to guide the choices of words in the generated "reviews". The only word following the pair "ad" and "hoc" in our source reviews, for example, was "tweaks"; thus once "ad" and "hoc" had been chosen, the next word had to be "tweaks". The pair "of the", on the other hand, appears numerous times in our source text, followed by words such as "field", "body", and "rapidly". However, "theory" is the most common successor, and, therefore, the most likely to be chosen to follow "of the" in the generation of new text. The generation of the "summaries" was similar, but based on the front matter of the book itself. See (Poli and McPhee, 2008a) for an application of these ideas in genetic programming.

---

[1] Adobe Photoshop is a registered trademark of Adobe Systems Incorporated

CPSIA information can be obtained at www.ICGtesting.com
Printed in the USA
BVOW08s1438150815

413401BV00001B/175/P